Love of the Sirens

On Composers, Compulsions, and Creations

Edith Zack

Translated from the Hebrew by Anthony Berris

Love of the Sirens

On Composers, Compulsions, and Creations

Written by Edith Zack

Translated from Hebrew: Anthony Berris

Illustrations: Roi Shinar

Design: Keren Amram

Produced by Notssa – www.nottsa.com

In memory of Israel Zack

with love

'*I carry your heart with me (I carry it in my heart)*'

(E.E. Cummings)

Contents

A PLAY LIST WITH SELECTED MUSIC IS AVAILABLE ON
WWW.EIDTHZACK.COM

Prologue

This book was conceived when my interest was piqued by
the stories of women down the centuries who chose music as
their métier, but were excluded from general history books
and, more surprisingly, from books on the history of music.
A short time after I began delving into the personal
correspondence of these women, and seeking every scrap of
contemporaneous information about them, I found myself
enthralled by their life stories, which were no less fascinating
than the compositions they wrote. Then I started asking
myself, how was it possible that these women, who lived,
worked and composed in different places and during
different periods in history, had disappeared from the
chronicles of history; their voices silenced? And how could
it be that the general public is unfamiliar not only with their
names, but also with their work?

"Women composers? Is there such an animal?" This was
repeated every time I raised the issue with my music
students. "Were there any women at all in the world?" I
replied. And the more deeply I researched the subject, the
more amazed I was by the total exclusion of women from
music history books in particular, and from the
consciousness of Western culture in general. In this book I
have chosen to focus on twenty women composers who were
active and prolific in the society and culture of their time.
And the question in my mind is still, "Why have we never
heard of them?"

For centuries the prevailing stereotypical concept was that men had a monopoly on creativity. The source of this gendered concept lay in the stereotyping and distortion of the term "creation." For men, creation is a mental and intellectual act that takes place in thought. Thus it is they who write, compose, paint and produce scientific inventions. Female creation, on the other hand, is a physical act that takes place in the womb, resulting in the birth of children and all it entails: a husband, a home, and their attendant spheres of responsibility.[1]

Judith Shakespeare

In Victorian society such differentiation between the sexes – which sounds so preposterous in the second decade of the twenty-first century – was extremely commonplace. In two lectures delivered at the Arts Society in October 1928, Virginia Woolf described the clear distinction between the sexes at the time. Woolf, who was acutely aware of women's inequality, wrote a satirical essay, at the center of which is a fictitious sister of William Shakespeare. Although not a documentary account, the story provides an excellent example of contemporary women's status as opposed to that of men in everything pertaining to professionalism and developing creativity. The story's central question is what would have happened had the Shakespeare family actually produced a daughter no less gifted than the famous William? Woolf's story is about a fictitious Judith Shakespeare, a gifted and inquisitive girl with a talent for writing and rhyme, a natural sensitivity for rhythm, and refined theatrical taste. Judith's brother William spent his days and nights poring over the works of the great Roman poets and writers, Virgil, Ovid and Horace. Unlike William, Judith did not attend school and was therefore denied the kind of education that would have enabled her to read the books that so intrigued her. And all because she was a woman. Still, Judith's curiosity surmounted all the obstacles society placed in her path, and she seized every opportunity to surreptitiously read her brother's books. But then her parents told her to mend the stockings and mind the stew and not moon about with books, or in other words, to perform all the tasks reserved solely for women.

Judith continued to dream of a world in which a woman could go for a walk in the street on her own without fear of compromising her reputation, a world in which a woman could write and publish a novel, act in the theater, direct a play, and write music. But the period in which she lived was not the right one for her. Soon after being informed that she was to be betrothed to the son of a neighboring wool-stapler, she packed her belongings and ran away to London to fulfill her dream of becoming an actress.

In London she met many men involved in various spheres of art – playwrights, novelists, actors, and producers. They all mocked her for her dreams, until one day she met a man who agreed to take her under his wing. Fate decreed that aside from the warmth and affection he gave her, he was also a theatrical agent. Her future seemed promising, but the fantasy was short-lived. One day her benefactor vanished and Judith found herself pregnant. All alone in the big city and too ashamed to return to her parents' home, she took her own life. Judith Shakespeare – as insignificant in death as she had been in life – is buried near one of London's gloomy crossroads.[2]

Art as a Feminine Ornament

According to musicologist Marcia Citron, the story of sixteenth-century Judith Shakespeare is no different from that of many other women involved in various spheres of creativity, even many years later. It is but one of many models that present the "masculine power of art" which dominated Western culture and created a schism between the sexes. Men were granted legitimacy to be intellectuals, to let their imagination run free, and to be responsible for creativity in its various forms. Thus they became poets, writers, composers, and artists; they were also conductors, philosophers, critics, and historians who documented the story of the Western world. In society's collective awareness, women, on the other hand, were consigned to salons and morning visits, to sewing, embroidery, flower arranging; and piano playing.

In 1820, the German-Jewish banker Abraham Mendelssohn wrote to his daughter Fanny on her fifteenth birthday, "Perhaps for Felix music will become a profession, while for you it will always remain but an ornament; never can and should it become the foundation of your existence." And he went on to note that Fanny's joy in Felix's joy is proof that had she been in his place, she would have enjoyed the same kind of recognition. Moreover, he counseled her to remain faithful to these feminine values, and only that which is truly feminine is a genuine ornament for members of her sex.[3]

The Mendelssohn family's gender-oriented perception, shaped as it was by German bourgeois society, dictated the fate of brother and sister alike – both possessed enormous talent and studied music together alongside their general education, until their father decided to separate his sons and his daughters. Fanny and her younger sister, Rebecca, learned the art of conversation, languages, religion and ethics, drawing and painting, dancing and music, as well as the efficient running of a household. At the same time, Father Mendelssohn hired the services of a senior lecturer in history from Berlin University, a classical philologist, and a senior mathematics teacher for Felix and their younger brother, Paul, to broaden their horizons and prepare them for their matriculation examinations. In music, the elder Mendelssohn had plans for Felix to become a great composer. He took the boy on an educational tour of England, Paris and Rome, and informed him that he would have to choose a city in which to settle, manage his professional life, and prepare for a life of travel, during which he would conquer the world's concert halls. Fanny, as we shall see, conformed with the gender codes dictated to her. She remained in her parents' home where, in her own private space, she continued to write music and present her compositions to invited audiences.

In the Absence of Professional Tutoring

Throughout history, gender codes have dictated the paths of women in everything connected to professional education. In the Middle Ages, life was conducted in accordance with the dictates of the Church, which held sway over births, marriages, deaths, sex, and even eating habits. It also set the rules for jurisprudence and medicine, as well as issues concerning philosophy and wisdom.[4] The social status of the head of the family dictated that of his wife and her role in the family and society. Women managed the household and were entitled by law to inherit and manage property. Aside from enlarging the family, they were expected to be polite and well mannered and know how to play chess and other fashionable social games of the time. Moreover, they were expected to know how to "tell stories, to recite, to solve riddles, to sing, to play a string instrument, and to dance."[5] Up to the age of seven, which in the Middle Ages marked the end of childhood, the mother, wet-nurse or nanny were responsible for the schooling of both boys and girls, and it was they who taught them the rules of language through songs, stories and their first prayers. From age eight onward, girls were transferred to a regime provided by a governess known for her erudition, or sent to a convent. However, the standard of women's education was limited, and even those considered educated were schooled at home by their mothers or governesses rather than by professional teachers.

Boys, on the other hand, attended cathedral or monastery schools where they studied seven different subjects in preparation for a higher education in philosophy and theology. The first stage of a boy's education consisted of Latin grammar, rhetoric and logic, followed by arithmetic, geometry, astronomy, and music in the second stage. These subjects were known as "the liberal arts" since only freemen were allowed to study them. Women did not fit this description.

Hildegard of Bingen was a nun, Benedictine abbess, poet, dramaturge, and composer, an autodidactic musician whose many works were published in her lifetime. Her parents had dedicated her to the Church when she was still in her mother's womb, and when she was eight years old she was sent to the Disibodenberg monastery where she joined Jutta von Sponheim, an anchoress (a nun enclosed from the world) only four years her senior. As we shall see in the chapter dedicated to her, Hildegard admitted that she was not fluent in rudimentary Latin grammar and had learned music through listening to the prayers and notes audible from the monastery adjacent to her cell. Thus when she decided to put her literary and musical compositions in writing, she was helped by monks whose education was broader and deeper than her own.

From the sixth century onward, European monasteries were responsible for training women to play an active role in prayer and religious ceremonies, and the knowledge they acquired conformed to this training. Among them were women who composed musical works but did not sign them, and they therefore remain anonymous to this day. In secular life, women were involved in musical activity at home if they were fortunate enough to have been born into either the aristocracy or to an affluent family. But there were some who joined guilds whose members were writers of secular poetry – wandering minstrels, members of mixed male and female troupes, and female troubadours who were poets and court singers.[6] For example, a minstrel by the name of Beatrice Maras is listed in the 1297 Paris tax register, and the fourteenth-century accounts of the Court of Burgundy include documents attesting to payments made to women who sang and composed music.[7]

Renaissance period guilds ruled that artists had to learn their trade by the apprenticeship method. Anyone who wished to specialize in the sphere of the visual arts, for example, was required to work with a "master" in order to learn all the professional aspects of the art, from grinding colors, through mixing pigments, and up to the final details of completing and signing a work. To avoid the risk of moral turpitude, women were not allowed to perform physical work alongside male apprentices.

European courts hired only a few women as artists and sculptresses. Those who did manage to break through the gender barrier were usually daughters of men who themselves were well-known artists. The stonemason Sabina von Steinbach, for example, was taught her craft by her father when she was still a child. Some years later he was commissioned to sculpt the façade of Strasbourg Cathedral in Germany. Unfortunately he died suddenly before fulfilling the commission, but his daughter was able to quickly step into his shoes and complete the work successfully. Artemisia

Gentileschi, one of the more famous painters of the Renaissance period, also learned the secrets of her profession from her father Orazio, the famous Italian painter of the period. Artemisia was captivated by portraiture and achieved fame after painting the portraits of England's King Charles I and his family.

Women who composed music, sang, and played instruments constituted an important component in the performances that took place in the various courts of Renaissance Italy, although most of their work was never published. An exception was Maddalena Casulana, who in her lifetime had the sixty-seven madrigals she composed published in three volumes. The first of her books, published in Venice in 1568, was dedicated to her benefactor, Isabella de' Medici, thus: "[I want] to show to the world (as much as is possible in the profession of music) the vain error of men that they alone possess intellectual gifts, and who appear to believe that the same gifts are not possible for women."[8] The direct reference to the gender ideology that shunted creative women aside is an expression of her daring, and also proves that Casulana understood that the publication of her work was not something to be taken for granted. Although her lineage is unclear and her biography obscure, it is known that she had connections in the Italian courts as well as the German court of Munich, from which she even received a commission to write the music for the wedding of William V, Duke of Bavaria, to Renata of Lorraine in 1568. Unlike male composers, Casulana was known for the sophisticated texts she composed for her madrigals, with erotic connotations and metaphorical allusions to sexual arousal.

The Women Musicians of Ferrara

More than a decade after Casulana wrote her dedication, a volte-face took place in the performances of women court musicians in Italy, especially in Florence, Mantua and Ferrara. On the initiative of Alfonso II d'Este, Duke of Ferrara, a group of virtuosa singers was formed, which became known throughout Italy as *Concerto delle Donne*. Each of these young women was a vocal virtuosa who, in addition to her singing talents, played an instrument and composed music. They began their careers as courtesans in the various courts, and only later managed to carve out a position for themselves as professional musicians. The fact that they had been ladies-in-waiting to duchesses freed them from the negative connotations that adhered to those courtesans who were skilled in conversation and knowledgeable in the arts, and who were the mistresses of noblemen. But to avoid any suggestion that the music was composed by a woman who might be perceived as a rich man's mistress, Duke Alfonso made sure that the *Concerto delle Donne* performed only the works of male composers. In addition, he ensured that each of the musicians in the group received a generous dowry and married a nobleman.[9] Laura Peverara, for example, one of the ensemble's three founders, was invited to live in the ducal palace.

Laura and her friends worked and performed in places denied to other women, and ostensibly enjoyed the kind of creative freedom of movement and handsome remuneration unavailable to their counterparts. In practice, they were controlled by their patron, who decided on the venues at which they would appear and the music they performed. The greatest achievement of the women musicians of Ferrara was their innovative compositional style which centered on solo voice with instrumental accompaniment. And like any owner of an innovational patent, the Duke zealously safeguarded the musical secrets of the *Concerto delle Donne*, and so only guests personally selected by him were permitted to listen to them. They therefore mainly appeared before invited audiences of aristocrats.[10] Nonetheless, despite the great secrecy that surrounded them, the singer-composers became known throughout Italy and beyond, inspiring male composers and performers, and similar groups of women singers established in other Italian city-states.

Courts at that time constituted a kind of large corporation that sponsored artists from various fields; very much like in modern times, and then as now sponsors vied to locate first-rate singers, artists and dancers. The fortunate ones who came under the aegis of the court were able to participate in the production of operas and other forms of musical entertainment, and did not miss an opportunity to promote themselves as performers and virtuosi.[11] Moreover, whatever happened at one court was immediately copied by another, so that there would be no disparity between the competitors. When, for example, Duke Alfonso of Ferrara took his court singers on a tour of Italy, Giulio Caccini, who was employed at the court of the de' Medici, saw to it that his women singers were given a similar perquisite. His wish was fulfilled in 1584, when he embarked on a tour, the crowning glory of which was a performance at the wedding of Eleonora de' Medici and Vincenzo Gonzaga, Duke of Mantua.[12]

Daughters of Famous Fathers

Among Giulio Caccini's female musicians were his daughters Francesca (see chapter Two) and her younger sister, Settimia. Francesca was a brilliant, intelligent young woman as well as a talented singer and musician, but like other girls of her time she was not allowed to attend a public school. Nonetheless, she was the only one of Giulio's ten children who received a basic humanist education. Francesca learned Latin, a little Greek, rhetoric and grammar, and she usually read and wrote independently. She studied music with her father, a leading figure in the *Florentine Camerata*, a group of intellectuals, writers, poets, musicians, and nobles who conceived the idea of opera and dictated a new style. Francesca grew up with this style and quickly gained fame as a singer and player of several instruments with a brilliant talent for improvisation. But despite her many admirers, and although her name was on many lips and other courts vied for her services, her first name was not mentioned until she was twenty-four. Until then she and her sister Settimia were known as "the daughters of Giulio Romano", since their father hailed from Rome. As the girls were not known by their first names, their fees were not paid directly to them but to their father, who transferred them directly into his household account.

Barbara Strozzi (see chapter Three) was also among the influential artists' daughters who were able to present their work by dint of their fathers' connections. She was the illegitimate daughter of Giulio Strozzi, a poet and intellectual with excellent connections in early seventeenth-century Venice. It was a period in which the academies flourished: learned societies, each of which specialized in a specific subject and enjoyed the support of an aristocratic sponsor. Unlike the universities where the focus was on teaching, the academies were concerned with research and discourse. Academy members were men who met to exchange ideas, opinions and new discoveries.

Giulio Strozzi was a member of the *Accademia degli Incogniti* (Academy of the Unknowns), a name derived from the fact that its members often wrote in a secret language and published their works anonymously. It was a learned society of intellectuals, some of them noblemen, who met to share their creative output and influence the culture and political life of mid-seventeenth-century Venice. Strozzi knew that if he wanted his daughter to progress as a musician, he had to establish an institution that would be identified with her and her art. Thus the *Accademia degli Unisoni* (Academy of the Like-Minded, and a pun on the musical term "unison") was founded, on whose stage Barbara presented the fruits of her musical activity. One evening, Barbara addressed her male-only audience from the stage of her academy and said: "I have no doubts as to your decision, honorable Sirs, to come here [to hear] my songs. I know full well that I would not have been graced with your presence had I invited you come to see me weep."[13]

Barbara was aware that she was risking the accusation of being the bastard daughter of a man who was also illegitimate, and because of her audacity in presenting her work in public. In her first book of madrigals, which she dedicated to Vittoria della Rovere, Grand Duchess of Tuscany, she wrote, "I have to dedicate to her the first work that I, as a woman, am daring to publish, in order that this – the creation – will find a safe place under a golden oak against the slander and ridicule that await me."[14]

Feminine Stratagems

Strozzi's reference to the fact that she, as a woman, was publishing her musical work might be interpreted as insecurity, a search for a refuge against criticism. But it is also a determined statement: "Yes, I'm a woman, and yes, I dare to publish my work". And she metaphorically places that work under the oak, the biblical tree symbolizing strength, daring, power and longevity (Amos, 2:9). Its roots are thick and wide, its trunk sturdy, its foliage dense, and it bears fruit.

Female composers employed a variety of stratagems to surmount the gender obstacle that excluded them from publishing their work. Hildegard of Bingen made a point of recording her visions which, according to her, appeared in the form of a male entity that addressed her directly, instructing her to convey its messages. Whereas the written works of men in the service of the Church and monasteries were based on their predecessors who were great theologians, Hildegard contended that the authority that appointed her was none other than God himself. In her writings, Hildegard reversed traditional male-female roles and related to time and knowledge as empowering feminine phenomena. In a letter to Henri Capet De Beauvais, Bishop of Rouen, she defines time as "feminine time" and pure knowledge as a female face filled with light, its eyes resembling the hyacinth, its dresses silken, and on its shoulders a velvet mantle like the one worn by the bishop.

Hundreds of years after Hildegard, women were compelled to employ various stratagems to reverse gender roles. In literature, we find George Sand and George Eliot who adopted male pseudonyms to enter public consciousness and pave their way into a hegemonic society. Amantine-Aurore-Lucille née Dupin (1804-1876), later Baroness Dudevant, reinvented herself as the French novelist and memoirist, George Sand. She became famous for expressing her political views in public, as well as for smoking cigars and her provocative dress, which included men's suits and trousers. This at a time when fashion dictated that women wear dresses over layers of petticoats and hoops to obscure their figure.

Victorian novelist Mary Ann (formerly Marian) Evans (1819-1880) followed the advice of her partner, George Henry Lewes, and assumed the name George Eliot to protect herself against Victorian prejudices. This tactic proved itself with the publication of her first novel, *Adam Bede*, whose realistic pastoral atmosphere is replete with painful scenes of seduction, unwanted pregnancy, and shame, which result in the heroine running away to hide from the world.[15]

Eliot gave freedom to the voice of a woman who, according to Victorian mores, had fallen from grace, and in her text she preaches tolerance, compassion, and forgiveness in their fullest humanistic sense. The book was a great success. Readers and critics alike were convinced that it was written by a man of the cloth, which helped them to accept and even applaud it. One day, however, Joseph Liggins, an erstwhile tutor, claimed credit for having written the text, and Eliot decided to reveal her identity in order to defend her literary reputation. Now the tone changed, and the same readers and critics denounced Eliot for her treatment of subjects like love and morality. An unsigned review in the *Dublin University Magazine* states that she had given free rein to her own passion, while in London she was accused of using a novel as a defense for her unmarried relationship with Lewes. In other words, the values of the novel's protagonists had to face the wrath of society, not because of their nature, but because of the way in which the author led her own private life.

As in literature, in music too, the irrelevant attitude to the works of women composers is manifested in derogatory comments on their femininity as well as their work. Any woman who presented her work outside of her private circle and achieved recognition was risking fierce criticism and accusations of various kinds. It was said of them that they are masculine, promiscuous, and even sexually unsatisfied. Augusta Holmès, a singer and composer who wrote dramatic works for large orchestras, was accused of writing works that were masculine in spirit (see chapter Twelve). Her colorful and lively personality fired the imagination and lives of many men, and the gossip that surrounded her ranged from speculation over her love affairs to articles written about her success as a woman of her time. Holmès harnessed the "masculinity" with which she was attributed to consolidate her position in a male-dominated society. Instead of being insulted she declared that she had a man's soul in a woman's body, and even possessed a "masculine coarseness" resulting from her strict education. The same was said of Clara Schumann, the first woman to be accepted as a teacher of piano at the Frankfurt Hoch Conservatory. On her acceptance to the position, the director of the conservatory which, until then had not employed women, said, "Regarding Madame Schumann, I think of her as a man."[16] His remark was intended to "compliment" this gifted musician whose career spanned many years, who worked full time and earned handsome remuneration that enabled her to financially support her children, and later, her grandchildren too. As we shall see in the chapter entitled "A Shining Light", ironically Clara was the most brilliant pianist of her generation, but when it came to composition, she often displayed a lack of confidence simply because she was a woman, as this diary entry attests:

> *I once believed that I had creative talent, but I have given up this idea; a woman must not wish to compose – there never was one able to do it. Am I intended to be the one? It would be arrogant to believe that. That was something with which my father tempted me in former days. But I soon gave up believing this.17*

Nevertheless, Clara continued to compose as she moved from one to the next of her eight pregnancies, family life, and the creativity that burned within her. In May 1849, when she discovered that she was pregnant with her fifth child, she wrote in her diary:

> *And so I have decided to face the difficult time that is coming as cheerfully as possible. Whether it will always be like this, I don't know.*[18]

Women's lack of confidence in their creative ability, and their reluctance to even relate to their works as their own made them dependent on the opinions of men who were involved in the same field, whether the man was their father, brother, close friend, or partner. "I continued to compose pieces for piano and, for the first time, I managed to complete one piece that sounded brilliant," Fanny Mendelssohn reported to her brother on June 30, 1836. "I don't know exactly what Goethe means by the demonic influence, but this much is clear: if it does exist, you exert it over me. I believe that if you seriously suggested that I become a good mathematician, I wouldn't have any particular difficulty in doing so, and I could just as easily cease being a musician tomorrow if you thought I wasn't good at that any longer."[19]

There is no doubt that the lack of confidence suffered by Fanny and the other women composers mentioned here was compounded in no small measure by personality traits as well as the issue of gender. Moreover, a woman was required to have a strong personality and a very high level of self-confidence if she were to surmount the obstacles placed in her path by centuries of male hegemony in all spheres of life. In Fanny's case, she made no attempt to leap over the gender barriers and maintained her "feminine values" in accordance with her father's wishes. She performed and presented her works only in the private space of the music salon in her Berlin home, and accepted the unequivocal opinion of Felix – who was already a famous composer – that she must not publish her work, because, he stressed, of her being a woman and a mother. And he convinced her. Her greatest source of pride was that she was her brother's professional advisor, critic, and leading admirer in everything pertaining to his composition. "…I have watched the progress of his talent step by step," she wrote in her diary with satisfaction, and added "and may say I have contributed to his development. I have always been his only musical adviser, and he never writes down a thought before submitting it to my judgment."[20] This last sentence contains echoes of some recognition of her self-worth from a professional standpoint, but it also reflects a delusion of her involvement in her brother's public success. But it was not so, since up to a year and a half before her death, when she decided to publish her works, Fanny accepted the restrictions imposed on women in the bourgeois society in which she lived, and which dictated that respectable women did not perform their work in public. Furthermore, to protect her from the embarrassment of social criticism, six of her lieder were published under Felix's name (as part of his Opus 8 and Opus 9). Eighteen years later, when he performed his Opus 8 for her, Queen Victoria told him that *Italien* was her favorite lied. Felix admitted that his sister Fanny had composed it.

Anima and Animus

Even today, in the early twenty-first century, the prevailing opinion on the non-publication of works by women throughout the ages derives from the quality of the works. Had they composed works like those by Haydn, Beethoven, and Mozart, we would have heard of them, for after all, music, like every other artistic genre, is gender-neutral.

Indeed, the nature of composition is a priori gender-neutral, and therefore the musical canon, which for centuries was exclusively male-dominated, should be reexamined. It should also be borne in mind that in every composer there are masculine and feminine elements which, in the course of composing, find their way into the work. Jung defines the feminine inner personality in the human psyche as *anima*; and the masculine one as *animus*. These two elements which coexist in the subconscious of each of us are like energetic transformers in the mental processes that all of us, men and women alike, undergo in the course of our lives.[21] They are manifested in the artistic language and create a culture that radical feminism has defined as "androgynous." The more extreme radical feminists interpret androgynous culture as a feminist culture that will replace the masculine one. In her book, *The Dialectic of Sex: The Case for Feminist Revolution*[22] feminist writer Shulamith Firestone declares that the way to achieve this is to release women from their biological totalitarianism by controlling their fertility (through birth control, abortion, and artificial insemination). In her opinion, women will never be liberated so long as they continue to be a group of sex slaves whose role is to release men and thus enable them to be free to do business.

Prizes for Men and Prizes for Women

Even if Firestone's words written in the 1970s sound extreme and perhaps even outdated, there is no denying the fact that women's representation in language and culture has not resembled that of men. The encyclopedia devoted to women composers[23] lists more than one thousand women who were engaged in instrumental or vocal composition, but aside from scholars of gender in music, who has heard of them? And who knows what difficulties they faced merely because they were women? The Conservatoire de Paris, for example, which was an important and highly respected center for music, excluded women from its composition classes until the second half of the nineteenth century. Later, women and men studied in separate classes. Violin and piano classes, too, were held separately according to gender, and there were different syllabuses for men and for women.

Additionally, only a few women managed to obtain a teaching position in this conservatory, and their terms of employment were different from those of their male counterparts. Take Louise Farrenc (see chapter Eight), for example, a composer who won numerous awards and taught at the Paris conservatory for fourteen years (1825-1839) and was noted for her professionalism and the fact that thirty of her Études were required courses for students of piano, yet her salary was consistently lower than that of her male colleagues.

An inseparable part of success was participation in competitions and winning prizes. Yet prior to 1903 women composers in France were not entitled to compete for the prestigious Prix de Rome – awarded by the French government in conjunction with the *Académie Royale de Peinture et de Sculpture* – which was awarded to French artists in the fields of music, painting, architecture, sculpture, and engraving. The prize – an annual bursary of 3,000 francs over five years – enabled artists of under thirty to study for five years without the burden of supporting themselves financially. The first two years of study were held at the Villa de Medici in Rome, and the third was spent in Germany. Until the 1930s no one questioned the fact that the prize was aimed solely at male contenders. The writer George Sand was the first to raise provocative questions about the *Académie* being an exclusively male institution. On 17 June 1892, the sculptress and women's rights activist

Hélène Bertaux submitted her candidacy for a newly-vacated seat in the *Académie*. Although her quest was unsuccessful, the issue fired fierce public debate and eleven years later, in 1903, the French minister of education made it possible for women to compete for the prize. Eight years later, in 1911, it was awarded to the sculptress Lucienne Heuvelmans (1885-1944), and in 1913 the winner was nineteen-year-old Lili Boulanger, the first woman musician to win it[24] (see chapter Sixteen).

Gender ideology devised a variety of beliefs, customs, and behavioral concepts which supported social norms and rules: what is appropriate to each gender, what are the expectations from them, what is permitted, and what is "accepted"? Women were consequently forced to fight for recognition of their work, while ignoring the fact that it was written by a woman. When Augusta Holmès composed dramatic works for symphony orchestras, her critics contended that her tone was masculine. Camille Saint-Saëns, one of the judges in the Prix de Paris competition, found Augusta's work to be worthy of first prize. Following the decision to award her the prize, on 26 March 1881 he patronizingly wrote: "Women are so intriguing and amusing. When they seriously devote themselves to art, they are so preoccupied with making us forget the fact that they are women and proving their masculinity beyond all doubt, without understanding that excessive occupation with the subject exposes them as women".[25] The fact that Holmès did not belong to a specific school led her critics to claim that her tone was not original. Holmès, who was fully aware of the difficulties involved in being a creative woman in the society in which she lived, said succinctly: "Don't believe that a creative career is more accessible to members of my gender. It's a big mistake. The way [for a woman] is much harder and the camaraderie [among men] that is of such benefit to so many artists, is closed to a certain extent to a woman who had the fortune – good or bad – to have been born a musician."[26]

The Music Salon

Women who studied or wished to study musical composition knew at the outset that their work would consist of small genres most suited to a private space. The concept of a music salon was similar to that of a painter's studio – a private space in which new compositions were first performed, where aesthetics and choices in composition were discussed, and the work analyzed. The common interest of all salon performers was in composing genres that were as ambitious as possible and performing them before as large an audience as possible. The repertoire depended on the character of the salon, which was determined by the person who headed it and the physical dimensions of the space. The most popular genres were compositions for voice and piano – the principal instrument in nineteenth-century salons – solo compositions for piano, and chamber music. Lieder, Études, Fantasias, Romances, and Variations are but a partial list. The large genres, which were too long and complex to be performed in a private space, were discussed on the basis of the libretto and score if they were available, and only selected segments were played in situ.

Regarding chamber music, it is important to note that string and wind instruments were considered inappropriate for women musicians. Wind instruments called for puckering the lips, which was considered indecent, whereas brass instruments were associated with street music or military bands. By contrast, female violinists left themselves open to criticism due to the belief that the instrument contorted the female body and demeaned her appearance. Thus, women's experience in orchestration was poor in comparison with that of their male counterparts.

In Paris of 1859 there was only one woman among the thirty-three soloists of the *Conservatory Concert Society Orchestra*, while in pre-1913 London they numbered eighteen of a total of 131. The violinist Wilma Neruda (1838-1911) was an exception in that period. Neruda, who came from a family of musicians, performed in thirteen concerts with the *London Philharmonic Orchestra* between 1849 and 1907, and was considered to have led to the elimination of the taboo against women violinists.

The music salon was a reputable cultural institution that determined the acceptance of a musical piece by a professional and non-professional audience, as well as its marketing. Rumors about new pieces and new composers spread through the numerous salons in the various cities. Two of the more notable musical salons were those of Pauline Viardot-Garcia and Fanny Hensel-Mendelssohn. In the mid-nineteenth century, every Thursday Pauline Viardot opened the doors of the music salon at her home at 50 Rue de Douai in the 9th arrondissement, which became one of the most important artistic meeting places in Paris. It was there in 1860 that the opera *Tristan und Isolde* was first performed, with Viardot as Isolde and Wagner singing Tristan. Viardot's villa in Baden-Baden was also a venue for art and assignations. Flaubert, Berlioz, Bizet, and Fauré were but a few of the many people who enjoyed the hospitality of Viardot's salon. Pauline impressed her guests with her unique personality, conversations about music, her singing and improvisation, and by voicing her opinion on virtuosi such as Liszt, Chopin, Thalberg, and Kalkbrenner. On Thursdays she hosted professional concerts attended by the crème de la crème of literary and cultural society. On

Sunday afternoons the meetings were more informal and attended by close friends and acquaintances who played, sang, and generally enjoyed themselves. In addition, Pauline organized concerts at her home, which enabled her students to perform before an audience. She composed more than fifty songs and five salon operas, which included complex roles for advanced singers.

The beginnings of Fanny Hensel-Mendelssohn's Berlin salon took the form of intimate groups of friends meeting on Sundays for conversation, light refreshments, and music. The salon soon evolved into Sunday matinées to which every self-respecting member of the Berlin bourgeoisie clamored for an invitation. It was this platform that enabled Fanny to showcase her own musical creations, her choral works, chamber music, and compositions for piano. Friday afternoons were devoted to rehearsals with her choir, which consisted of eight sopranos, four altos, and two tenors, as well as the small orchestra that she conducted. Indeed, it was this place that significantly boosted her self-confidence in her voice as a composer, but as we shall see in the chapter devoted to her (Nine), all this took place close to her sudden death. Fanny, who composed more than four hundred works, did not live to enjoy the public approbation her labors brought her.

Isolated yet Involved

Do women composers in the twenty-first century feel any differently from the ones mentioned here? Do they enjoy equal representation? Should the same criteria be employed when judging the music of female and male composers? The composer Sofia Gubaidulina who did not experience exclusion as a female musician under the Soviet regime, discusses the feminine disposition that distinguishes her from her colleagues. Every new idea she discovers or learns, as she attests of herself, deprives her of vast resources of energy. Although she is able to work through entire nights in order to submit a work on time, her physical powers are rapidly depleted.[27] By contrast, others posit that with regard to the arts and creative processes there is no difference between men and women. "'Music does not suffer definitions, fences, or gender [distinctions]' I was told by one of the composers I talked to, "which is why there is no reason to distinguish between men and women". That is the ideal situation. Today, women in music are indeed heard, but in the reality of Western culture women composers have been excluded not only from the public space but also from anthologies, history, and literature. And that, as scholar Nancy Reich contends, should be a matter of concern for us.[28] And what of research? Musicology was far slower than literature in exposing women and their works. It was only in the 1980s that women's studies scholars called for the rediscovery of women composers from the past, for the publication of their biographies, recording their works, and researching them in depth. With regard to publication, scholars' opinions are divided. Musicologist Susan McClary, for example, contends that addressing women composers as a discrete group is tantamount to declaring them different and inferior in comparison with the mainstream. In other words, the quality of their works is not on a par with that of men.[29] On the other hand, Marcia Citron proposes a pluralistic approach to the canon. According to her, there is no need to try and adapt the works of women composers to the extant canon, but rather to relate to their music as enriching it.[30] Therefore there must be a reconceptualization of the history of music, to be followed by reconstruction based on a canonical addendum. This mandates a unique methodology which will not be based on comparative research, but on awareness of the restrictions imposed on women composers, on a critical approach, and on a sociological understanding of the context in which their music was created.[31] Needless to say, like any other historical or archeological discovery, the importance of rediscovering women composers and their works lies in the knowledge of their having existed. Thus, only by exposing these composers and their works, by performing them, and conducting in-depth studies on them, will we be able to include these works in academic and public discourse. Only then will we obtain a more accurate picture of history in general and of the history of music in particular.

One

The Priestess of the Rhine Valley: Hildegard von Bingen (1098-1179)

On her forty-second birthday Hildegard was assailed by a fierce headache that worsened as the day wore on. In the evening, a beam of light pierced her vision, and shining meteors that filled space blackened as they struck the ocean. Her eyes were closed and unintelligible sounds escaped her lips. Her novitiates milled around her, physicians were called to her bedside, various herbal compounds were mixed, but all to no avail. Suddenly, an inhuman cry escaped her lips and she lost consciousness.

Tithe

This episode was preceded by weeks of sleeplessness. When she was wide awake she was beset by visions of the kind she had experienced in her parents' home in the village of Bermersheim in Germany. She was the tenth child of the Burggrafs, a well-to-do family in the Rhine Valley. Her parents, Hildebert and Mechthild, named her Hildegard, which in Old High German means "protectress against war".

Hildebert and Mechthild lived their life in accordance with the codes dictated by the Church in its capacity as consoler, protector, and healer. The Church's patrons supported its believers in times of trouble, while the Virgin Mary and the saints protected them against harm and enemies. The Church controlled birth, marriage, sex, eating habits, and death. It made the rules concerning legal and medical matters, and even defined with which subjects philosophy and wisdom would engage. The sinners that strayed from the straight and narrow path laid out by the Church were destined to burn in Hell and suffer torture and agony.[1]

When their tenth child was still in her mother's womb, her parents promised her to the Church as a tithe, a common practice in the Middle Ages aimed at proving devoutness and profound faith. Yet it was not only faith that guided Hildegard's parents, but also practical considerations, the most notable of which was financial and status advantage. By placing some of their offspring into the service of the Church and its monasteries, the parents thus obviated a larger division of the family assets, thus ensuring that the other children would receive a larger portion of the family property, and in the case of daughters, the ones that were sent to a convent gave their siblings a better chance of marrying well. There were also other considerations deriving from concern for children who were physically or mentally different: parents would send a particularly weak or out of the ordinary boy or girl to a monastery to ensure the family's peace of mind. In a monastery, so they believed, the child would be in safe hands and be well cared for in every way – physically, mentally, and financially.

Hildegard's parents promised her to the Church before she was born, but they soon realized that their youngest child was different from other children. She was a tiny, feeble infant, and the older she got the more time she spent in bed complaining of severe headaches and lassitude. Hildegard would later relate that at a very early age, when her bones and nerves were not yet sufficiently strong, she would be taken abed by terrible headaches. Her vision became blurred, she said, and then, in a state of complete wakefulness she would be overwhelmed by a world of sights and visions.[2]

When she was three she went for a walk with her nanny in the fields, where they saw a cow calving. As they watched, the little one told her nanny what color the unborn calf would be, including the color of the patches on its hide. When the calf emerged and the nanny saw that the child had accurately predicted what it would look like, she ran all the way home and told Mechthild the story. The mother smiled, calmed the agitated nanny, and gave her a gold coin. As a result of the prophetic powers attributed to her, many years later Hildegard became known as "the Sibyl of the Rhine Valley".[3]

Asceticism

The girl's poor health spurred Mechthild's decision to give her to the Church. As a nun she would be freed from marriage, childbearing and raising a family, and the monastery would provide for all her needs. After seeking a suitable place for her, her parents decided on the Disibodenberg Monastery, not far from their home. The monastery was named after Disibod, a wandering monk from Ireland who came there in the seventh century and was later canonized, and settled on a mountain overlooking the confluence of the Nahe and Glan rivers.

There, in a cell built adjoining the southern wing of the monastery, in complete seclusion, lived Jutta von Sponheim, the daughter of a noble family of Gallic extraction, who became known throughout Germany because of her personal story. Hildegard's father was in the service of the Count Stephan II of Sponheim, Jutta's father, and the two families were on friendly terms. On her thirteenth birthday Jutta became gravely ill. In her distress she vowed that if she recovered and was able to stand, she would abandon the vanities of the material world and dedicate her life to God. Within a few weeks her prayers were answered and she made a rapid recovery. Her pallor was replaced by rosy cheeks and she was full of life. It seems that once she rose from her sickbed her beauty became striking, and her reputation spread throughout the Rhine Valley. Young suitors came from all over the country to try and win her hand, but Jutta had not forgotten the vow she made when she was sick, and resisted their advances. Now she directed her zeal and love of life toward religious studies, and despite her family's protestations she abandoned the material world and entered the isolated cell from which she did not emerge until her death in 1136. She was joined in her cell by Hildegard.

There is some speculation regarding her age at this time. According to a gilded plaster relief made in 1895 to commemorate her 800th birthday, her noble parents whose attire attests to their wealth, handed over a girl of seven or eight who is splendidly dressed – she is wearing a decorated golden dress with a pink lining and fur-trimmed hem – to a nun with a motherly appearance. Beside them is another small figure holding a bundle with the personal possessions of the anchoress-to-be.

Another version has it that on reaching age eight, Hildegard moved to a regime of tutoring and religious studies on the Sponheim estate, where she remained until she was fourteen. Her governess there was Uda of Gollheim, an educated, aristocratic widow and devout Catholic, who taught her the New and Old Testaments and basic Latin, which enabled her to read classical texts.

When she reached age fourteen she was taken to the monastery by her parents in the company of others. There a ceremony was held in which she took her monastic vows with all the commitments they entailed. A black coif was placed on the altar before which she knelt. Bishop Otto of Bamberg, who conducted the ceremony, blessed her as she rose and slowly approached the altar. The bishop then took the coif from the altar and placed it on the head of the novitiate, while exhorting her to quickly progress along the path of purification and quelling of lust.

At the conclusion of the ceremony Hildegard took her leave of her parents and family, crossed the threshold of Jutta's cell, and the door closed behind her for several decades. The only person allowed to visit the cell was the abbot, and then only when the two women sought to consult him on spiritual matters, or when they needed medical attention. Today a cell and a life of seclusion might be automatically associated with a jail, but it should be borne in mind that many female hermits came from affluent families and lived in these cells in quite comfortable conditions. Some even had servants so that physical discomfort would not divert them from their devotions.[4] Moreover, they were allowed to keep jewelry and, some say, fine clothes and expensive cloth. Many years later Hildegard would face criticism to the effect that she and her nuns enjoyed an excessively high standard of living, which she would rebut, saying that wearing jewelry for worship meant reverence for God.

The cell built specially for Jutta adjoined the south wall of the chapel inside the all-male Benedictine monastery. It was spacious, with one door and two heavily-curtained windows. The larger window was opened at fixed times during the day to allow food to be passed inside and the removal of waste. Once a week visitors from affluent families would come to this window, families whose daughters wished to join the beautiful nun known throughout Germany as a mystical and romantic figure. Jutta would speak to her visitors through the heavy curtain, so they could hear but not see her face. The other window was small and narrow, and through it the nuns could see the chapel altar, hear the prayers offered up eight times a day, and listen to the plainsong.

According to Benedictine rules, the monastery's day was divided into two parts: one for manual labor, and the other, longer period, for devotions. Prayers during the day were shorter than evening prayers. The None service was held while it was still daylight, and Vespers at sunset. Throughout the night monks ensured that prayers were said at the appropriate time.

At three o'clock in the afternoon, with the end of the day's work, Hildegard and Jutta had their first meal of the day, which was passed through the big window. According to

Benedictine monastery custom this was their main and only meal in winter. In summer, on the other hand, they were entitled to two meals, the main one consisting of beans, eggs, fish or cheese, fruit of the season, and bread. Meat was expressly forbidden, except in cases of extreme weakness when the body needed it to survive. Children, the elderly, and the infirm were given a light breakfast of bread and a drink. Meals varied according to the season of the year. On feast days the enclosed women were given a boiled onion and cake instead of beans, and also water.

The attacks Hildegard had experienced in her parents' home recurred in the cell too: fierce headaches, beams of light piercing her vision, and convulsions followed by fainting. One day, on recovering consciousness she confided in Jutta and told her about the visions that had beset her since she was three years old. "From the very day of her birth," she writes of herself, "this woman has lived with painful illnesses as if caught in a net, so that she is constantly tormented by pain in her veins, marrow and flesh. This vision has penetrated the veins of the woman is such a way that she has often collapsed out of exhaustion and has suffered fits of prostration that were at times slight and at other times most serious."[5] Were these visions the result of childish moods in which she daydreamed, or perhaps an optical disorder? Perhaps it was all an unconscious strategy her young psyche employed in order to continue existing? Did her physical sickness enable the little girl to escape from her crowded home into a fantasy world in order to alleviate the fear of abandonment? Neurologist and psychiatrist Oliver Sacks[6] interprets the headaches and the consequent visions as migraines, whereas Charles Singer, a historian of science, technology, and medicine, contends that Hildegard's movement between total dysfunction and sudden, complete functionality indicates a neurological disorder.[7] In normal times Hildegard immersed herself in reading and study, and absorbed the liturgical singing she could hear from the chapel. Jutta taught her everything she could, but her own education was limited and thus she was unable to answer her young charge's many questions, especially about Latin rhetoric.

A Monastery of Her Own

After thirty years together, Jutta passed away on a cold January day in 1136 and was buried by the monastery's main altar. While the enclosed nuns were deep in mourning, the thirty-eight-year-old Hildegard was ready and willing to take up the mantle of leadership. The plan she formulated in her mind was to disengage from the male monastery and establish one exclusively for nuns. Abbot Kuno vehemently opposed her idea, which meant losing the handsome income from the nuns' families, but the young nun persisted. She enlisted her contacts with the nuns' families, most notably Archduchess von Stade, mother of Richardis who would become her personal assistant and confidante.

The pressure they exerted on the abbot did its work, and the resolute Hildegard was granted permission to leave the monastery and look for suitable land. This took years, in the course of which she raised funds, purchased land in Rupertsberg, an isolated mountainside location some thirty kilometers from Disibodenberg, played an active role in planning the new monastery and its budget, and even personally supervised the building work.

In 1152, together with twenty nuns and two servants, she moved to their new home in Rupertsberg. In the evenings she would sit with her "girls" and compare her happiness with how an infant felt after feeding from its mother's breast.[8] Did she have some faint memory of her infanthood?

We do not know. In all her writings there is no mention of her childhood feelings in her parents' home nor of the moment she parted from them when she crossed the threshold of Jutta's cell. But when she dictated her memoirs to her personal secretary, the monk Volmar, she told him that her parents had vowed to dedicate her to the Church with a painful sigh. Was this the rationalization of an adult woman who, from the time of her earliest memories, had known that her parents had decided to give her to the Church as a tithe? There can be no doubt that she was aware of the possibility of breaking a vow such as this by making an offering to the Church in exchange for which the parents could keep the child at home. She apparently kept her personal pain locked away, but in *Scivias* (Know the Ways of the Lord), her first major theological work which she wrote later, she specifically states that children should be asked if they consent to dedicating their life to the Church, and if they say no, they should not be forced to do so.

Compulsion and Creation

Hildegard's assertiveness was manifested in her every action. She ran the monastery with an iron hand, delegated responsibility, and heightened motivation to improve it and increase its income, while fostering mutual respect and loyalty among the nuns. On weekdays the nuns held workshops where they copied books, wove, embroidered, and sewed, while some tended the garden. On feast days they would gather in the cloister, sit quietly and practice reading and singing. Hildegard functioned as both a spiritual and administrative figure. She displayed generosity and conviviality towards them all, dispensed advice, resolved problems, instructed on various matters, and guided anyone she felt had sinned back into the fold.

But all this did not fulfill her. Creativity burned in her very bones and gave her no peace. She wanted to share with the world the music, songs, and the many ideas that filled her, but she was conscious of her own limited education. When she compared her writing and oratorical abilities with those of learned men she was assailed by anxiety, a cold sweat broke out over her body, in her ears her heartbeat sounded like an unchecked galloping horse, and she was beset by a feeling of imminent fainting. The pressure in her head increased, and she would awaken in the morning with a severe headache, her neck and arms stiff, and she had difficulty getting out of bed.

Know the Ways of the Lord

As Hildegard passed her forty-second birthday she again experienced visions with a vengeance, the headaches became more intense, and she was more or less paralyzed. The nuns fluttered around her bed in an effort to ease her pain, but in vain. Then one day a miracle occurred. After many weeks of suffering, she suddenly rose from her sickbed and went back to her daily work as if nothing had happened. To her fellow nuns she related that a beam of light that blinded her brain and warmed her heart had brought her a message from God: she must share with the world the cosmic-mystical knowledge she had been given.

Hildegard related the visions she experienced to Volmar, her confidant from Disibodenberg and the Rupertsberg nuns' father confessor. He urged her to document her visions, and together with her personal assistant Richardis von Stade, assisted her with the writing.

Over a period of five years she dictated her first great work, *Scivias*. Today *Scivias* is defined as "the complete guide to Christian doctrine",[9] and consists of three volumes spanning a wide range of subjects which are all based on Hildegard's visions, with her own interpretation of them. The last volume, *Ordo Virtutum* (Order of the Virtues), is a musical drama in which the writer voices clear views on family values and upholding a conservative Christian way of life. This includes sexual intercourse solely for having children in accordance with the Adam and Eve model, proscription of intercourse during pregnancy and menstruation, and of infidelity and not being given absolution for committing it. In Hildegard's view, in order to atone for infidelity the couple must either join a monastery or send their children to a life of abstinence and chastity. She also advised widows to espouse abstinence. In the course of their work on the first volume of the three, something happened between Hildegard and her personal assistant, which led to a grave crisis and Richardis leaving the monastery. With the help of her brother the archbishop, Richardis moved to the monastery at Birsim (today, Bassum), a long way from Rupertsberg. What transpired between the two women remains a mystery, but Hildegard was beside herself when the nun she loved so deeply left the monastery. She begged her to stay, and even wrote to Richardis's mother, Archduchess von Stade, who had helped her in the past, to her brother, and even the Pope himself, pleading with them to help her change Richardis's mind, but in vain. In her grief she also wrote to Richardis: "...my grief flies up to heaven. My sorrow is destroying the great confidence and consolation that I once had in mankind," and she goes on: "I so loved the nobility of your character, your wisdom, your chastity, your spirit, and indeed every aspect of your life that many people have said to me: What are you doing?"[10] In her letters she admitted that she had erred by crossing the line with her love for the noble woman, and was convinced that the beloved nun's leaving her was God's way of showing her that she had sinned. "Why have you forsaken me like an orphan?" she asks in a letter to her former protégé. In her despair she was not to know that Richardis, too, was suffering great longing, and a year later would suddenly fall ill. After her death, Hildegard received a letter from Richardis's brother, the archbishop of Bremen, who told her that from her sickbed his sister had confessed that she yearned for Hildegard and her monastery, that she was unable to remain far from her, and that she intended to go back there. But before she was able to fulfill her wish, she fell ill and died.

Hildegard did not reveal her personal feelings over her beloved friend's death, but completely immersed herself in the work she intended to publish, so that the whole world would come to know her ideas. Before she completed *Scivias* she sent a letter to Bernard of Clairvaux, one of the authoritative figures in the Church hierarchy in Europe. She told him of her visions, while moving with virtuosity between a display of feminine weakness bordering on self-effacement, and praise of a man in a high position in the religious-political establishment.

Sun, Moon

"Venerable father Bernard," she wrote, "I lay my claim before you, for, highly honored by God, you bring fear to the immoral foolishness of this world and, in your intense zeal and burning love for the Son of God." This was at the time of Germany's defeat in Turkish territory in the Second Crusade, and Hildegard, who was well-versed in politics, reminded him of his great power and how much she, a seemingly weak woman, needed him as a spiritual protector. "[You who] gather men into Christ's army to fight under the banner of the cross against pagan savagery. I beseech you in the name of the Living God to give heed to my queries."[11]

She went on to tell him that two years previously he had appeared in one of her visions, "I saw you in a vision, like a man looking straight into the sun, bold and unafraid. And I wept, because I myself am so timid and fearful." Once she had prepared the emotional ground, she told him of the burning flame descending from on high and teaching her the profundities of the Holy Scriptures. She described how, when in her sickbed, she heard the voice of God revealed in her vision as a monstrous worm whose body is made of five differently-colored sections, all of them poisonous: green, white, red, yellow and black. This creature, whose colors symbolize the senses of Man which are attracted to sin and licentiousness, is the alter ego of the Serpent in the Garden of Eden. Like the Serpent, the creature lies in wait for the believer and diverts him from the straight and narrow path.

Bernard read this missive and shuddered. Whereas the writings of men in the service of the Church and the monasteries were based on the works of their predecessors, Hildegard was now claiming that the authority guiding her was none other than God himself. He was no less impressed by her humility, piety, and political eruditeness, and he replied in a short letter encouraging her to continue writing. In 1148, while still working on *Scivias*, Hildegard's work was brought to the attention of Pope Eugene III who appointed a commission to decide whether or not her visions were indeed inspired by the Holy Spirit. The commission visited the monastery, and after reporting that the visions were indeed divinely inspired, the Pope declared her a prophetess and visionary. In fact, Hildegard was the first woman to gain the approval of Christianity's highest authority to write theological works.

After receiving the Pope's blessing she quickly became a sought-after counselor, preacher, and charismatic speaker who appeared before mixed audiences. Her sermons were attended by men and women from the entire social and intellectual spectrum, and kings, nobles, diplomats, and leading figures in the Catholic establishment waited to meet her. At a time when women were not allowed to stand on a platform and address an audience, Hildegard's voice was heard through every means available at the time, from correspondence with the high social echelons, artistic writing and its publication, to travels in which she voiced harsh criticism of both secular and religious Christian society, and their moral values.

In the sermons she delivered on her travels, she knew her audience and spoke accordingly. She would begin by introducing herself as a little, sickly woman, lacking both courage and education, whose only vocation was to serve as a conduit for conveying messages from God to the faithful. She described a wind that passed over Rupertsberg that carried her, a tiny, powerless feather, to convey the Divine Word. By turning the subject into a spiritual-religious one, she made the world around her take her seriously.

Wherever she went, Hildegard was given a warm and loving welcome as befitted a spiritual mother, even though her sermons were critical and sometimes conveyed an apocalyptic vision. At a convocation at Trier Cathedral she warned that the city would be obliterated like Nineveh because of the irresponsible deeds of its priests. She announced to the bishops that she would pray for the city's salvation through love of the Holy Spirit, but added that she harbored doubts about it. To her audience she reiterated that the vision of the monstrous worm was revealed to her so she could present it to them and warn them lest they stray from the straight and narrow path. It was in Cologne that she delivered her famous sermon in which she berated the city fathers who had abandoned their flock, leading them to follow a false cult that opposed the Catholic priesthood and Church.

Sacred Technology

Hildegard did not stop at sermons and the letters she dispatched from Rupertsberg. For her nuns she wrote texts and music aimed at increasing their self-confidence in the role they had taken upon themselves, and at strengthening their ties to the monastery. In some of these works the Church appears as a beautiful woman imbued with power, whereas the monastery is depicted as a particularly striking building in Jerusalem.

For Hildegard, music was not only the highest form of worship, but also a technique for guiding the human mind and heart and for bringing Man back to stand firmly on the ground. According to her, we lose our way on the path to perfect balance several times a day. Singing and playing an instrument help us to unify body and soul, and it is this unification that is the secret of harmony in human existence. It was in this context that she wrote the *Symphonia Armonie Celestium Revelationum* – a collection of seventy-seven chants whose texts are based on verses from the Old and New Testaments. Some of them are songs of praise to local saints, while others engage with questions of modesty, obedience, and chastity.

Although she claimed never to have been given a musical education, Hildegard's composition is characterized by some unique elements, one of which is a recurring motif that appears in all her works, and which is in fact her musical signature.[12]

Causae et Curae

But Hildegard was not solely occupied with music. She also wrote on science and medicine, and did not shy away from subjects considered taboo, such as sexuality from the woman's viewpoint, including female orgasm. "When a woman is making love with a man," she wrote, "a sense of heat in her brain, which brings forth with it sensual delight, communicates the taste of that delight during the act and summons forth the emission of the man's seed. And when the seed has fallen into its place, that vehement heat descending from her brain draws the seed to itself and holds it, and soon the woman's sexual organs contract, and all the parts that are ready to open up during the time of menstruation now close, in the same way as a strong man can hold something enclosed in his fist."[13]

Her male audiences did not escape her sometimes scathing criticism, and she voiced her opinion on gender issues employing metaphors from the world of flora. The man, she said, possesses greater physical strength than the woman, but his spirit is like a tree from which human murderers and the bearers of evil into the world emerge. This tree is dried up, and it is this that has made the world a dangerous place ruled by male power, which spreads danger, fear, injustice, and cruelty. The woman's spirit, on the other hand, stretches between heaven and earth, its face is suffused with light, its eyes are like the hyacinth, its dress silken, and it wears a velvet mantle inlaid with rubies like the mantle worn by a bishop. The woman who inhabits the entire universe and wears a garment signifying male hegemony is part of Hildegard's strategy to intensify the feminine image.

Like the dramas, poetry, and music she wrote, her writings on scientific subjects were originally aimed at her nuns. However, her work quickly gained a reputation outside the monastery, and she received many requests for help from travelers who stopped at Rupertsberg seeking her advice. Her two medical works reflect an extraordinary level of observation, which today would be called holistic medicine. In her *Physica* she describes and identifies over two hundred medicinal herbs and plants, as well as the characteristics of birds, fishes, mammals, trees, metals, and precious stones. The second of these books, *Causae et Curae*, discusses the cause and treatment of illnesses, and is based on her own experience with medicinal herbs and plants. She reviews the symptoms of more than two hundred illnesses, including leprosy, psoriasis, acne, and allergies, and suggests possible treatment for a complete cure. She also suggests ways of treating lice, scalds and burns, and hair loss in young men. The various curative herbs she used and were later proved to have anti-inflammatory and antibiotic qualities, appear in the recipes she shared with her readers.

Over the years the Rupertsberg monastery flourished economically, and in 1165 Hildegard founded another smaller one in Eibingen, a verdant region on the banks of the Rhine and near Rudesheim, a UNESCO World Heritage Site. Today the monastery is known as "The Benedictine Abbey of St. Hildegard". In her final years Hildegard found herself in conflict with the Church authorities. She agreed to bury in the abbey graveyard a young man whom the Church had decided to excommunicate because he had refused to confess on his deathbed. To explain her position she met with her superiors, stubbornly insisted that she had clear proof that the young man had been given absolution, but to no avail. She returned home, went to the young man's grave, and despite his excommunication, blessed it. Together with her senior nuns she swept away any sign of a grave to prevent discovery of the body. Consequently, she and her nuns were punished and were forbidden to celebrate Mass and say their daily prayers aloud, including the accompanying chants. In a letter to her superiors in Mainz, Hildegard demanded that their right to pray and sing at prayer be restored, and eloquently explained the significance of music in religious devotions. She did not stop there, and made it clear to her superiors that she doubted the sincerity of their intentions in silencing them. Moreover, she even adopted a threatening tone, saying that anyone attempting to silence praise of God would find themselves in the place without music, the place where Satan dwells.

Hildegard passed away in Rupertsberg on 17 September 1179, at the age of eighty-two, and was buried in the Eibingen abbey. Reports of the miracles she worked continued even after her death.

Two
La Cecchina – The Songbird:
Francesca Caccini
(1587-1638)

She held a prestigious position with the de' Medicis, and of all the court musicians her remuneration was the highest. Her music so enchanted her audiences that even heated political arguments were stilled when she began to sing and play. Before concluding her service in the de' Medici court, she asked the poet and librettist Andrea Salvadori to write a libretto for her, but he refused and wrote satirical poems about her instead. The bad relations between them began as a consequence of her claim that he harassed her singers, and in retaliation he wrote the misogynistic poem "Donne musiche parlano dall'Inferno" (Women musicians speak from Hell).

A Secular Love Song

Francesca Caccini was born in September 1587, the first daughter of a musical family. Her mother, Lucia Gagnolanti, was a soprano and music teacher, and her father, Giulio Caccini, was a well-known singer and composer, an admired teacher, and a gifted player of several instruments. He was a central member of the *Florentine Camerata*, a group of intellectuals and nobles whose number included professional and amateur musicians, composers, and music theoreticians, who gathered at the home of Count Giovanni de' Bardi to discuss matters of culture, science, and current affairs. The main thrust of these discussions was the consolidation of a new musical style that would be close to the music of ancient Greek drama. Francesca grew up within the new style dictated by the Camerata, at the center of which was solo voice with accompaniment aimed at expressing the content of the libretto and its changing atmosphere. When she was four years old her sister Settimia was born, and a year later their mother passed away. Their father quickly remarried, his second wife also being a musician, and life in the Caccini household continued from the point at which it had stopped with Lucia's death. Francesca was a highly intelligent girl with a great thirst for knowledge, but like other girls of her time she was not allowed to attend a public school. Nonetheless, she was the only one of the ten children born to her father from three different wives who was given a basic humanistic education. She learned to read and write on her own, as well as grammar, rhetoric, Latin, and some Greek. She possessed an impressive ability to improvise music for poetry originally written in Latin, Italian, French, Spanish, and German. Additionally, she was interested in mathematics, astrology, and philosophy, but as a young girl in a hegemonic society she was unable to further develop her knowledge in these spheres.

As a young woman who grew up in court culture, Francesca traveled a great deal with her family throughout Italy and Europe to participate in betrothal, wedding, birth, and funeral ceremonies, and other events held by the ruling class. On 6 October 1600, when she was thirteen, she appeared with her stepmother Margherita and her sister Settimia in a grand production of the opera *Euridice*, at whose center is the love story of a beautiful nymph and Orpheus, the musician whose playing mesmerized the entire universe. Her father Giulio was in charge of the production celebrating the marriage of Maria de' Medici and Henry IV of France. This was the second opera staged in Florence and first performed in Palazzo Pitti. The intensive performance schedule demanded of Francesca was exhausting. Three days later she sang a leading role in the opera *Il Rapimento di Cefalo* (The Abduction of Cephalus) to her father's music, which was staged at Palazzo degli Uffizi before an invited audience of hundreds.

In 1604 the family traveled to Paris, where the women appeared as a family ensemble called "The Daughters of Giulio Romano" (since Giulio hailed from Rome). When they played before Henry IV, the king was so amazed by Francesca that he offered her a position in his court. As was customary at the time, her father conducted the negotiations, and it was he who received her salary and transferred it to his household account.

The de' Medicis were renowned for their grand balls and grandiose theatrical performances, between whose different parts *Intermedi* (Interludes) were performed, allegorical scenes from mythology which included music, songs, dances, costumes, sets, and choreography. This genre was so loved by them that it became a dazzling production in its own right. At an event marking the marriage of Cosimo de' Medici and Archduchess Maria Maddalena of Austria, the librettist, a producer, a choreographer, and five famous composers, including Francesca, collaborated. The performance, which was staged at Palazzo Pitti, was attended by guests who ascended a spiral staircase connecting the stage with the auditorium. In the center of the auditorium the open space for dancing was filled with male and female dancers who, at the end of their performance, stood on the dance floor in a choreographed arrangement of the names of Cosimo and Maria Maddalena.

The evening continued with a spectacular performance that included choreographic inventions, extravagant costumes, choruses of mythological figures, and spectacular theatrical effects that enthralled the audience. The opening scene showed the harbor of Porto-Veccio, which was of great importance to the de' Medicis. Silver paint, corals, and seashells all helped to create a perfect illusion, and the composer Jacopo Peri, who played Neptune, emerged from the sea with blue hair and a crown of pearls. The Tuscans were overjoyed when Neptune sang the aria in praise of their region. Sirens and tritons emerged from the sea and formed a chorus that sang a canzona, a love song in honor of the bride and groom; nymphs sitting astride dolphins lifted their tails from the water. Meanwhile, behind the scenes the three women composers who also played nymphs, got ready. The sea filled up with ships and the three nymphs came onstage to sing three madrigals, each of which was composed by its singer. At the end of the performance they all sang a piece by Francesca Caccini, at the conclusion of which they descended into the auditorium and distributed to the seated ladies gifts concealed in silvered shells[1]

La Stiava (The Maidservant)

When the de' Medicis offered Giulio's daughter a well-paid position, he was only too happy to oblige. But Francesca was single, and her new patrons preferred married court musicians (of the fourteen women composers employed by the de' Medicis over two hundred years, at least eleven were married). Consequently, Christina de Lorraine, Grand Duchess of Tuscany, arranged Francesca's marriage to court musician Giovanni Battista Signorini. The betrothal document was signed by the two men – Giulio who viewed his daughter's virtuosity as his personal property, and the impoverished and ambitionless Signorini who was indebted to the Grand Duchess for finding him a talented, educated wife who would improve his financial standing. On 4 November 1607, the marriage was consecrated in the bride's home, and a week later the dowry was transferred to Signorini.

That same year Francesca composed her first work for the stage. *La Stiava* (The Maidservant), was written to lyrical texts by a family friend and court poet Michelangelo Buonarotti, and was for castrati voices. The person responsible for the de' Medici court journal described the music as "amazing" and "tremendous". Giulio Caccini's letters document how Francesca worked: First she sang the lyrical text, then she wrote the music, and finally asked her father to go over the work and revise it as he deemed fit.[2]

Io veggio i campi verdeggiar fecondi (I see the fertile fields turn green)

Francesca was in the service of Christina de Lorraine, Grand Duchess of Tuscany, a well-known patroness of the arts, for twenty years. The duchess resided in her husband Ferdinand II's palace outside the city, and there, far from hectic political life, she awaited his visits and raised his eight children.[3] With her daughter-in-law Maria Maddalena of Austria, she ran the world of the de' Medici women, caring for orphans, widows, and women in unhappy marriages, but she would also harshly criticize anyone who disobeyed her. She was an undisputed ruler who conducted negotiations on matches, even on the marital problems of the women who lived under her aegis, and she understood her power and her commitment to live in accordance with social conventions, even if they frequently clashed with her personal wishes.[4]

Francesca provided the services of a virtuosa musician and composer. She sang in church and at the concerts held in the palace's halls, improvised and produced plays, composed new pieces, and conducted rehearsals, playing various instruments including the lute, harpsichord, and any other string instrument required for her performances. Apart from the music lessons she gave to the royal children, she also taught composition to girls and young women, thus inculcating the *stile nuovo* (new style). Her daily schedule was overloaded, and despite her undisputed professionalism she was regarded as just another one of the royal family's servants. She was sometimes summoned without warning to play for one royal personage or another, and in some cases she was forced to wait for hours, sometimes days, even in the harsh winter. As the court musician and musical director she was sometimes called upon to critique the first, non-professional pieces written for amusement. She also had to teach people totally unskilled in music, which went against her grain. It is said that she once shouted at and hit one of her pupils because she did not learn her part in the time she was given.

Non sò se quel sorriso (I don't know if that smile)

Francesca did not live in the palace but in the city, in a large house with an inner courtyard that was her and her husband's only property. As a woman born into a patriarchal society it was she who managed the household, ordered food and clothing, and was in charge of and supervised the servants. She also kept track of the household's income and expenses, gifts, jewelry, and wages, whereas it was her husband who managed financial affairs requiring contact with external bodies such as banks, notaries, and government offices. Their house, which was situated in an area populated by affluent artists, was also her workplace. It was crowded with musical instruments: a harpsichord she had inherited from her father, a double lyre in a leather case, a bass flute, and sordellinas. There was also a music library which housed copies of her works and printed manuscripts of her own and of others, and she used them constantly, both to learn from them and for teaching her students. It was there that she composed and received mail several times a day. Messengers would often have to wait to take her to whoever had commissioned a work until she completed it. In the mail she also received information on rehearsals, costumes, and the progress made by her students for various performances. Her work called for constant negotiations which usually took place in the city, and she either walked or rode in a horse-drawn carriage to teach or perform in Palazzo Pitti or at the imperial villa across the Arno.

The court formed a sort of additional family framework, and Francesca moved between it and her own home in the course of her daily work during which she composed music in commercial quantities. On top of this she accepted invitations from other Italian courts, and thus she traveled to Pisa to present her works to Ferdinando Gonzaga, later Duke of Mantua. Gonzaga hoped to hire her services, but she speedily returned to Florence to appear in the spectacular performance at Cosimo de' Medici's wedding. In her late thirties Francesca was credited with a large collection of songs, and on 17 November 1614 her salary was significantly increased, making her the highest earner in the Florentine court. The high salary was given to her for her works, but no less for being a leading teacher with a clear pedagogical approach to both composition and improvisation.

Apart from being impressive musical pieces, her songs were also exercises in the art of improvisation, and they included breathing control, coordination between hands, voice, and melody, and their combination. Francesca was renowned for her ability to perfectly combine all these techniques. Her music and the way she performed it swept her audiences up to sublime spiritual spheres, hearts changed the order of their love on hearing her singing and playing, and moods swung in accordance with the changing colors of her music.

Lasciatemi qui solo (Leave Me Be)

In contrast with the sublime music she composed, according to biographical evidence written by one of her court colleagues, Francesca Caccini was a productive but talkative woman lacking both personal charm and aristocratic manners. She demanded perfection from her students, and was wont to fly into a rage when work was not ready on time or was not pleasing to her discerning ear. Toward the end of her service in the de' Medici court she asked the poet Andrea Salvadori to write a libretto for her, but he refused and wrote satirical poems about her instead. The bad relations between them began when she criticized him for choosing his singers according to his intimate relations with them. She thought that he harassed them, and in retaliation he wrote the misogynistic poem "Donne musiche parlano dall'Inferno" (Women musicians speak from Hell) which was performed at the court as part of the 1621 Epiphany celebrations.[5] As a result Francesca bore a grudge and waited for her chance for revenge, which only came four years later when Salvadori was working on an opera for Margherita de' Medici's wedding. She took her revenge by convincing Margherita and her mother, Grand Duchess Maria Maddalena, that the subject of the opera might be interpreted as reflecting Margherita's desire to control her new husband. Salvadori thus had to write a new libretto at very short notice.[6]

In August 1618, the year her father died, Francesca Caccini's first book of music, *Il Primo Libro delle Musiche,* was published. It was dedicated to Cardinal Carlo de' Medici, and was the biggest compilation in the new style that had appeared so far. It is a collection of thirty-two short pieces for solo voice, or two voices accompanied by basso continuo, a harmonious instrument that plays the bass line and chords. The works were coded by the composer by the first line of each song and classified by form.[7] In addition to the music, this unique collection also contains the libretti (with the exception of three works) written by Francesca herself.

Women, Men, and Sorcery

On 9 February 1622, and after fifteen years of marriage, Francesca and Signorini's only daughter was born. She was christened Margherita the following day, and we know that like her mother and grandmother she was a singer, but unlike them she chose to become a nun. From that year onward the composer signed her letters "Francesca Signorini Malaspina", the double-barreled surname her husband had used since 1619. The reason behind this signature is unclear, but it was perhaps aimed at preserving the unity of the family name; perhaps it stemmed from a desire to glorify in the ancient Roman lineage connected with the D'este family, and perhaps it was the birth of her daughter that spurred Francesca to sever her ties with her father's name and image.

While Margherita was growing up, her mother continued her intensive work and reached the peak of her creativity with the opera-ballet, *La Liberazione di Ruggiero dall'Isola d'Alcina* (The Liberation of Ruggiero from the Island of Alcina).[8] Of the five operas she wrote and called "balletos", only this one remains.[9] It was first performed in Florence in 1625 and was dedicated to the woman who commissioned it, Grand Duchess Maria Maddalena. It was commissioned for a special carnival whose objective was to make a match between her daughter Margherita and her cousin, Crown Prince Wladislaw Sigismund of Poland.

In Florence the opera gained great acclaim from some, and opprobrium from others. There were those who compared Francesca to the renowned Claudio Monteverdi whose work was considered revolutionary and marked the transition from Renaissance to Baroque, while others lambasted the work. At the end of the carnival the proposed match came to naught, but we are left with significant pieces of this work, which contains social criticism of the monarchic-patriarchal world in which Francesca Caccini lived, a world ruled by men, a world in which two sorceresses, Alcina and Melissa – one a good androgynous character, and the other an evil sexual one – fight for the heart of Ruggiero, who is supposed to rule by logic, knowledge, and intelligence – his manly powers which will save him from the dark forces of sensuality and emotion. To sway Ruggiero, Melissa dons men's clothes and assumes a role that is completely inappropriate to her nature. Only this way is she able to come close to his rational world and triumph through lies and deceit, whereas Alcina is defeated due to her overly feminine love and emotions.

Feminine Identity in the Mirror of Bereavement

On 29 December 1626 Signorini died after passing a black kidney stone the size of an egg. After her husband's death, the thirty-nine-year-old Francesca's life changed. According to the laws of Florence, her first obligation was to take care of all her husband's funeral arrangements, including, shaving and washing the body, removal of the coffin, and organizing a group of women mourners from his family. At the center of the latter's keening stood the widow's sexual abstinence. But if that was not enough, Florentine law also stipulated that the widow must shave her head so that the whole world can see that she is asexual. Furthermore, immediately after the funeral she had to decide whether she would continue living with her husband's family together with her daughter, or return to her own family, or whether she wanted to remarry and thus forego her children by her late husband. Francesca felt that there was nobody to take care of her interests, but she resolved not to give up her only daughter, Margherita. She wanted full custody of her. Now her years as part of the de' Medici court came to her aid, and Grand Duchess Christina de Lorraine ensured that Francesca was given custody of the child instead of her late husband's family. Ten months after her husband's death Francesca remarried, this time to Tomaso Raffaelli, a wealthy nobleman and amateur musician from Lucca at the foot of the Apennines. She bore him a son who was named Tomaso after his father. The family lived well and happily for only a short time, for in April 1630 Tomaso senior passed away and the forty-three-year-old Francesca was widowed for the second time.

Three months later, on 15 June, plague broke out in Lucca and Francesca was unable to leave the city. By August 1631 8,000 souls had perished and public life moved into private homes where the women stood in the windows praying for their families. In 1634, after three years of sequestration, Francesca and her children – eleven-year-old Margherita Signorini and five-year-old Tomaso Raffaelli – returned to Florence, and although they did not live in the palace they were involved in the women's coterie that centered round Christina de Lorraine.

The end of Francesca Caccini's life is shrouded in mist. We know that in 1643 her name disappeared from the documents of the three communities in which she lived (Rome, Lucca, and Florence), and that in February 1645 she was no longer her son Tomaso's legal guardian. Perhaps by then she was no longer alive, perhaps she remarried, and perhaps she continued to live privately, devoting herself to the studies she had dreamed of in her youth.

Three
His Chosen Daughter:
Barbara Strozzi
(1619-1667)

The above portrait, "The Viola da Gamba Player" is
apparently of composer, singer, and lutist, Barbara Strozzi.
The portrait, which currently hangs in the Dresden
Gemäldegalerie, was commissioned by Giulio Strozzi and
painted by Bernardo Strozzi, who despite having the same
surname was no relation. The woman's very revealing dress

and the flower in her hair are an allusion to Flora, the Roman goddess of flowers, a symbol both of fertility and a courtesan. Like the Roman Flora, the commonly held assumption is that Barbara Strozzi, too, was a courtesan, the dictionary definition of which is a prostitute, especially one with wealthy or upper-class clients.

His Chosen Daughter

There were two types of courtesan, each according to their social status: those born into either noble or grand-bourgeois families, and those of a lower class. The grand-bourgeois courtesans were involved in glamorous, sophisticated, and charismatic activity. They were celebrities, companions of kings and emperors, government and treasury officials, writers and painters, and were consequently the subject of gossip about where they were seen, what they wore, and what they talked about. They were usually not faithful to only one man, and it was perfectly acceptable for them to have several lovers who contributed to their upkeep. Their relations with one or more benefactors were not a single episode, but an open and long-lasting relationship. The men proudly presented them to all and sundry, and they accompanied the men to public places: coffee houses, eating houses, balls, the opera, and even entertained the men's friends in their homes. They frequently received gifts of apartments, estates, even palaces, as well as expensive fashionable furniture, porcelain tableware, jewelry, a regular allowance, and as we shall see, living arrangements for their children born out of wedlock.

According to the records of Santa Sofia Church in Venice, Barbara Strozzi was born to Isabella Garzoni and an unknown father. The story behind her birth is that she was the illegitimate daughter of Giulio Strozzi and his

housekeeper. Giulio, one of Venice's most eminent savants –
a poet, dramaturge, and librettist who wrote the libretti for
numerous operas staged in the city in the 1630s and 40s –
never publicly declared that Barbara was indeed his
daughter. Nonetheless he informally adopted her, called her
"my chosen daughter", and bestowed his family's name on
her.

In Venice's narrow streets, where the balconies almost
touched one another, everybody knew that the infant lived
with parents who had never married. Illegitimate children in
Italy's city-states were often perceived as children of sin, and
although they had no part in the decision to be born, they
themselves were considered sinners. Some fathers
abandoned their illegitimate children, whereas others chose
to embrace them and raise them under their own name.

This was what Giulio Strozzi did. He made sure that Barbara
was given the best possible education, like that of the
daughters of noblemen. It appears, however, that her mother
Isabella played a significant part in the discussions and
decisions regarding the girl's education. The three of them
living together for so many years coupled with the fact that
nothing is known of Giulio having relationship with other
women – like many of his friends – suggests that the Strozzi
family unit worked well.

When Barbara was still quite young it was clear to Isabella
and Giulio that their daughter, who sang and played several
instruments, possessed extraordinary musical talents, but as
far as her early childhood goes, very little is known. In 1635,
when she was sixteen, her father organized a concert at their
home to which he invited musicians and critics to hear her.
The concert was a huge success and the happy father, who
was no stranger to celebrity life in Venice, approached the
Italian composer and organist, Nicolò Fontei, with a

proposal that they collaborate on writing songs for Barbara. This proposal yielded two volumes of songs.

When Barbara reached eighteen, her father founded a private academy, *Accademia degli Unisoni* (Academy of the Like-Minded). This institution's main objective was to serve as a musical and social stage for Barbara. At this point in her life she was a beautiful and charismatic young woman, a talented conversationalist with a broad education, well-versed in literature, history, and the arts. In the academy she was able to appear as a singer and instrumentalist with works she had composed, and also to meet influential men and make use of their connections to advance herself in Venetian society.

Privately-founded academies outside the universities were common in Italy since the fifteenth century. They were actually groups of male intellectuals, each of which was organized under the aegis of a patron who funded it. They engaged in a wide range of subjects, from music, literature, poetry and theatre, through architecture, languages, history and archeology, to hunting, equestrianism, and martial arts. The academy founded by Giulio in their Venice home was, to a great degree, a musical subgroup of another renowned Venetian academy, *Accademia degli Incogniti* (Academy of the Unknowns) whose name, as mentioned above, derived from the fact that its members – all men – wrote in a secret language and published their works anonymously. Among them were philosophers, writers, historians, and clerics, and in fact any self-respecting Venetian viewed it an honor to be among their number. Barbara frequently sang before them, and was also a hostess considered a talisman by the men who attended. But despite her connections, and since she was a woman, she was never accepted as an official member of this august body.

A Woman Comes of Age

By contrast, at the *Accademia degli Unisoni* she was the leading light. Giulio was in charge of the academy's public relations, while Barbara managed the events held there and was responsible for their content. It was she who drew up the agenda for the various meetings, and at the end of the discussions it was she who decided which subject was worthy of appreciation. The main topic discussed at her academy was love: the connection between love and its attendant pain, the polarized relations that swing between weeping and tears on the one hand, and poetry and the music written for it on the other. She concluded one of the musical soirées at the academy by saying to the all-male audience: "I do not question your decision, gentlemen, in favor of song; for well I know that I would not have received the honor of your presence at our last session had I invited you to see me cry and not to hear me sing."[1]   With this blunt statement Barbara publicly revealed the limitations imposed upon her as a woman engaged in a "male" profession. But aside from the gender issue, Barbara's remarks raise questions about her own life. Were tears and pain merely aesthetic means to express passion in a musical piece? Or were they part of her personal life? And if so.did she suffer heartbreak as a result of unrequited love?

A Golden Oak

Seven years after the opening of *Accademia degli Unisoni*, Strozzi's first book of madrigals, *Il Primo Libro de' Madrigali* was published. The composer dedicated it to Vittoria della Rovere, Grand Duchess of Tuscany, and on 12 October 1644 she writes to her benefactress:

Most Serene Highness,

I have so frequently received such affectionate aid through the generosity of one scholar-vassal of Your Highness in guiding me to the use of these, and of other most harmonious compositions. Therefore I must reverently consecrate this first opus, which I, as a woman, too rashly bring to the light, to the most august Name of Your Highness, in order that under an oak tree of gold it rests protected from the lightning bolts of slanders prepared for it.

The choice of the lyric verses will help me somewhat, which are all trifles of he who from my girlhood has given me his name and material comfort. These will relieve the boredom of anyone who does not remain entirely pleased with the poor harmonies of my songs.

But favored by the protection of Your Highness, I flatter myself to believe that you will harbor none who vilify these, my works, if they come to be seen in those royal hands, and to be heard by those most discerning ears, that never do other than hear with Heroic kindness when receiving others' devotion. In this regard I profess myself not last in the line of affection, I am not inferior to any who revere the great worth of Your Highness.

Thus, bowing deeply, I pray for the sublime privileges of the divine wisdom of Your Highness, each additional one a more suitable bliss.

Your Most Humble and Devoted Servant,

Barbara Strozzi[2]

The uniqueness of this dedication is in its direct woman-to-woman approach as a sort of declaration of an alliance at a time when women's artistic works were considered inferior to men's. Barbara's gender-rhetorical strategy in the dedication is ambivalent. On the one hand she is defending herself in advance lest her work not be well received because it was composed by a woman, while on the other she declares that her professional abilities are not inferior to those of other composers. The golden oak beneath which she lays her musical offering is a symbol of sturdiness and courage – hers perhaps, perhaps the duchess's, and perhaps of them both. Like Hildegard of Bingen before her and other women composers who came after her, she lauds the sublime wisdom of her patroness that will truthfully guide her in discerning the professional quality dedicated to her. And if that is not enough, she cites the authority of an eminent man, noting that the texts are her father's, and that her composition teacher is the singer and organist Francesco Cavalli, one of Venice's leading composers at the time.

If You Loved Me

In 1644, the year her book of madrigals was published, Strozzi gave birth to her daughter Laura. The father's name is not documented, and we know that she never married. Conventional wisdom holds that like her older brother Giulio Pietro who was born three years earlier, and Barbara's middle daughter Isabella who was born in 1642, Laura was the fruit of the composer's long-lasting relationship with Giovanni Paolo Vidman, a close friend of her father's who was many years older than her, and a married man with children.[3]

Barbara raised her children on her own in a house in Corte del Remer that belonged to the Vidman family. In the course of the years in which she gave birth to her children, Barbara published no new works but after seven years went back to working intensively, which yielded three volumes of

Cantatas that were enthusiastically received.[4] Their uniqueness is in the new monody style – solo voice with instrumental accompaniment[5] that emulates and stresses the natural inflections of speech and underscores the meaning of the word. The texts she chose deal with the suffering and sorrow resulting from unrequited love:

> *Sleep, sleep, o my sorrow,*
> *slumber, o my suffering,*
> *hold back sighs and laments,*
> *repose in a quiet heart.*
> *Be at peace, o hopes,*
> *Still yourselves, o desires,*
> *exile yourselves, o torments,*
> *into the eternal distance.*[6]

The sense of deceit and heartbreak combines the private and personal with the religious:

> *...oh, how many times at your altar*
> *I have scattered with devoted sighs*
> *tears, prayers, and oaths;*
> *and I do not realize, alas,*
> *that I worship a statue and invoke stone.*[7]

When Laura was four, Paolo Vidman died leaving a will that he finalized only five days before his death. He was generous with his bequests to his legitimate children, and added a rider stating that the will should be executed "exactly, confidentially, and faithfully". He instructed that two thousand ducats (gold coins whose current value is approximately 200,000 dollars), a loan he had taken from Barbara a few years previously, be returned to her. Additionally, he made bequests to each of his three children born out of wedlock. Ironically, the executor of the secret rider was his widow, Camilla Grotta, who made sure that the girls, when they reached a suitable age, would be sent to the

San Sepulcro nunnery that was administered by one of her relatives. The money left by their father was used as a dowry given to the nunnery. The son, who chose a secular life, also received his part of his father's estate.

In 1652, a year after the cantatas were published, Barbara's father died and she, his sole heir, discovered that he had left almost nothing. The little money that was left barely covered the cost of his burial, not to mention covering the cost of perpetuating his name as he thought Barbara should do.[8] In his will he hinted that his daughter had money of her own, and requested that she use it to perpetuate his memory. "How much I have done for her by raising her and setting her on the path of virtue."[9]

Despite Time

And indeed, Barbara grew up splendidly. She was a prolific musician, and her approximately one hundred works were published in eight volumes, Opuses 1 to 8. Seven contain secular music and one is devoted to liturgical music. From the standpoint of the number of Cantatas she published she was almost certainly the leading composer of her time in Venice. But anyone dipping into the various encyclopedias and dictionaries published in the second half of the twentieth century will find only Giulio Caccini and Jacopo Peri among the composers engaged in this genre. Not one of these books mentions Strozzi, whose works include three volumes of compositions for voice of this type, and who can boast the title "The Secular Cantata Composer". Strozzi's music was published together with the works of the great composers of her time. Side by side with their innovative style, clearly evident in her works is the growth process she underwent from girlhood to middle age. If she dedicated her Opus 1 to her teacher Cavalli, and alluded to the special privilege accorded to her as a woman to publish a work, then in Opus 5 she succeeded in shedding her fears and expressing her confidence in her professional endeavors. "...since feminine weakness restrains me no more than any indulgence of my sex impels me," she wrote, "on lightest leaves do I fly, in devotion, to bow before you."[10] And perhaps it was not by chance that this opus was written three years after her father's death.

Twilight

Strozzi's emotional maturity is also clearly evident in her choice of texts for her compositions. One example is *Until Death*, which opens Opus 7, [11] and engages with longing for love to remain in old age. The Italian text was written by Sebastiano Baldini:

> *Until death parts us*
> *I insist*
> *that I shall love you,*
> *I want to love you*
> *with no regard for time and fate,*
> *until death parts us.*
> *Let the curly hair*
> *that shines blonde in a golden mass*
> *turn silver through the hand of time.*
> *The amorous ruins*
> *of your beauty that I so adore,*
> *let time trample them and try to consume them.*
> *Let the light be extinguished*
> *from your pupils and let the purple and vermilion*
> *of your cheeks and lips become impoverished.*
> *Even against the thought*
> *that nourishes the soul,*
> *the victor's palm will be taken*
> *by the blind archer...*[12]

Barbara Strozzi fell ill in 1677, and on 8 May she was still in Venice. A short time later she traveled to Padua for an unknown reason, perhaps to find a cure for her illness. She died in Padua on 11 November 1677.

Four

The Goddess's Vengeance: Élisabeth-Claude Jacquet de La Guerre (1665-1729)

Élisabeth Jacquet was born on the picturesque Ile Saint-Louis in the River Seine. Today this romantic island, a few hundred meters walk from Notre-Dame Cathedral, is a fashionable tourist site. Its past residents included celebrities such as the poet Charles Baudelaire, sculptor Camille Claudel, Jewish politician Leon Blum, a three-time prime minister of France, and former French president Georges Pompidou.

A Child Prodigy

Élisabeth was the second daughter of Anne (née de La Touche) and Claude Jacquet de La Guerre, of the upper bourgeoisie of Paris. From her first marriage her mother Anne had connections with the royal house,[1] her father Claude was a master builder of harpsichords and a professional organist who was appointed the first organist of the Saint-Louis en L'Ile church, a post he occupied until his death in 1702. One of the instruments he built in 1652 is currently housed in the John and Mabel Ringling Museum of Art in Sarasota, Florida.

The family's children – the brothers Pierre and Nicolas, Élisabeth, and her older sister Anne – were given a musical education from infancy. At the time an education of this kind for young girls was important among the nobility and the upper bourgeoisie, but schools were also established for the lower classes, the best known of which was Saint Cyr, founded in 1686 by Madame de Maintenon who was later the second wife of King Louis XIV.

All the children engaged in music as a profession in their adulthood. Anne, known as "Nannon", was a protégée of Marie de Lorraine, Duchess of Guise (a first cousin of Louis XIV), and earned a high salary as a musician in her court, Pierre was an organist in Paris, and Nicolas played the same instrument in Bordeaux. Élisabeth studied singing, the harpsichord, improvisation, accompaniment, and composition, in the clear knowledge that like her sister and brothers, her father was preparing her for a professional career. And although all four were talented, Claude Jacquet was so impressed by his second daughter's singing and playing that he decided to present her to the king.

At the Royal Palace

When she was only seven years old Élisabeth was presented to Louis XIV. The king, who coined the phrase, "L'État, c'est moi", was the sole decision maker on everything that went on in his kingdom, from foreign and internal policy, through taxation, to war and command of the army. To ensure his complete control he compelled the nobles and high clergy to live in the Louvre Palace in Paris. He awarded them high offices with a commensurate salary, but without governing authority. During his reign, magnificent buildings, expansive squares, and impressive gardens were built in Paris, and the city became the most splendid in Europe. The city walls, which were extended during the reign of Louis XIII, were pulled down and replaced with wide boulevards, including the lower part of the Champs Elysées. He built Les Invalides and the Pitié-Salpêtrière Hospital for the needy, and perpetuated his military victories with two triumphal arches, Arc St. Denis and Arc St. Martin.

This total control was also evident in the arts. When Louis succeeded to the throne, the French lacked confidence in everything pertaining to their own culture, feeling as they did that Italian art was superior to theirs. This picture changed when the king converted his palace into a magnificent center of culture and the arts. He founded the academy that engaged in research and definition of French literature and language, and in 1667 established the *Acadèmie Royale de Danse*, aimed at fostering professional dancers. The Acadèmie was in fact the world's first school of ballet, and it employed leading dance teachers as well as choreographers and musicians. Since his youth Louis himself was an enthusiastic dancer. He was dubbed "The Sun King" following his role in the last act of *Ballet of the Night* that was staged at The Louvre in 1653 and lasted for twelve hours, starting at sunset and finishing at daybreak. He was fourteen at the time and played the role of the Sun, wearing a magnificent golden costume that gleamed in the setting and rising sun. Dancing with him was the Florentine-born French composer Jean-Baptiste Lully, the man who held a monopoly over the court's musical life.

In 1669 he founded the *Acadèmie Royale de Musique* whose opera house on rue Saint-Honoré presented its operatic performances. Lully was the chief composer and choreographer of all these works, and also appeared as a dancer and actor in plays by Moliere and Racine. As a man who had amassed great power, he was behind numerous intrigues, and later apparently influenced the music composed by Élisabeth, but we shall cross that bridge when we come to it.

The king's health deteriorated, and two years earlier he consequently forsook his dancing roles in the big productions staged in his court. Despite this, the court and its music which joined forces during the "Sun King's" heyday were still prominent in the Parisian scene. On first hearing Élisabeth he was amazed by her voice and the way a seven-year-old girl accompanied herself on the harpsichord, her sight reading, and the fact that she immediately accompanied anyone around her who broke into song. He urged her father to develop the little one's talent, and Claude went back home and devoted himself to this task. Five years later, in July 1677, the following announcement appeared in the *Le Mercure Galant* literary periodical: "For four years a wonder has appeared here. She sings at sight the most difficult music. She accompanies herself, and others who wish to sing, at the harpsichord, which she plays in an inimitable manner. She composes pieces and plays them in all the keys asked of her... and she still is only ten years old."[2]

When she was twelve Élisabeth moved into the royal court as a protégée of the Marquise de Montespan, Louis' mistress at the time, who was responsible for the organization of chamber recitals in his private apartments. For four years she was educated together with Louis' and the marquise's four illegitimate children.

In Honor of the Victory

The daily schedule under the marquise included singing, dance, liturgical and instrumental music, and work on producing plays, but all this came second to playing the harpsichord, a specialization reserved for particularly gifted girls. Although we do not know from whom she learned to play, we do know that the chief teacher of this instrument was the composer Jacques Champion de Chambonnières, who was considered the French school's father of the harpsichord. He was also an excellent dancer who sometimes appeared with the Royal Ballet, but he was too single-minded and opinionated to survive under the court musician's regime. When he refused to play in a Lully opera, he was forced out of his post and consequently his pension was revoked. De Chambonnières then found an original way of recouping his losses, and sold his title to his student, the harpsichordist Jean-Henri d'Anglebert. The latter understood full well what the king wanted, and unlike others who found working with Lully difficult, he had a good relationship with him.

As an outstanding student, Élisabeth grew up in a world of ballet-opera in which dance was part of the plot. She witnessed the popularity of the lyric tragedy that engaged with subjects from mythology and folktales which also included elements of ballet. Similar to other musicians in the court of Louis XIV, her dream was to compose a work in one of these two genres. But as a result of Lully's absolute control over court music, she, like other French composers up until the eighteenth century, had very little experience in this sphere. Still, as we shall see, she resolved to try her hand at composing a dramatic work of her own.

When she was sixteen she was granted a bursary by the king which enabled her to study composition, a profession that thus far had been a male domain. That year Lully's ballet, *Le Triomphe de L'Aamour* was staged in Paris, and for the first time in the history of dance in France a female dancer took the role danced by the king before his health deteriorated.

In the fall of 1683, Louis secretly married the Marquise de Maintenon, governess of his illegitimate children with the Marquise de Montespan. He transferred his residence to Versailles, and the eighteen-year-old Élisabeth who wanted to distance herself from the intrigues of musical life at the court, requested that she continue to live in Paris. With extraordinary regret the king acceded to her request, and as a mark of his esteem for her professional endeavors granted her a pension in perpetuity, and also permission to dedicate her works to him. In Paris she met Marin de La Guerre, an organist at the church of Saint-Séverin, one of the oldest in the Latin Quarter. They were married in September 1684 and moved into a house on rue Le Regrattier. It was at this point that she decided to combine her surnames, and was thenceforth known as Élisabeth-Claude Jacquet de La Guerre.

As a woman who had spent her youth in the royal court at which spectacular operas were staged, it was Élisabeth's burning ambition to stage a theatrical work. Following the

War of Devolution that consolidated the borders of Louis XIV's France, she asked permission to dedicate to the king her ballet-opera *Les Jeux à l'Honneur de la Victoire*, in which dance is part of the plot. While still working on the composition she knew she had to meet the standards set by Lully,[3] and this with the little experience she had in writing an opera. Moreover, she realized that her work would almost certainly raise eyebrows not only because she was a woman, but also because she would seemingly be invading the exclusive territory of the domineering, hot-tempered court composer. At worst, her work would be rejected out of hand. To protect herself against this kind of reaction, Élisabeth appended a personal letter to her dedication in which she adopted a strategy similar to that employed by women composers before her – self-effacement, and giving all the credit to the man possessing the political power and to whom the work was dedicated:

> *Presented at your court at the most tender age (this memory will be eternally precious to me), where I had the honor of staying for several years, I have learned, Sire, to consecrate to you all my waking hours. You deigned to appreciate the first fruits of my genius, and you have been pleased to receive more of its productions as well. But these particular signs of my zeal have not been enough for me, and I longed for the happy occasion in which I could bring them before the public. This is what has brought me to make this ballet for the theatre. Women before today have produced excellent works of poetry for the theatre, which have had great success. But until now no woman has tried to set an entire opera to music; and I gain this advantage from my enterprise, that the more it is extraordinary, the more worthy it is of you, Sire...[4]*

The Goddess's Vengeance

On 1 July 1685, the pastoral work *Les Jeux à l'Honneur de la Victoire* was presented in the apartments of the Dauphin at Versailles. It was harshly criticized and although Élisabeth had prepared herself for this eventuality, the failure was a bitter one, and she went back to performing and writing for the harpsichord, her specialty. Two years later her first work for the harpsichord, *Pièces de Clavecin*, was published and it demonstrated both her personal taste and talent for the art of improvisation.[5] But Élisabeth did not rest. She aspired to create a lyric tragedy, an operatic genre established by Lully that engaged with subjects from mythology. The tragedy usually opened with a traditional prologue devoted entirely to praise of the king, and it combined music, singing, and dramatic activity that aroused interest throughout the entire piece. Onstage there were dragons and sea-serpents in pursuit of the protagonists, and sea creatures of huge proportions (eighteen feet long and six feet wide) that gurgled menacingly. Ballet played an integral role in the drama. The audience saw the protagonists flying through the air in a jeté, but the dancer's name did not appear in the program in order to create the illusion that it was the singer who was performing this feat.

In March 1694, two years after the birth of her only son, her lyric tragedy *Céphale et Procris* was performed at the *Acadèmie Royale de Musique* in Paris. The work, at whose center is the vengeance of the goddess whose womanly honor has been besmirched, is loosely based on a story by Ovid, with a libretto written by an almost unknown poet named Joseph-François Duché de Vancy. The tragedy was performed several times that year, and then taken off. This was seven years after Lully's death. Like other composers in Paris, Élisabeth, with her music, attempted to fill the void left by the man considered to be the representative composer of dramatic music in France at the time. But the fact that she was the first woman to write an opera in France made no impression on the Parisian audience. The chilly reviews claimed that the libretto, the poetic text, was weak, and that Élisabeth's dramaturgical ability was inadequate. Today, on the other hand, different opinions can be heard. Thus, for example, researcher Wanda Griffiths who re-edited the music and published it in 1998, contends that the composer was a sensitive and professional dramaturge. In her view the librettist also did a fine job.[6]

Yet Elisabeth's unsuccessful foray into opera made her give up this genre and she went back to composing cantatas and pieces for harpsichord. At the same time she began taking an interest in a new style that had emerged in Italy and taken Paris by storm, at the center of which was the sonata – an independent instrumental work with social functions. Every self-respecting keyboard musician deemed it proper to write and perform a sonata of several contrasting movements. Side by side with this captivation there was also opposition, with some accusing the new genre of unbridled exhibitionism (in contrast with the "royal" vocal works of the seventeenth century). But the power of the new genre was unstoppable, and it became the bon ton of both the Parisian soloists and social events. People hummed the themes they heard at private and public recitals, and were eager to hear sonatas old and new, discuss them, and nurture and enhance their composition. The favored venue for these recitals was the home of the priest Nicolas in the Latin Quarter, where the audience was eager to hear sonatas which had not yet been publicly performed. This somewhat obsessive preoccupation was aptly summed up by the French writer and intellectual Bernard Le Bovier de Fontenelle, who wrote, "Sonata, what do you want of me?"[7]

Élisabeth's sonatas were published in 1695-96 and were among the first examples of the genre in France. Her model was the famous French composer François Couperin, or "Couperin le grand" as he was known, who was renowned for his style that combined the Italian and French styles much to his audience's satisfaction. In her sonatas, which are among the first examples of their kind, the composer discarded the basso continuo and the affect declaring a singular mood in the music of the Baroque period in favor of balance and symmetry on the one hand, and contrast between a flowing melody and accompaniment on the other. Ironically, even though her work was influenced by Couperin, it was he who criticized her musical language as being "too Italian".

A Lyric Tragedy

Although the eminent composer's criticism did not halt Élisabeth's prolific musical life, the vicissitudes of her personal life did. At the turn of the new century, when she was at the peak of her musical activity, she suffered a series of personal tragedies. Her and her husband Marin's only child – who was also a promising musical talent – fell ill and died aged ten. A short time later her father, to whom she was very close, also passed away, and he was followed two years later by her husband. These multiple bereavements left her shrouded in grief and unproductive in her work. After a long period she made up her mind to return to her professional and social activity, but this time she apparently decided that she needed company around her. She opened a music salon in her home, which fitted in with the tradition of the salons that flourished in Paris of the time, and there she held recitals and gatherings at which music was performed and discussed. Professional and amateur musicians and intellectuals from Paris and beyond viewed an invitation to her home as a signal honor. And there is no doubt that compared with other salonniéres of her time, her uniqueness was in her being a leading professional musical authority who had gained fame at an early age.

Together with these activities she went back to composing. In 1707 her first collection of pieces for harpsichord was published, which could also be played on the violin.[8] She dedicated these works, which call for a high degree of professional skill and improvisation, to the king who, in the final third of his life took pleasure in quiet, intimate gatherings in his apartments at Versailles. Influenced by his wife, Madame de Maintenon, he became a devout Catholic and subsequently revoked the Edict of Nantes issued by his grandfather, King Henri IV, which granted freedom of religion to the Calvinist Protestants of France. In its place Louis announced the Edict of Fontainebleau, which declared Protestantism an illegal religion. This measure led to a mass exodus of Protestants from France to Britain, Prussia, and the Low Countries, and caused great damage to France.

Élisabeth composed her biblical cantatas inspired by the atmosphere in the palace, and perhaps they were commissioned by Madame de Maintenon. Three were dedicated to the king, and it is a reasonable assumption that they were performed before him and a select invited audience. Although these works focus on biblical subjects they were written for secular objectives, and thus the original Latin text was replaced by a freer French version.[9]

It was during this period that de La Guerre also wrote music for the exhibitions and fairs held in the Théatre de Paris. After her retirement in 1717 she attended public performances of the first series of concerts that began in 1725 and ended in 1790. The aim of these concerts was to provide entertainment during religious festivals when the

Opera de Paris, La Comédie Française, and La Comédie Italienne were closed. The concerts, which were performed in the Salle de Cents Suisses (Hall of the Hundred Swiss Guards) of the Tuileries Palace, began at six in the evening and were attended by the wealthy bourgeoisie, aristocrats of the lower order, and tourists.

Over the years the composer maintained contact with the royal family, and 1721 saw the performance of her last composition, *Te Deum*, to mark the recovery of King Louis XV from smallpox.

In the twilight of her life Élisabeth lived in the parish of Saint Eustache in the 1st arrondissement of Paris. The magnificent Church of Saint Eustache, which houses a splendid sixteenth-century organ and Rubens paintings from the seventeenth century, was where Louis XIV celebrated holy communion, and it was there that eminent personages such as Cardinal Richelieu, Madame de Pompadour, and Moliere, were baptized. There, on 27 June 1729, Élisabeth-Claude Jacquet de La Guerre was buried. That year a commemorative medal bearing her image was struck, with the reverse side bearing the inscription: "With the great musicians I competed for the prize".

Five

Dixit Dominus:
Marianna Martines
(1744-1812)

Marianna Martines was born in a spacious six-room apartment in a five-story building on the Michaelerplatz, at 11 Kohlmarkt Street in the old city of Vienna. She was the sixth child of Maria Teresa, who was Austrian, and Naples-born Nicolo Martines, who lived in Vienna in his capacity as major-domo at the papal nuncio. Marianna was baptized Anna Catherina but chose to use the name Marianna.

Vienna

The house on Kohlmarkt Street was a microcosm of eighteenth-century Viennese life. On the first floor lived the dowager princess of the wealthy Esterhazy family; the second floor housed a bourgeois family; the Martines family lived in a spacious apartment on the third floor; and in the fourth-floor attic, which did not even have a stove to heat it in the bitterly cold winter, lived Joseph Haydn, a struggling young composer and music teacher. The building's residents maintained personal, social, and professional contact, and for some of them the house was a steppingstone to the center of Vienna's cultural activity. For example, Princess Esterhazy befriended Haydn and through her good offices he was offered a post by her sons who later became his patrons.

Marianna was a gifted girl who spoke fluent German and Italian at home, and she also spoke English and read and wrote in French. Her education was put into the hands of Europe's most famous court librettist and poet of the time, Pietro Metastasio, who had come to Vienna in 1730 to take up a post on the court of Emperor Charles VI.[1] He and Marianna's father Nicolo had known one another in their youth in Naples, and when Metastasio came to work in Vienna he was invited to live in the Martines home, where he became one of the family and remained part of it until he died.

As early as her childhood Marianna gained the attention of the Viennese court with her singing and playing the harpsichord, and at age seven won praise from Nicolo Porpora, a Neapolitan composer who was considered one of the greatest music teachers in Europe. Among his students were Metastasio himself, Haydn, and some great singers including Carlo Broschi, who performed under the stage name of Farinelli. In 1754, when Marianna was ten, Metastasio decided to add the eighteen-year-old Joseph Haydn to her team of teachers. The young composer, who had just been dismissed from his post at the St. Stephen's Choir School, moved into the attic on Kohlmarkt Street and had his meals with the Martines family in return for teaching the talented young girl to play. Haydn and Marianna formed a close relationship that lasted until Haydn's death in 1809. For Marianna this relationship yielded musical thinking similar to Haydn's, based on a deep understanding of the arts of imitation and the fugue.[2] As a harpsichordist she was influenced by Carl Philipp Emanuel Bach, one of the founding fathers of the classic style, and she composed works of several movements based upon a similar musical concept.[3]

Keyboard music captivated audiences in Vienna of the time, the city that was home to the royal court, aristocrats who were enthusiastic patrons of the arts, and public concerts. Composing for the Hammerklavier (Fortepiano), the precursor of the modern piano, which in the eighteenth century was something of an attraction, flourished concurrently with the discourse on equality and liberty, and the reexamination of all the institutionalized ideas, including the existence of God.[4] Merchants, physicians, and government officials were earning more than ever before, which enabled them to buy big houses, wear the finest clothes, eat the finest fare, and host musical soirées in their drawing rooms. Aristocrats and wealthy commoners played instruments together with professional musicians. The owners of private homes often looked for servants who were also musicians, and advertisements in the vein of "Wanted for a respected household, a servant au fait with the (name of the instrument)" were not out of the ordinary in the city's newspapers. Light and popular music was heard in the city streets, string and wind instrument ensembles played at garden parties or under the windows of the citizens who threw coins down to them, and in the streets on summer nights Serenades and Divertimenti, short gay pieces, could be heard for people's delectation and which were suitable for social events.

She Never Left Vienna

As a hobby and pastime, music was at the center of the lives of middle-and upper-class girls and women. Most of them played the piano, the harpsichord, or the harp, and sang as well. Some possessed great talent, studied professionally, and in their adulthood became teachers, performers, and composers. Marianna was frequently invited to sing and play at the court of Empress Maria Theresa who was only four years older than her. Marianna, familiar as she was with the musical taste of Golden Era Vienna, composed and played using techniques which impressed her audiences as she demonstrated her mastery of the keyboard. When she was seventeen, the third Mass she composed was performed in St. Michael's Church adjacent to her home – a work for orchestra, choir, and one male and two female soloists. Over the years she composed some two hundred other works, of which only seventy have remained intact.

It is said of Marianna that she maintained a conservative lifestyle. She never married, never left Vienna, and after the death of her parents she continued living in their apartment with her sister Antonia and Metastasio. The two sisters cared for the eminent poet to his dying day, and he, as a token of his esteem, willed his entire estate to the Martines children.

Marianna's close relationship with the poet, who was forty years her senior, aroused much speculation and set evil tongues wagging. At the time he was the most famous poet in Europe, and for Marianna he was a father figure, her mentor, and helped her to establish connections with the leading cultural lights in Vienna and Italy. The most important of these was Giovanni Battista Martini, known as "Padre Martini", a composer, theoretician, and music scholar, who was considered the greatest teacher of his time and supported her compositional work from his residence in Bologna.[5]

Urged by Martini and backed by Metastasio, Marianna submitted her candidacy to the *Accademia Filarmonica di Bologna*, a prestigious music education institution among whose students were Farinelli and Mozart.[6] At the time she was more a pianist than a harpsichordist, and frequently played at leading social events in Vienna. There is some conjecture that Mozart composed a piano concerto for her to play at a social gathering in the garden of Doctor Franz Mesmer, a German physician resident in Vienna who theorized that there was a natural energetic transference that occurred between all animated and inanimate objects that he called 'animal magnetism'.[7]

Before her thirtieth birthday she was admitted to the Accademia, thus becoming the first woman member to be admitted in the institution's 108 years of existence, since its founding in 1666. Up to the end of the eighteenth century only five other women were accorded this honor. To gain this prestigious appointment she composed *Dixit Dominus*, a cantata based on the opening verses of Psalm 110 ("The Lord said unto my Lord, sit thou at my right hand, until I make thine enemies thy footstool"). According to the academy's rules, the composer must be present at the performance of his work, but in Marianna's case she was not present and all the correspondence and transfer of the score were done through Martini and her mentor Metastasio. Was she afraid of travel and its attendant hardships? Was she perhaps loath to part from her sister with whom she had lived all her life, and to whom she was particularly attached? We shall never know.

At the Accademia assembly held on 25 May 1773, the eighteen members voted unanimously to admit her. They noted the interest that Martini and Metastasio showed in her, and added that her election bore a political dimension, whose aim was to gratify Empress Maria Theresa.[8] Her admission was granted in absentia, and Padre Martini conveyed the certificate from the Accademia in Bologna to her home in Vienna.

But despite this prestigious title Marianna did not obtain a professional post in the sphere of music. It may be reasonably assumed that the reason for this was that a professional position was considered "not respectable" for a woman of her standing. Her milieu, too, reacted accordingly. On the one hand her talent and professionalism were a byword, and she was invited to play and sing her works, while on the other she was categorized as an amateur of a high standard. When the English musicologist Charles Burney visited Metastasio when gathering material for his book on the history of music, he heard her and even wrote about her enthusiastically in his travel journal published in 1775. Burney's writings are an important historical document.[9] His writing is replete with humor and fully expresses the special relationship he had with leading figures from the world of music of his time. But like other music historians, Burney too chose to commemorate only men. It is therefore hardly surprising that despite his enthusiasm over

Marianna's work, her name is absent from his book, which is a most important reference source for eighteenth-century musical life and its connection with European culture.

A Prestigious Salon

After Metastasio's death Marianna began holding musical soirées in her home, which rapidly became one of Vienna's most prestigious institutions. The city's elite gathered there on Friday evenings to listen to their hostess's works, and those of other musicians like Mozart, Salieri, and Michael Kelly.[10] Kelly, an Irish tenor and actor who came to Vienna to perform, relates that at the Martines salon he heard her and Mozart playing one of the sonatas for four hands that Mozart had written to perform with her.

In 1796, when she was fifty-two, she opened a school for singing in her home. Through teaching and training a new generation of male and female singers she continued to cement her place in the musical life of Vienna in its first Golden Era. But in the nineteenth century Martines's voice fell silent, and in 1844, she was publicized in the memoirs of Caroline Pichler, a writer who hosted a literary salon and who in her youth had been a musician. Pichler mentions Martines and the blind pianist, Maria Teresia von Paradis as composers whose music lacked merit.[11] And as in numerous cases in which women hurt other women more than men harm them, according to Pichler no woman musician succeeds in reaching the standard of their male counterparts.

Antonia Martines died on 11 December 1812. The sudden death of her beloved sister, who was three years her junior, badly affected Marianna, and two days later, she too passed away.

Six

The Chorus Line:
Maddalena Laura Lombardini-Sirmen
(1745-1818)

On a cold and wintry night in early November, the seven-year-old Maddalena was tossing and turning in her bed. Her roommates were fast asleep, all of them girls from affluent families whose parents had done everything they could to ensure that they studied at the prestigious *Ospedale dei Mendicanti*. Together with twenty-nine other candidates she had taken the entrance examination earlier that day. Each of them underwent a meticulous screening process before thirty-three grave-faced examiners who ultimately accepted four of them, including Maddalena.

Venice: The Beginning of the Road

Nothing is known of her childhood up to age seven, and also unknown is who put little Maddalena into the Ospedale. It was possibly her parents, Gasparina Gambirasi and Pietro Lombardini, or perhaps only one of them. Perhaps her father had died and one of the ways in which her widowed mother was able to ease her financial situation was to place her daughter in the boarding school, where life was similar to that of a convent. *Ospedale dei Mendicanti*, the beggars' hospital, was one of four famous charitable institutions which began as hospitals to all intents and purposes, and later underwent a change which led to them becoming prestigious, desirable institutions of learning. From hospitals the ospedali were extended and became infirmaries for the penurious elderly and orphanages for abandoned and illegitimate children. For the unfortunate children to whom fate had dealt a harsh blow in their early childhood, these institutions were paradise on earth where they found a roof over their head, a bed, hot meals, and professional education.

In both living quarters and education there was total separation of boys and girls. The boys learned the ins and outs of commerce, and a large number left the ospedale in their early adolescence and joined the merchant navy. The girls on the other hand were given an in-depth professional musical education, and some joined the faculty of one or other of the institutions. In terms of its approach to girls' education, the Mendicanti was ahead of its time. Side by side with the physical conditions which were similar to those of convents, the girls studied music at a high professional standard with the best teachers; the rationale was to enable them to acquire a profession that would give them the possibility of working and making a respectable living. Yet there was a paradox between their ascetic lifestyle and the thinking about a professional future and financial independence for the young women.

In eighteenth-century Venice a large part of musical life took place in the ospedali. The city had neither soccer fields nor playgrounds where children could play, and so at a time when there was no radio, television, internet and electronic games, music occupied a central place. Venice boasted eleven theaters devoted to opera, four music conservatories, and the hundreds of musicians who lived in the city, studied, taught, and performed on every available stage. We call their music "classical", but in fact it was music which from the popularity standpoint is reminiscent of today's pop and rock. When the public liked certain performers or composers, they would stand in line for hours to obtain tickets and filled the auditoriums.

On the face of it, Maddalena should have been happy when she was accepted into the prestigious institution, but it may be assumed that once she realized that her success in the entrance examination meant leaving home for good, she was not happy at all. On her acceptance a contract was signed whereby she would remain in the ospedale until she was eighteen. Until that time she would see her family once a month, but not alone, since there was always one of the women staff members in attendance. Every present she received, every message or letter, would be opened by the Signora Priora, the holder of the institution's highest office. At eighteen she would only be able to leave if she had decided to marry, and then she would receive a dowry from the ospedale, a sum of money that would enable her to be financially independent.

The Chorus Line

On her first day at the ospedale Maddalena was selected to be one of the "figlie del coro", the choirgirls, a title that set her and her young colleagues apart from the others who had no musical aptitude. Together with her specialization in violin, she also learned singing and theory with a skilled team of teachers mainly consisting of professional women musicians, most of whom were graduates of one of the Venice ospedali, while the rest were composers who held respected posts in one or more of these institutions. The most famous of these was Antonio Vivaldi who for most of his life worked at the *Ospedale della Piêta* as a teacher and composer.

On the day the figlie del coro appeared, there was a long line of people who had come in the early hours of the morning to buy tickets. The audience consisted not only of locals, but also visitors to Venice who had heard about the girls choir. A contemporaneous saying had it that, "if you have never heard at least one ospedale choir, then it is as though you have never visited Venice".

Maddalena's musical talent stood out, and she quickly became the ospedale's star. She took part in dozens of concerts both as an instrumentalist and vocalist. The performances were held in a hall in the ospedale, and the young musicians were placed in the upper gallery, where they were separated from the audience by a large distance that made it difficult to see them clearly. To ensure that they were well hidden, they appeared behind an iron lattice. Edward Wright, who documented his travels in Italy between 1720 and 1722, attended one of these concerts and wrote: "Their Performance is surprisingly good; and many excellent Voices there are among them: and there is somewhat still more amusing, in that their Persons are conceal'd from view."[1] Aside from the music, a suggestion of mystery attracted the men in the hall: "They sing like angels," it was said of them, "all of them are girls – illegitimate, orphans, or those whose relatives are not able to care for them."[2] From behind the lattice Maddalena and her companions could hear the thunderous applause and see the audience on its feet, but at the end of the performance they left the gallery without being seen and went back behind the institution's walls.

Maddalena was a brilliant student, and when she was fourteen joined the faculty and began teaching the violin. Additionally, she composed music and conducted one of the choirs: she led the choir dressed in white, with a cluster of pomegranate flowers behind her left ear to distinguish her from the singers. But despite her success she felt she wanted more, albeit she knew she would be unable to get it from the ospedale, outside whose walls was a whole world of musicians she wanted to meet. In particular she dreamed of specializing in the violin with Giuseppe Tartini, a virtuoso violinist and teacher of international repute who was the first to teach students in his home as part of the school for violinists he established. To this school flocked virtuosi violinists from France, Holland, Sweden, Germany, and even more distant countries like the island of Java in what is today Indonesia.

Dreams for Duet and Trio

One morning, after a night spent thinking and daydreaming, Maddalena made up her mind to write a personal letter to Tartini. In it she asked his advice on how she could improve the sound of her violin, and told him a little about herself. To her delight, the great violinist and teacher's reply was not long in coming, and signaled the start of a close correspondence between them.[3]

She quickly decided to submit to her superiors a request to study with Tartini. In her rationale she wrote that apart from the fact that this would be a great advancement for her and her contribution to her students would be significantly greater, the news that she was studying with the eminent violinist would enhance the ospedale's reputation. In other words, she tried to persuade the committee that giving her permission to travel was a long-term economic consideration, not to mention its attendant prestige, since the Maddalena after Tartini would be worth far more to the ospedale than the Maddalena prior to him. Parents all over the country would hear of her specialization with the famous violinist and would want her to teach their daughters. Furthermore, mention of her specialization with the professor from Padua in concert brochures would surely attract large audiences.

The committee approved her studies in Padua, and the happy young woman, accompanied by her tutor Chiara Variatti, set off for two months of specialization. Chiara's specific instructions from the Mendicanti administration were to return to Venice so as not to overburden Maddalena's family that was paying her wages and expenses while she was away from the city. During the two months she spent in Padua, a special relationship was cemented between teacher and student. The childless violinist treated her as the daughter he had never had, and fostered her as if she were his own child.

On her return to Venice, Maddalena knew that her life was about to change, but did not know how. For six years beginning in 1760, she traveled to Padua to study, with each such journey being the start of a quest for personal and creative freedom. Each time she went, her ambition to make this freedom permanent heightened, albeit she knew that according to the rules of the Mendicanti only marriage could release her from her contract with the institution.

In this case, too, Tartini came to her aid. Through his wide network of students all over Europe, the composer arranged a meeting between Maddalena and Ludovico Sirmen, a violinist from Ravenna who was performing in Venice. Exactly where the two met, and under what circumstances, is unknown, but they quickly decided to marry. Was their decision driven by love? We do not know, but as we shall see, there is no doubt that it was a marriage of convenience for both parties. Maddalena met Ludovico when she was twenty-two, and ripe for a relationship that would lead to marriage, a condition to her leaving the Mendicanti. For her, meeting him was the ultimate solution: he was a professional violinist, unmarried, and her senior by only a few years, and not only that, he was Italian and thus suited to her both culturally and socially.

Quartet

Three months before her twenty-second birthday, Maddalena was given the Mendicanti's approval to marry. She left the ospedale with a dowry of three thousand ducats, and the couple married and went on their honeymoon. The dowry enabled them to work for two years on a joint musical program, to establish contacts that helped them raise the funding required for a tour, and enjoy financial independence. Through Tartini they met Count Benvenuto di Raffale, the Savoy minister of education and a well-known violinist who was also a former student of Tartini's. The Lombardini-Sirmens dedicated Six String Quartets to the count, which were later published in Paris and consequently Maddalena became the first woman to compose for this kind of string ensemble.

One very interesting fact is that the couple were accompanied by the priest Dom Giuseppe Terzi who Maddalena had met at the Mendicanti when she was very young, and with whom she had a profound emotional relationship. According to the gossipmongers of the time Terzi regularly accompanied her wherever she went, including the young couple's honeymoon. Although the true nature of their relationship is unknown, we do know that only nine days separated their passing.

The first way-station on the journey of Maddalena, Ludovico, and Dom Giuseppe was Turin, the capital of Piedmont which was then part of the kingdom of Sardinia and an important musical center. The local audience welcomed them enthusiastically, but it was clearly the gifted woman violinist who moved and captivated them. In her style she was considered the great teacher Tartini's successor, and the audiences gave her a standing ovation.

Between concert tours in 1769, at the age of twenty-nine Maddalena gave birth to their only daughter, Alessandra. A year later the Lombardini-Sirmens embarked on another concert tour of Europe, and once again it was Maddalena's virtuosity that garnered great acclaim throughout Italy and the capitals of Europe. Between 1770 and 1773 she lived in London where she performed in some two hundred concerts and enjoyed fame as a composer with her violin concerti in an orchestral version, and in an adaptation for harpsichord.[4]

The couple continued their joint concerts and gained great acclaim, due mainly to the string quartets they composed together. On the face of it, this was a family idyll of a pair of artists, but it transpired that this was not really the case.

During their stay in London Ludovico felt he had had enough of living abroad, and the couple decided to separate their careers: Maddalena continued with her concert tours as a virtuosa violinist and composer in the international arena, while Ludovico returned to Ravenna to teach and continue his career there.

His marriage to the famous composer-violinist coupled with his connection with Tartini helped him to enhance his reputation, and he became a pivotal point in the city's musical life. Maddalena continued on her travels accompanied by Terzi, and over a thirteen-year period the Lombardini-Sirmens met only rarely, and some say that they did not meet at all. During this period Ludovico formed an intimate relationship with Countess Zerletti, and the two became known as a permanent couple. This was a very convenient arrangement, mainly due to the fact that Maddalena functioned as a sort of private bank for her husband. Every now and then she sent him money so he could invest it wisely, and thus increase the Lombardini-Sirmen family assets. But Ludovico preferred the good life with Countess Zerletti, and gave no thought to his expenses. Furthermore, he even bought his lover another house, apart from the one he lived in with her, and gave her expensive jewelry.

Solo Decline

Maddalena lived outside of Italy for thirteen years, taking care of her career, undertaking concert tours accompanied by Terzi, while knowing that in Ravenna her husband was living with another woman. It seemed that her husband's private life did not bother her, but that was not so. Maddalena was jealous and angry about the squandering of the financial resources of which she was the source, and deep down she blamed Countess Zerletti for not allowing her husband to accompany her on her tours. She was filled with feelings of duality originating in subconscious drives, and although she had a permanent escort she wanted her husband to be with her, which would have happened had he not had a mistress. Her relationship with the countess was based on a latent competition coupled with the two women's mutual curiosity. When Maddalena arrived in Ravenna she rented a cottage where she entertained the countess for lunch, an invitation the countess reciprocated by inviting her to lunch on St. Martin's Sunday. The atmosphere between the two was difficult, and Maddalena left Zerletti's house with Terzi as soon as the meal was over.[5] And Ludovico? Although he was living with Countess Zerletti it appears that he was unable to completely ignore his wife's anger. When Maddalena embarked on a concert tour to Russia he resigned his post at the college where he taught, left his home in Ravenna, and joined the tour, due either to Maddalena's pressure or perhaps it was professional considerations that guided him.

Maddalena gained fame due to her unique style that emphasized the tonal beauty so that it would sound as close as possible to the singing voice. The audience loved her, and when she and Ludovico performed together, the attraction was even greater.

But in style as in style, there are always periodic innovations driven by new schools which are more innovative than their precursors. In Maddalena's case this was a new concept in bowing that in the 1780s was led by composer-violinist Giovanni Battista Viotti.[6] He came to Paris in 1762 from the Turin court orchestra, and instead of the lyrical style that was dominant up to that time, Viotti spoke about a brilliant style in which dexterity and technical control are the measure of quality and execution of a work. On the eve of the French Revolution the audience was ready to welcome the revolutionary style in which virtuosity is the essence. Maddalena's style was no longer relevant.

The turnabout occurred in Paris, of all places. The city that had taken her into its warm embrace for a decade, now put an end to her brilliant career. On 7 May 1785, the *Mercure de France* published the following review:

> *Mme. Sirmen, the woman violinist who was such a sensation when she first performed here 14 years ago, played again but the reaction was less favourable.* **She preserves the characteristics of the Tartini school – charming tonal quality, and a playing style that is full of grace and emotional intensity, especially since she is a woman – that are, perhaps, somewhat neglected nowadays.**, *[My emphasis, E.Z.] Her playing style, however, is just the same as it was when she appeared here 14 years ago and, is therefore, extremely out of date. For some time now, violinists have placed more importance on speed of playing instead of tonal quality and on feats of skill instead of in imitating the singing voice. Unfortunately Mme. Sirmen may have been able then to astonish her listeners' ears, but she can do so no longer. While far from intending to criticize artistry, the reviewer believes Mme. Sirmen would do well to change her playing style so that it conforms to what is fashionable today. If she does, then we do not doubt that she will again receive the same enthusiastic applause that she did heretofore.*[7]

Three months after this review was published, and apparently in an effort to regain the support of the Parisian audience, Maddalena performed in a concert in which she decided to play a Viotti concerto. But the audience was far from moved, and she decided to stop performing on the international stage. In the meantime the French Revolution broke out, and public attention was diverted to war, not art.

In the late 1890s Maddalena Lomardini was a wealthy woman living in comfort in Venice. She lived in her own house at 3117 Fundamente Nuovo with her adopted daughter Angela. Ludovico lived in Ravenna until his death on 18 January 1828. Their daughter Alessandra married, had six children, and lived in Virgiano, fifteen minutes drive away from Rimini. In May 1797 Venice was conquered by Napoleon, and in January 1798 was annexed to Austria, thus putting an end to the magnificent republic. The occupation adversely affected the Italian currency, and on 15 May 1818 Maddalena died almost penniless.

So far twenty-six of her instrumental works have been published.[8]

Seven

Capriccio:
Maria Agata Szymanowska-Wolowska
(1789-1831)

She divorced her wealthy husband because he was not enamored of the fact that his wife wanted a profession. She made sure she had custody of their children and built herself an impressive musical career from which she made a good living. Some who have written about Maria Szymanowska like to relate the story of an evening in St. Petersburg when she sat down to play the piano, and asked composer John Field to turn the pages for her. Field declined, saying that her pretty white shoulders would distract him from the score.

Polonaise

Maria was born to a family of merchants that was among Warsaw's famous late-eighteenth-century bourgeoisie. The ancestry of her father, Franciszek Wolowski, a wealthy merchant and brewery owner, goes back to Jacob Frank, a Jew who founded a messianic movement and was considered the successor of Shabbetai Zvi, the noted false messiah. Like most Frankists, Wolowski converted to Catholicism and then married Barbara Lanckorońska, an educated Polish woman who bore him five daughters and five sons and raised them in affluent conditions. Maria was the couple's seventh child.

Warsaw of the time was a vibrant cultural center whose theaters presented operas, most of which were in Polish and a few in Italian, plays, ballet, and concerts. In 1795, when Maria was six, King Stanisław II August Poniatowski, the last of the Polish monarchs, abdicated, whereupon a large influx of Germans came to the city, among them operatic groups, with some coming from Italy too. Over four years the population of Warsaw quadrupled, and at the same time the demand for musicians and actors also grew. The private music teacher profession flourished, and this in fact signaled the start of musical education in Poland.

The Wolowski salon was well known as a meeting place not only for Warsaw's who's who, but also for travelers passing through the city either to perform there, or for those who were on their way to the royal court in St. Petersburg. The Wolowski's impressive list of regular guests included Jozef Elsner, founder of the first national conservatory in Warsaw; Franciszek Lessel, a Polish composer who went to Vienna to study with Haydn; Angelica Catalani, the Italian soprano who gave the young Frédéric Chopin a gold watch in appreciation of his musical talent; Prince Antoni Radziwill, a cellist and close friend of Chopin who was there with Kappelmeister Ferdinando Paër who was in charge of musical life in the court of Napoleon Bonaparte, and many other famous names. The Wolowski's sought to present to their guests the musical talent of their daughter, who had surprised the family with her improvisational skill on the keyboard. It was clear to the parents that they would do all they could to advance her professionally, and they hired the services of Antonin Lisowski to teach her piano and composition. After two years the teacher announced to the surprised parents that they would do well to put their daughter into the hands of a teacher of a higher standard. Surprisingly, despite belonging to the upper bourgeoisie the parents approached Tomasz Gremm, a teacher not considered to be of the top rank. Maria felt she was not progressing at the proper rate, so side by side with her studies with her new teacher she learned new material on her own, delved into new performance and compositional methods, and organized private master classes with leading musicians for herself.

In 1809, when she was twenty, Warsaw's first school of music was opened – for men only. Maria realized that she stood very little chance of studying in her hometown, so she packed her belongings and moved to Paris. After a year in which she performed in private recitals in the homes of acquaintances and friends of her parents, she went back home resolved to continue her progress. She enrolled for private tuition with the three well-known teachers who were leading musicians in Warsaw at the time, the director of the school for music – the school that had not accepted her because she was a woman – Jozef Elsner; composer

Franciszek Lessel, and Karol Kurpinski, conductor at the national theater in Warsaw.

In 1810, the year she returned to Warsaw, she married Józef Szymanowski, a wealthy landowner with a substantial estate, with whom she had three children: Helena (1811-1861), and the twins Celina (1811-1861) and Romuald (1812-1840). The most famous of the three is Celina who later married Poland's national poet Adam Mickiewicz. Her pregnancies and confinements did not hinder Maria in continuing to perform, but her husband – for whom music was an alien world – did not like his wife performing either privately or publicly. In any case, his main interests were managing his properties and breeding horses.

The rift between the two deepened to a point at which Józef voiced his total opposition to Maria playing in public. For five years, until she was twenty-six, she only performed privately before invited audiences, but her husband was determined that she give up her occupation completely. Maria, however, had no intention of relinquishing her career, and moreover, the marriage was in trouble in any case, so she decided to divorce her husband. She signed a divorce agreement whereby she had no financial claims on her husband, and all she asked – and was given – was custody of the children. When she embarked on her new life she experienced freedom the like of which she had never known, and she buckled down to establishing herself and her career as a pianist and composer.

Nocturne

Between 1815 and 1828 Maria had a brilliant concert career that took her all over Europe. These were the years that saw artistic music flourish, years in which court patronage began giving way to sponsors of art who were also tycoons engaged mainly in the purchase and sale of land. Wealthy propertied men built their own chapels and often maintained a private orchestra, choir, and even theaters in which they held concerts and staged operas.

Maria performed in England, Germany, France, Austria, Belgium, Holland, and St. Petersburg. Each of her programs included works of her own, and she also lectured on the art of piano. Some of her performances were at private recitals arranged by noble families, while others were commissioned by distinguished institutions such as England's Royal Philharmonic Society which booked her for a number of concerts in 1824. As a woman raised on European piano-playing, she was naturally drawn into the virtuoso piano trend both as a pianist and composer. Robert Schumann, who was considered an exacting critic, described her Etudes as innovative pieces that presented a professional quality rare in women composers of the time, or freely translated: any self-respecting male composer would consider himself blessed if he could attain the professional standard of Maria Szymanowska 's etudes. Chopin and Liszt, both piano virtuosi in their twenties, met her in St. Petersburg and lauded her playing. In 1823 Tsar Alexander I appointed her "First Pianist of the Royal Princesses Elizabeth and Maria", the first appointment of a woman to such a senior musical office in a court.

Notwithstanding her myriad admirers, Felix Mendelssohn did not like her playing. He claimed that Maria Szymanowska's playing made him think more about her pretty face rather than her execution.[1] But even this comment by the man considered to be the professional authority in the sphere of piano-playing and composition did not deter Carl Friedrich Zelter, himself a musical activist and teacher of both Fanny and Felix Mendelssohn, from becoming one of the most active supporters of Szymanowska's piano career. One of the best-loved stories quoted by everyone writing about Maria the accomplished pianist is the one about Johann Wolfgang von Goethe falling in love with her. They met when taking the waters at Marienbad where, at the curative springs frequented by the Bohemians, both a cultural and a turbulent social life flourished. Holidaying at the famous spa towns was not solely for taking a cure, but also for rubbing shoulders with the right people at the right place, and the springs whose curative powers became known as early as the thirteenth century were frequented by crowned heads, politicians, scientists, diplomats, and artists from every sphere. The magnificent buildings erected in the first half of the nineteenth century hosted, inter alia, King Edward VII, Mark Twain, Henrik Ibsen, Franz Liszt, Johann Strauss, Ivan Turgenev, Frédéric Chopin, Antonin Dvořák, Richard Wagner, Rudyard Kipling, Thomas Alva Edison, and many other celebrities who were regular visitors. Many of Europe's famous affairs also took place at these spas, and legend has it that the great German poet fell hopelessly in love with the gifted musician, and even dedicated his poem *Aussőhnung* (Reconciliation) to her. But as we know, Goethe's career was filled with inspirational women, and Maria Szymanowska is not among those mentioned in the various sources dealing with him and his great loves.

Maria worked very hard to advance her career. As an autodidact she made sure that she maintained an association with the leading teachers, performers, and composers of the time. Thus, for example, in Paris she met the famous Italian composer Luigi Cherubini and sought to learn his concept of music. Cherubini was an ardent supporter of absolute music that expressed itself and only itself, and which did not rely on extra-musical content or ideas. In the wake of this meeting he dedicated his *Fantasy for Piano in C Major* to her. Among the many personal contacts she established were personalities such as Prince Michal Oginski, the writers Adam Mickiewicz, Ivan Krylov, and Julian Korsak, the poet Alexander Pushkin, painter Aleksander Orłowski, writers and composers John Field, Gioacchino Rossini, Johann Hummel, and Mikhail Glinka. Furthermore, since as well as being a consummate professional she was also beautiful, intelligent, elegant, and a lively conversationalist, both she and the men who surrounded her were the subject of many and varied stories.

People who have written about Maria like to relate the story of an evening in St. Petersburg when she sat down to play the piano, and asked the composer and piano virtuoso John Field to turn the pages for her. Field declined, saying that her pretty alabaster-like shoulders would distract him from the score. Like Goethe, Field was renowned for his complex relations with a considerable number of women, but his relationship with Maria was a professional one and went far deeper than the revealing dress she wore that night. In aristocratic St. Petersburg the two played duets at private recitals, and he gave her a letter of recommendation to the leading music publishing house of Breitkopf and Härtel.[2] Field's letter was particularly flattering not only because he was her teacher, but because of his reputation as a rigorous music critic.

Capriccio

Maria traveled all over Europe with an intensive performance schedule. Whereas in the early years of her career she was invited to perform on the strength of the letters of recommendation she made sure to obtain, now, thanks to her strenuous work, her contacts, and critical acclaim, her reputation preceded her.

One of the attractions was her playing by heart. At a recital she gave in Poznan in 1823 she performed her Capriccio from memory which made her an overnight sensation in the local press. At the time this was something of a phenomenon, and in fact Maria was the first piano virtuosa to perform her works by heart. Famous for this after her were Clara Schumann and Franz Lizst who set the virtuosic norm for playing from memory.

Maria's piano compositions published in her lifetime are of great significance in the history of artistic music in pre-Chopin Poland. Retrospectively, her work represents the early Romantic style in music for the piano. The central characteristic of her works is a flowing, lyrical, and melodic line combined with forms originating in local folklore. It is a representative sample of Szymanowska's wonderful capability to bend with the audience's taste on the one hand, and to preserve her professional compositional desires on the other.

Whereas Maria spent much of her time outside her native Poland, she remained absolutely patriotic. Although the musical world regards Chopin as the composer whose works represent his country, it would only be proper to say that Maria Szymanowska preceded him in the use of musical forms and content which originated in Polish folklore. Thus, for example, the Nocturne with which Chopin is usually identified is a miniature composed by Maria well before Chopin was perceived as the uncrowned king of this genre. And it should be borne in mind that Maria was a student of John Field, who was considered the father of the genre.[3] Her two Nocturnes demonstrate early piano poetry. The first, *Le Murmure* (The Murmur),[4] became one of her most popular works, while by contrast the second,[5] published in 1825, is different in style from everything she had previously written.

It demonstrates how a coherent structure grows from within a simple, direct style. The beginning of the melody which moves slowly, almost pensively, is accompanied by a Barcarole tempo imitating the sweep of the Italian gondoliers' oars, and is immediately followed by a darker part that heightens the tension and leads into a section that is nationalistic in character.

Ballade

From 1828 until her death Maria lived permanently in St. Petersburg with her two daughters, Helena and Celina, and her sisters Julia and Kazimiera. At thirty-eight she decided that she had had enough of traveling all over Europe, sleeping in carriages and wayside inns, separated from her family and home for weeks, sometimes months on end. Her regular income was now assured by the Romanov family who had been her patrons since 1823, and aside from her position as their court pianist she was given a post in a unique institution under their aegis that was exclusively for women. Considering that up to the 1840s women did not hold positions in respected music institutions, this was a golden opportunity to enhance her pedagogical talents. At the same time she continued to perform and give private lessons to women from noble families, including to the Tsar's daughter.[6] As well as the concerts, operas, and other theatrical events attended by the composer and her family, she prepared for the concerts in which she performed. But despite being a magnet for the audiences that came to hear her in public and private concerts alike, she was only part of the program and as was commonly accepted she performed together with other artists, and frequently accompanied them on the piano or organ. An example of this appears in the program of a concert held on 18 April 1827 at the palace of Countess Daria Dierzhavina in St. Petersburg:

1. *Overture from Cherubini's* **Anacreon**, *performed on two pianos and four pianists: Reinhardt, Meyer, Hartknoch, and Madame Szymanowska*
2. *Naderman's harp concerto performed by Mr. Schulz*
3. *Fields'* **Nocturne** *No. 1 with text from a Petrarch sonnet, sung by Miss Gebhardt*
4. *Hummel's well-known* **Rondo** *performed by Madame Szymanowska*
5. *Violin solo performed by Mr. Boehm*
6. *A "Romanse" from* **Othello**, *sung by Miss Gebhardt*
7. *Potpourri from* **Der Freisschütz**, *performed by Madame Szymanowska*[7]

At her home at 48 Sadova Street, near St. Michael's Palace, Maria held a salon that attracted the elite of Russian society. Among the guests were princes and diplomats, the exiled Polish poet Adam Mickiewicz who married Maria's daughter Celina; Alexander Pushkin; and poet-attorney Franciszek Milewski, a friend of Mickiewicz, who married her daughter Helena. At the Szymanowska salon *tableaux vivants* were staged by one participant or a group on a subject taken from poetry, popular operas, ballet, or famous paintings on show at The Hermitage.[8] These performances were actually fully-fledged plays complete with costumes, sets, and lighting and sound effects of the time.

As well as being a well-known figure in St. Petersburg society and the city's cultural scene, Maria was also occupied with organizing her music, copying her compositions and arranging them in a signed album. Together with her own works, the album also contains short pieces by Clara and Robert Schumann, Chopin, Liszt, Beethoven, John Field, Rossini, and Meyerbeer.

Szymanowska wrote more than 110 works and they include vocal and chamber music, and of course numerous piano compositions. Her works were published by leading publishing houses such as Breitkopf and Härtel in Leipzig and others in Paris, Warsaw, St. Petersburg, Moscow, Kiev, and Odessa.

In the summer of 1831, a cholera pandemic that began in India and cut a swathe through Europe, reached St. Petersburg. On 22 June riots broke out in the city, with the rioters calling upon the government to revoke the quarantine as they attacked the hospitals where the afflicted lay in isolation, and accused the market sanitary inspectors of poisoning the city's wells. Cavalry were called in to restore order, but in vain. It was only when the Tsar himself appeared in the market square and ordered the crowd to fall to their knees and doff their hats to him that the rioting was quelled. A short time later Maria fell ill, and on 25 July died in her home at the age of forty-two.

Eight

The Curator:
Louise Farrenc-Dumont
(1804-1875)

She was born in the prestigious Sorbonne arrondissement in Paris, the preserve of artists who enjoyed the patronage of the rulers of France. Her parents, Jacques-Edme Dumont and Marie Elisabeth Louise Courton, were both scions of Flemish families engaged in painting and sculpture. Her father Jacques, whose works are still on show in the Louvre, was a sculptor who insisted on maintaining freedom of thought and creativity, and consequently was not elected to *L'Académie Française*.[1] After his marriage to Marie the couple were granted the right of residence in the Louvre, a right granted solely to artists in the service of the royal family and their relatives. Following the birth of their first son, Auguste, the family was forced to move since the Louvre wing in which they lived was due to be renovated. Together with thirty other families they moved to an arrondissement designated for government officials, where they led a vibrant social and artistic life.

Food, Wine, Dancing

On summer nights the neighbors would gather in the inner courtyard garden to enjoy the fragrance of the blossom, fine wine, and good food. Besides the gatherings in the garden events were also held in the studio of one neighbor or another, and on wintry Sundays there were dance evenings at the Dumonts. Louise and her sister were born into this creative environment, and like their older brother were guided by the parents to acquire a broad education and specialize in one of the artistic professions.

Louise's great talent as a pianist and painter began to emerge at an early age. Even though in a family of artists like hers it was reasonable to assume that she would take up visual art, the girl's heart was set on music in general and the piano in particular. The woman who endowed her with this love was her godmother and first piano teacher, Anne-Elisabeth Cécile Soria, a skilled pianist and teacher who Louise's father had met in Rome and who became a close family friend. For Louise, Soria opened a window onto the world of piano and laid the foundations not only for her future professional career but also for the very essence of her being.[2] The turning point in the direction of a professional career came when she was fifteen, when she began studying composition under the tutelage of the flautist, composer, and theoretician Anton Reicha, a native of Bohemia who was a visiting professor at the Paris Conservatory. Louise was a diligent and industrious student, and her studies were of paramount importance to her. And then one evening when she sat down to play, listening attentively in the audience was Aristide Farrenc.[3] Farrenc was a flautist of repute in the city, and as we shall see their relationship led her to suspend her studies for a number of years. He had come from Marseilles to further his career as a musician, was accepted as a flute professor at the Paris Conservatory, and served as a flautist at the city's Théâtre Italien. Following their first meeting, Aristide came to play music regularly with the seventeen-year-old girl who was ten years his junior, shy and introverted, yet extremely intelligent and talented. He told Louise about his merchant family in Marseilles, about the future they had planned for him in commerce, and his decision to leave his hometown and family at the age of twenty-one to pursue his dream of becoming a professional musician.

Their long conversations and playing together led to romance, and on 29 September 1821 the couple were married. Louise suspended her studies at the conservatory, and she and Aristide honeymooned in France, which included trips combined with joint concerts, occupying themselves with music, and strengthening a deep emotional bond. Despite the age difference, they succeeded in building a relationship that was special for their time, at the center of which were mutuality and collaboration, but at the same time each of them maintained their personal and professional independence.

It took four years for Aristide to tire of their wanderings, and the couple decided to return to Paris. They took a house on Boulevard Poissonnière, which was home to numerous artists including Frédéric Chopin.[4] Louise resumed her studies while carrying their first child, and Aristide devoted himself to publishing, opening Éditions Farrenc which quickly gained him a fine reputation as a publisher throughout Europe.

Aristide was the more extroverted and entrepreneurial of the two. Conscious of his wife's shyness and introverted personality, he decided to help her by taking action. His first step was to hire a small concert hall near his publishing house where he arranged "a room of her own" for Louise in which she could compose and practice. Additionally, it was he who published her early works for piano which she wrote between 1825 and 1839, and ensured that they were published in London and elsewhere in Europe.[5]

Birth and Rebirth

In 1826, five years after their marriage, their daughter Victorine was born. After her confinement Louise devoted most her time to the baby, thus curtailing her musical activity. But when Victorine reached the age of four Louise felt it was time to resume her composition and orchestration studies. She began under the tutelage of Johann Nepomuk Hummel, a former student of Mozart's and Salieri's, who over the years became one of the most significant mentors in her professional life. In addition to the personal friendship that flourished between the Farrencs and the Bratislava-born composer, Aristide also saw the commercial potential in their relationship. He acquired the publishing rights to Hummel's music and didactic work, a man famous as a composer and piano virtuoso who developed a new fingering technique for the piano, and thus Aristide provided his publishing house with fresh impetus. When Hummel came to visit them to iron out the contractual details, the couple held a festive dinner at which the eminent composer announced his retirement from the concert stage.

Theme and Variations

As a woman with two parallel professional personas, one of a performer and the other a composer, it is hardly surprising that of the fifty-one opuses composed by Louise, thirty-two are for piano. But she did not stop there. Side by side with these works she also wrote chamber music in which she accorded the piano and woodwinds a leading role. Her affinity with these instruments, the flute in particular, was the result of her studies with Reicha in her youth, and no less due to the fact that Aristide was an accomplished flautist. From this standpoint Louise was a groundbreaker since the flute only appears in French chamber music much later in an ensemble similar to that employed by the French composer Francis Poulenc. This is manifested in her two *Piano Quintets*, in which the ensemble comprises piano, violin, viola, cello, and double bass.[6] The uniqueness of this ensemble, which is reminiscent of Schubert's Quintet *The Trout*, is the use of the double bass instead of two violins. It is assumed that like many other composers who wrote parts for certain instrumentalists (or singers) they knew, Louise, too, wrote this special part for a brilliant double bassist who played with the Paris Opera, and whom she evidently knew personally. She frequently performed her two Quintets at soirées – musical evenings for invited audiences – or at matinees in the early afternoon. The Quintets gained her professional notice among both critics and music lovers who were the regular consumers of music in Paris of the time.

The Opera Craze

The musical aesthetics of Paris of the time revolved around virtuosity, character pieces aimed at presenting mastery of the piano and enthralling the audience. This was Paris of the Cancan, Mazurkas, Nocturnes, and amusing satirical songs whose tunes were hummed by the masses; the Paris that was captivated by descriptive elements and program music was swept up in the opera craze as well. The audience was swamped with libretti, and newspaper reports, and also with ideas of how music should be listened to, and how it should be sung. Piano reductions that could be heard at performances in private homes changed the way in which audiences experienced listening to opera. The playing and singing enabled lovers of the genre to re-experience what they had heard with a full ensemble, and those possessing basic piano skills and sight singing could also experience performing.

To some extent Piano Fantasies composed during those years were responsible for shaping audience taste. One of the operas on which Fantasies were written was *Norma*, by the Italian composer Vincenzo Bellini. At the center of the story that unfolds in ancient Gaul – France of today – is a female character, Norma, who is torn between her duty as a high priestess and as the daughter of the Archdruid, and her forbidden love that yields two children. Like other composers in Paris at the time, Louise composed *Theme and Variations for Piano on three Cavatinas*, short songs of simple, restrained character, from the opera that had taken Paris by storm.[7] She expressed Norma's conflictual state of mind with melodies differing from one another in character, and the atmosphere they create, from restless perpetual motion, through expressive pensiveness in a gentle lilt to an assertive statement, concluding in the style of a moderate dance.

Between 1825 and 1840 Louise mainly composed music for the piano that was reviewed by leading critics of the period. However, the critics – all of them men – could not refrain from making comments rooted in prejudice regarding the works of women. Robert Schumann, for example, wrote in his paper about her Variations on a Russian Air:[8]

> *Were a young composer to submit to me variations such as these by L. Farrenc, I would praise him highly for the auspicious talent and fine training everywhere reflected in them. I soon learned the identity of the author rather, authoress, the wife of the renowned music publisher in Paris...[9]*

Despite the highly laudatory opening, he goes on to express his complete lack of belief that a woman could compose such a work:

> ...so finished that one must fall under their charm, especially since a subtle air of romanticism hovers over them.10

Louise continued composing, devoting herself to instrumental music that was outside the mainstream. In its form and content her music embodied the continuation of the classic school: works for the piano, symphonic works, and chamber music, which in retrospect were the harbingers of the style of the 1870s. Like the French-born composer of English descent George Onslow, who before her had been dubbed "the French Beethoven", she too raised the banner of instrumental excellence that was the antithesis of the fashionable Romances, the Quadrille (a square dance performed typically by four couples and containing five figures, each of which is a complete dance in itself), and other works whose declared aim was to amuse the audience.

The 1840s were kind to Louise and her family. Her daughter Victorine followed in her mother's footsteps, progressing along the road of piano virtuosity, and in 1842 Louise herself was appointed professor of piano studies at the Paris Conservatory. Beyond her acceptance to this prestigious post, it was the first time in history that a woman was given a chair in the renowned institution, and it was an outstanding achievement.

As mother and daughter progressed professionally and were happy, Aristide decided to embark on a new and satisfying career. He gradually wound down his publishing business and began devoting his time to researching seventeenth-and eighteenth-century music. As a publisher he had some rare manuscripts in his possession, including a sizable repertoire of works for keyboard. He decided to gather these manuscripts and convert them into a single rare collection he called *Le Trésor des Pianistes* (The Treasure of Pianists).

Success, Awards, and Crises

Louise took a great interest in her husband's musicological project, and she included works from this unique anthology in her concert programs. During this period in which women were excluded from establishment orchestras and ensembles that played in public, she organized concerts for herself in the private arena. At the same time she continued composing chamber music, including her famous Nonet that became her most-performed work.[11] Its first performance was in 1859 and drew a large audience. Among the musicians for this premiere was the famous violinist Josef Joachim who at the time was not yet nineteen, and the performance was a resounding success.[12]

Following the dizzying success of her Nonet, Louise requested that her salary from the conservatory be on the same scale as that of her male colleagues. Her request was approved, but the wheels of bureaucracy turned very slowly, and she received her salary increase only after a time which in her view was far too long.

Her contribution to chamber music is undisputed, and on two occasions, in 1861 and 1869, it gained her the prestigious *Prix Chartier* of the *Académie des Beaux-Arts*.[13] This was a totally unexpected and extraordinary event considering that throughout the nineteenth century the academy was male-dominated.

Together with composing chamber music Louise wrote three symphonic works. Her *Third Symphony in G minor,* op. 36, opened the Paris Conservatory's subscription concert season in a concert featuring Beethoven's Fifth Symphony. Her deep-seated fear that the eminent composer's symphony would overshadow her own in its first performance was proved unfounded when the audience responded enthusiastically.

But all at once her happiness with her success and the joy of creativity were cut short. Louise's world collapsed in ruins when her daughter Victorine contracted tuberculosis and died aged thirty-two. The anguish that engulfed the family home was unbearable. Louise shut herself off from the world, and grief became her constant companion. She stopped composing and ceased to play at concerts. Her only regular activity was teaching and helping Aristide to complete his enterprise – collecting and editing the keyboard repertoire.

But that was not the last of Louise's travails. In 1865, seven years after their daughter's death, Aristide also passed away. To overcome her grief this time she decided to complete her husband's project herself. The decision to work and not sink into a slough of despond filled her with renewed vigor, and she worked energetically, classifying and cataloguing, editing and proofreading. At one point she enlisted the aid of some of her students: each of them played pieces from the repertoire before they were published, and together they discussed the stylistic and execution issues of the music. At the conclusion of the ten-year process, *Le Trésor des Pianistes* was published. This unique anthology, comprising twenty-three volumes of early keyboard music written over a period of 300 years is currently housed in Hunter College, New York.[14] In the extensive introduction to the first volume Louise presents her professional conclusions, including the dilemmas and questions which emerged in the course of the classification and editing, and also subjects raised by her students who participated in the historical concerts she held.

Adagio Cantabile

Side by side with her musicological endeavor Louise continued teaching composition and piano, albeit her declared preference was composition. At a certain point she realized that the number of students in her classes was dwindling, whereas the classes of her male colleagues were full. At first she was angry, thinking that this was because she was a woman, but after a while she realized that she was facing discrimination of a different kind, this time against the backdrop of her advanced age. Because she did not have enough students she found herself in financial straits, and toward the end of her life she was compelled to put Aristide's rare books and manuscripts up for auction.

She retired from the Paris Conservatory in 1872, but her music was played in the city until her death in 1875. At her last concert, on 14 February 1875 at the *Théâtre du Châtelet*, she played the *Adagio Cantabile* from her Third Symphony.

Seven months later, on 15 September 1875, Louise Farrenc died aged seventy-one.

Nine

Minerva: Fanny Cécile Hensel-Mendelssohn-Bartholdy (1805-1847)

On a fine spring day, Friday 14 May 1847, Fanny Hensel-Mendelssohn was sitting at the piano accompanying her private choir. They were rehearsing for the Sunday concert at which her brother Felix's *Die erste Walpurgisnacht* was to be performed. All at once her hands dropped to her sides and she lost consciousness. Someone ran to call Sebastian, her sixteen-year-old son who was having a painting lesson in the adjacent summerhouse, and he summoned a physician. Examination showed that she had suffered a massive brain hemorrhage, and she passed away without regaining consciousness at eleven o'clock that night.

That Sunday, which should have been a joyous musical occasion, turned into a day of profound grief. The piano in the spacious hall at Leipziger Strasse 3 in Berlin was replaced by Fanny's coffin. The newly-widowed Wilhelm sat stunned beside the coffin, but still his hand sketched yet another drawing of his wife. He recalled that a week earlier Fanny had a nosebleed, but she had viewed it as the result of her excitement about the forthcoming concert, and had continued rehearsing.

"In their lives and in their death, they were not divided"

Felix Mendelssohn did not attend the funeral of his eldest sister, his soulmate and the person closest to him. The news from Leipziger Strasse reached him at a time when he was suffering from chronic fatigue and hypertension. On 28 October 1847, some five months after his beloved sister's death, he and his wife Cecile were out for a stroll, and on their return home he collapsed on the doorstep. On his recovery from what was a stroke he hastened to send some of his sister's works to the music publishers Breitkopf and Härtel, as if in atonement for his years of opposition to her publishing her music.[1] A short time later he became paralyzed, and six months after Fanny's death, he too passed away. In retrospect it seems likely that the Mendelssohn family suffered from a genetic defect. Aside from Fanny and Felix, their grandfather Moses and their parents Abraham and Lea all suffered strokes, as did their sister Rebecka who died of a stroke when she was only forty-seven.

Perfect Fingers

Fanny Hensel-Mendelssohn was born at 6.30 in the morning on 14 November 1805, the first child of Lea and Abraham Mendelssohn and granddaughter of Fromet (née Guggenheim) and Moses Mendelssohn, the Jewish Enlightenment philosopher. It was a cold wintry morning in Martens Muhle near Neumühlen in the Hamburg district. The birth was difficult and the new mother was exhausted, but when the midwife congratulated her and showed her new daughter to her, Lea exclaimed that her tiny fingers were "perfect for playing Bach fugues".[2]

Lea, a daughter of the enlightened, affluent Salomon family, was a delicate, kindhearted, shrewd, and educated woman. She was fluent in four languages – including Greek – and took great pleasure in reading Homer in the original. However, she did this in secret lest it be said of her that she occupied herself with matters inappropriate to a woman of her standing. She did not conceal the fact that she was an amateur pianist of high standard, since the piano that stood in the center of any self-respecting nineteenth-century bourgeois home was considered a suitable instrument for women.

Abraham joined his brother Joseph's banking house of Mendelssohn & Friedlaender in Hamburg, and was the first Jew to be elected to the city council. He was an educated man, a confirmed music lover, and a pillar of German society. Like many others in the Jewish community who were not Orthodox, he did his best to assimilate into German society, and wanted to be seen as just another human being and not be labeled by the religious faith into which he was born.

"Male and Female Created He Them"

Fanny was a serious, obedient child who acted strictly in accordance with her parents' dictates. In the afternoon as she played with her dolls she listened attentively to her parents' conversations as they planned her educational future: she would study languages, literature, history, mathematics, science, and of course music. As an only child she dreamed about the company of other children, a dream that came true on 3 February 1809 with the birth of her brother Felix. The house was filled with the sound of the baby crying and the laughter of his happy sister.

Six months later, when she was only four years old, Fanny was given her first piano lesson by her mother. Lea, too, had learned to play at a young age, and in her room in her parents' home there was a piano at which she spent many hours every day. Fanny's first lesson lasted five minutes, to which her mother added a few more minutes with each successive day. She demonstrated to her daughter the position of the hands on the keyboard, what the forearm does when the fingers are busy striking the keys, and how to hold her posture. Baby Felix was also in the room, but he kept quiet during the lesson as if he already understood that in his mother's strict study regime there was no place for his voice.

At the end of the lesson Lea sat at the piano and played works by famous composers, first and foremost Johann Sebastian Bach, her favorite. As Fanny watched her mother she daydreamed: in her mind's eye she could see herself, a beautiful young woman dressed in the height of fashion (but not flauntingly so), sitting erect, legs together, and a soft smile on her face – proof of her good upbringing – playing wonderfully, just like her mother.

After lessons Fanny would amuse herself with Felix by telling him stories and singing to him. She proudly introduced him to relatives, friends, and guests who came calling, and her joy was boundless on hearing their admiration of the beautiful baby with a face like those of the cherubs in Renaissance paintings. "At long last there's a beautiful child in the family," she heard one of her aunts say, "the girl is talented and intelligent but not at all beautiful". Fanny was chubby and somewhat ungainly, with a slightly hunched back she had inherited from her grandfather Moses, which lifted her right shoulder, but her angelic smile and the love that Felix radiated to her helped her feel strengthened, and for a moment, beautiful too.

Flight to Berlin

The bond between them was reinforced further, and on 11 April 1811 they were joined by their new sister, Rebecka. The baby with her alabaster face bore a strong resemblance to Felix, but unlike her brother she seemed particularly fragile and delicate. She was born in the shadow of political change in Hamburg, Germany's largest port city at the time. As a result of the maritime blockade imposed by Napoleon, Hamburg became a center for the smuggling of sugar, coffee, cocoa, oil, wine, cotton, and other goods forbidden for importation. The Mendelssohn family bank thrived on undeclared revenue on which it did not pay tax, but with the arrival of the new French governor in 1812, the two brothers decided to flee the city before being exposed to the authorities.

They left in the dead of night and on reaching Berlin went to the home of Grandmother Fromet at Neue Promenade 7, near the Garnisonkirche. Fromet, already widowed, lived on the ground floor. The second-floor apartment was rented, and

Fanny and her family were housed on the "aristocrats' floor" that included four rooms, and servants as befitting their standing.

Neue Promenade was populated by Jewish and Christian families, and also numerous Jews who had converted, and good relations and mutual respect were maintained between them. The Jewish Enlightenment movement provided the Jews with an alternative way of living, and on the face of it there was nothing to distinguish them from the non-Jews. But the parents were concerned about their children's future career. They made sure that their Jewish faith would not hinder their children's talents and achievements. The missionary activity taking place around them together with suppression of the Reformists, added to the fact that coveted offices were open solely to converts led many of the Mendelssohn family's friends to the conclusion that converting to Lutheranism was the right strategy for them. On this subject, Dr. Leopold Zunz, a scholar considered the father of Jewish studies, wrote: "...But I consider it below my dignity and indeed a blot on my name to have myself baptized in order to enter upon an office in Prussia... We live in gloomy times. The scoundrel becomes respected, whereas respectable men are coerced into villainy."[3]

1815 was the year that witnessed the largest number of Berlin's Jews converting to Lutheranism.[4] Lea Mendelssohn was contemptuous of the Jews that converted during this period, calling the phenomenon "this hypocrisy". But she too was concerned about her children's future professional career and social standing. Moreover, her brother Jakob, who had converted and changed his name from Salomon to Bartholdy, persuaded her and her husband that anti-Jewish prejudices would only hinder his nieces' and nephews' progress in life. After long deliberations it was decided that

Lea and her husband would remain Jewish, while Fanny and her three siblings would be baptized in a private, intimate ceremony. In 1822, the parents would also convert, but in the meantime their decision to have the children baptized was kept secret from Lea's mother Bella, an Orthodox Jewess who had disowned her son Jakob immediately after his conversion.

On Thursday, 21 March 1816, the family attended the *Jerusalemkirche*, where Pastor Stegman awaited them. There, in the empty church, at a private ceremony attended only by the parents and Uncle Paul Bartholdy, Fanny, Felix, Rebecka, and baby Paul were baptized into the Lutheran Church. Thenceforth their surname would be Mendelssohn-Bartholdy.

Prelude

That same year the family traveled to Paris so that Fanny and Felix could study under the tutelage of the well-known teachers Mlle. Marie Bigot and M. Pierre Baillot. Bigot was a well-known composer and pianist who specialized in performing the works of her personal friends Joseph Haydn and Ludwig van Beethoven. Baillot was among the first faculty members of the Paris Conservatory, and his reputation as a virtuoso and expert on chamber music preceded him.

After a few months in Paris the Mendelssohns returned to Berlin, and the children entered a strict regime of study. Their timetable began at five o'clock in the morning, and only on Sundays they were allowed to sleep in until six. It was expected of Fanny and her brother that they work hard to enhance and develop both their intellect and professional talent.

In April 1817 Fanny and Felix began studying under Ludwig Berger, an interpreter of Beethoven's works and a leading Berlin pedagogue. After her first year Fanny surprised her parents on their wedding anniversary by playing for them – and the family audience that had gathered in their home – the twenty-four Bach preludes from *The Well-tempered Clavier*. She played from memory, and the rumor of her talent spread, reaching her Aunt Henrietta, Abraham's sister and Lea's closest friend, who at the time was living in Paris. Henrietta wrote to Lea that the child's achievements were indeed amazing and aroused respect for her mother who had ensured her musical education at such a high standard. But she added that despite her respect for and admiration of the talented Fanny and her ambitious mother, she criticized the strict regimen that her sister-in-law imposed in the home. "The extraordinary talent of your children," she wrote, "wants direction, not forcing."[5]

Fugue

Lea was used to criticism from her sister-in-law, a governess by profession, and was not offended by it. She was well aware that her Fanny had a thirst for knowledge, that she had a profoundly inquiring mind, and that study was utter pleasure for her. To consolidate and expand the knowledge that she and her brother had already acquired, the services of senior lecturers and scholars seeking extra work were hired. When the parents' relationship with certain teachers became untenable, Abraham did not hesitate to put his children into the hands of better ones. Thus, for example, when tension arose between Berger and the Mendelssohns, the latter hired Berger's rival, Carl Friedrich Zelter, an admired teacher of composition.

Aside from her lessons in playing and composing, Fanny also studied history, basic mathematics, and possessed good knowledge of the map of the world. But more than anything she loved the great classics of literature, especially Shakespeare's plays. Standing at the center of her and Felix's extramural activities were home theatrical productions, and the two worked assiduously at this pastime, presenting their work to their parents, the extended family, and friends. Their favorite play was *A Midsummer Night's Dream*. Additionally, she and Felix produced a paper whose summer edition was called "Garden Time", whereas the winter one was called "Teatime and the Snow".

An Ornament for Her Sex

In the afternoon the family gathered in the living room, reading aloud and watching *tableaux vivants*, costumed displays of popular paintings which at the time were considered the most sensational "last word". Fanny sat at the piano and played the gavottes she had composed over the last year, twelve pieces based on a dance of moderate tempo originating in the Dauphiné region of France, and which was popular in the court of Louis XIV.

But despite the girls' success, and particularly Fanny's progress in composition and piano, and the other subjects she studied, at a certain point the sisters and brothers were separated. Abraham hired the services of a senior lecturer in history from Berlin University, a classical philologist, and a senior mathematics teacher for Felix and Paul, to broaden their horizons and prepare them for their matriculation examinations. By contrast, Fanny and Rebecka learned the art of conversation, languages, religion and ethics, drawing and painting, dancing and music, as well as the efficient running of a household.

As on every birthday, when she reached fifteen Fanny received a letter from her father in which he wrote, "Music will perhaps become his [Felix's] profession, whilst for you it can and must only be an ornament, never the root of your being and doing. We may therefore pardon him some ambition and desire to be acknowledged in a pursuit which appears very important to him, because he feels a vocation for it, whilst it does you credit that you have always shown yourself good and sensible in these matters; and your very joy at the praise he earns proves that you might, in his place, have merited equal approval. Remain true to these sentiments and to this line of conduct; they are feminine, and only what is truly feminine is an ornament to your sex."[6]

The girl did not rebel, but continued composing artistic songs and pieces for the piano, albeit the separation of the boys from the girls aroused Lea's opposition. She kept a close eye on her daughters, and as far as she was concerned it was crystal clear that their talents were not inferior to those of her sons. Moreover, on different occasions she saw Fanny stealing along the corridor and eavesdropping on the lessons taking place in the next room. One evening Lea spoke to Abraham and persuaded him that they should allow the two girls to join Felix and Paul's lessons at least once a week. Abraham consented, and thenceforth the four children gathered to study together on the appointed day every week. What went unnoticed to the parents was the fact that Felix, who missed Fanny's presence in his lessons, devoted two extra hours every week to going over with her whatever he had learned with his history teacher, another two hours to what he learned in mathematics, one hour to geography, and another hour to German conversation. Thus the two studied together for six extra hours.

Together with her regular studies, Fanny's playing progressed and her composition matured. For her father's birthday she played a song she composed for the occasion, and the enthusiastic family lauded her work. For a brief moment she managed to forget the troubling thoughts about Felix's impending journey. The plan was that Zelter, who taught them both, would accompany Felix to Weimar where he would present him to Goethe, the supreme authority of assessing writers and artists.

Felix and Zelter left for Weimar while Fanny remained at home, drawing strength from the Lieder she composed of which she had already written more than twenty, as well as a piece for piano. Did the reports received at the Mendelssohn home about the great poet waxing lyrical over the talents of the boy with the golden curls rouse envy in her? If they did, she kept it to herself.

A Fateful Encounter

In the course of 1821 the Mendelssohn family were invited to a *tableau vivant* staged by King Friedrich Wilhelm III of Prussia and the Russian heir-apparent Archduke Nicholas, who was visiting with his wife, Grand Duchess Alexandra Petrovna. Petrovna (formerly Princess Charlotte) was Friedrich Wilhelm's eldest daughter, and the visit to her family in Berlin was to raise her spirits after she suffered a stillbirth. Fanny and her family were invited to the festive event and the exhibition of paintings that preceded it. A young painter, Wilhelm Hensel, was retained to paint the royal performers in their oriental costumes. While looking at the paintings, Fanny caught Hensel observing her.

Next day Hensel called at the Mendelssohn home and much to Abraham and Lea's displeasure, began courting Fanny. He was fourteen years her senior, the son of a poor clergyman from Brandenburg, and they suspected that he was after her money. They did not voice their opposition to his calling on Fanny, but received him with outright coolness. By contrast, Fanny was amused by her ardent suitor and was happy to discover that they had a common language. Their meetings became part of her schedule, and the more she got to know him, the more she was impressed by his ambition and talent.

And indeed, Wilhelm informed her one day that he had been granted a prestigious bursary from the *Royal Academy of Arts* in Berlin that enabled him to study classical art in Rome. Fanny's heart missed a beat, but outwardly she displayed great joy. Wilhelm confided to her that he was concerned that in his absence someone else would win her affections, and so to safeguard his status he asked her parents to betroth her to him.

Lea and Abraham did not hesitate for a moment before refusing point blank, and keeping his proposal secret from Grandmother Bella who was a pious Jewess. Their concern heightened when they discovered that Wilhelm was considering converting to Catholicism in the footsteps of his sister Louise. Even though two of Abraham's sisters had converted to Catholicism – one of whom lived in their home – Lea was shocked by the idea. In her consciousness the Catholic religion was akin to fanaticism. To make sure that Wilhelm fully understood their opposition to his proposal she wrote him a letter in which she explicitly stated that her daughter was too young to be a grass widow, yearning for her love who would be so far away. Furthermore, Lea did not allow the two to correspond, thus imposing silence and longing on Fanny and Wilhelm.

Summer Roses

After Wilhelm left, Fanny expressed her mood in a Lied she composed to the words of a poem by his sister Louise:

> *Summer roses are blooming*
> *and wafting fragrantly around me,*
> *I see them all dying away,*
> *I'll have no more flowers.*[7]

With Wilhelm away, Fanny helped her mother prepare for opening their home for the Sunday concerts. Lea wrote personal invitations and the children were busy rehearsing for their first performance in the private domain, which would quickly become one of Berlin's cultural centers. Among the guests who attended the Mendelssohn musical salon were the poets Wolfgang von Goethe, Ludwig Tieck, and Henrich Heine; historian Leopold von Ranke; folktale collector Jacob Grimm; composer and critic E.T.A. Hoffmann; salonniere and poet Rachel Varnhagen; philosopher Wilhelm Friedrich Hegel; scientist Alexander von Humboldt; and leading lights from the world of music such as violinist Eduard Rietz, composers Ferdinand Hiller, Carl Maria von Weber, and other well-known personalities from Berlin and beyond.

For Fanny and her siblings these musical gatherings provided a stage for demonstrating their musical talent. Fanny and Felix played the piano, Paul the cello, and Rebecka demonstrated her professional singing. All this was ostensibly perfect familial harmony, but seething beneath the surface were jealousy and conflicts between the siblings. Paul and Rebecka felt they were being discriminated against, and Rebecka would later state unequivocally that "My older brother and sister stole my reputation as an artist… Next to Felix and Fanny, I could not aspire to any recognition."[8]

Joy and Melancholia

In the summer of that year, on the morning of Saturday 6 July 1822, the Mendelssohns set out on a three-month grand tour of Switzerland. The declared intention of the tour was to travel through green landscapes dotted with lakes so that Lea could recover from the deep depression she was in following a stillbirth. But behind the excursion there were also practical considerations. It was a fine opportunity to open a window onto the big world for the children, since there is nothing like new places and people for enriching one's personal and musical repertoire. One of the high points of the tour was Fanny's meeting with Goethe, in the course of which she played for him and gained his approbation. But like all those around her, Fanny knew that as a woman in a bourgeois family like hers she would be unable to advance like her brother.

The Mendelssohn family returned home in the fall, and behind the scenes the relationship between Fanny and Wilhelm became more firmly cemented. For Christmas he sent her a six-part anthology containing seventy-six poems by his good friend, the renowned poet Wilhelm Müller. To the bound book he attached a portrait of his poet friend, a poem from the anthology, and a dedication to her:

> *This book full of joy and melancholy*
> *in a motley dream of lieder*
> *I hang in quiet humility*
> *on your Christmas tree.*
> *And if I had created it,*
> *Thou dear one, believe me,*
> *it would speak much of thee,*
> *much of it would be for thee.*
> *May its contents, then,*
> *be dedicated to thee,*
> *and as proof,*
> *I myself am signatory.*[9]

And here he appended the portrait as his signature.

The gift reached its destination and was immediately returned to the sender. Lea wrote to him that she did not wish to cast a pall over the Christmas festivities, but she took a dim view of a young man sending his portrait to a young lady. She had therefore decided to return the gift so that he could resend it in a more appropriate manner.

Her mother kept Fanny apprised of everything pertaining to Wilhelm, and she was happy to hear that a letter had come from Uncle Jakob Bartholdy who had met Hensel in Rome. Jakob, an enthusiastic patron of the arts, wrote to Lea telling her how impressed he was by the young man's talent and work, and added that he had commissioned him to paint a fresco for a whole wall in his home. Lea, who was considerably influenced by her brother, began thinking that she had perhaps been mistaken about her daughter's young suitor.

For his part Wilhelm did not sit twiddling his thumbs, and resolved to win over his beloved's parents. He sat down in his studio in Rome and did a pencil sketch of each of the Mendelssohn family members, with Fanny taking pride of place. He sent the sketches to Lea with a personal letter. She looked at the figures and was forced to admit that they had been executed with great sensitivity and in meticulous detail by the hand of a master. She was particularly moved by the sketch of Fanny. For the first time she saw her daughter as a young woman whose beauty radiated from her. There was no doubt in her mind that the man was an artist of great perception. She sat down at her escritoire and wrote to him again, this time in a somewhat softer tone.

Women's Work

Fanny's professional life was given a boost with the family's move to their new residence at Leipziger Strasse near Potsdamerplatz. The main house had a row of rooms with arched windows overlooking a big garden in which there was a small summerhouse. Around them there were seven acres of parkland and gardens and a small farm that supplied the house with fresh milk and butter. The house also boasted a spacious music room that could seat over a hundred.

Every day Fanny spent many hours at the piano practicing for her next concert in their home. The new house quickly became a small temple at which a large audience thirsting for art and music gathered every other Sunday. Fanny's work gradually matured. Her style was a combination of eighteenth-century classic form and innovative harmonies in the spirit of the Romantic period, with the piano in her lieder playing a duet with the voice in the best tradition of artistic song. Yet despite her compositional progress, her parents felt it inappropriate for a lady to publish her works.

To save her from embarrassment, her parents decided that six of her songs would be published as part of a collection of Felix's songs (Felix Mendelssohn, opp. 8 and 9).[10] The decision allayed Fanny's fears, who sought to avoid the trenchant criticism that stemmed from a stereotypical perception of creativity. This perception held that the feminine creative process is manifested solely in the creation of new life, whereas the male version is expressed in the public domain and takes place in material and sound, the written word and the spirit. Ironically, eighteen years later when Felix performed Opus 8 before Queen Victoria, she confessed that *Italien* was her favorite, and Felix was forced to confess that it had been composed by his sister Fanny.

Following the Mendelssohn family custom, Fanny received a letter of greeting from her father on her twenty-third birthday. Together with his good wishes he expressed his satisfaction with her, while not forgetting to remind her of her vocation in life: "...You must become more steady and collected, and prepare more earnestly and eagerly for your calling, the *only* calling of a young woman – I mean the state of a housewife. True economy is true liberality... Women have a difficult task; the constant occupation with apparent trifles, the interception of each drop of rain, that it may not evaporate, but be conducted into the right channel, and spread wealth and blessing; the unremitting attention to every detail, the appreciation of every moment, and its improvement for some benefit or other – all these and more (you will think of many more) are the weighty duties of a woman."[11]

And Fanny fulfilled his expectations. She mainly concentrated on the events held in her home, while making sure that she didn't rock the family boat. She called herself "Minerva of the house" after the Roman goddess who zealously safeguarded her chastity and was responsible, among other things, for poetry, wisdom, and the invention of musical instruments. This comparison with Minerva reflects the duality of Fanny's soul. On the one hand she fulfilled her role as a woman for whom the home is the center of her world, and on the other she was an active composer and performer of a high musical standard. The two sides come together when she advises her brother on professional matters: "I have watched the progress of his talent step by step," she wrote in her diary, "and may say that I have contributed to his development. I have always been his only musical adviser, and he never writes down a thought before submitting it to my judgment."[12]

The correspondence between them, and her brother regarding her as the supreme authority on composition, deluded her into thinking that she was a full partner in his professionalism and public success even outside Berlin. But it was only an illusion, for Felix traveled the length and breadth of Europe and progressed as a composer and conductor in the public arena, whereas she remained behind at home. And thus, despite her creative work, for Fanny the future seemed bleak and shrouded in mist.

he Wheel

Wilhelm's return to Berlin and his appointment as the Prussian Royal Court Painter sparked hope of a brighter future in the young Miss Mendelssohn. Although her friends and relations joked at her expense, saying that she would marry only Felix, and despite her parents' displeasure over her relationship with Wilhelm, she was now determined to follow her heart. She responded to Wilhelm's wooing, and when he asked for her hand she made it perfectly clear to her parents that she intended to marry him.

But even after their engagement was announced, the Mendelssohns still perceived Hensel as an outsider who had burst into their familial intimacy. In one of her letters to Felix, Rebecka described how on the previous evening Fanny had been sitting with her ardent fiancé by the light of an enchanting moon, and the young lady had fallen asleep. Why had she dozed off, asked Rebecka, and answered her own question: Because you are not here.[13] At the time Rebecka was in high spirits since her elder sister's engagement had opened the way for relationships of her own. Prospective suitors flocked to her door, and her reputation as a beauty who was both wealthy and amusing preceded her, so much so that Heinrich Heine, for example, declared that he only called on the Mendelssohns when Rebecka was at home, otherwise he became bored.

And Wilhelm? He continued with his art in order to win over the Mendelssohn family. Aside from the portraits he drew of them all, he also did a pencil drawing called *Das Rad* (The Wheel) depicting the Mendelssohn family circle. In its center is Felix in traditional Scottish costume, an allusion to his intended journey, while the sisters Fanny and Rebecka embracing form the spokes as otters (Felix called them his "fish-otters"). Hensel himself is outside the closed wheel, chained to Fanny's right hand, an allusion to the fact that at the time he was still unsure of his future as part of the family. Yet an important fact is that he drew himself as a winged Ixion, a medieval symbol of wisdom and fame. This drawing, together with one of Fanny, he sent to Felix, himself no mean artist, and in return received a letter replete with admiration of the notion of the wheel. He was less pleased with the drawing of his sister, since to his taste Hensel had not captured the rare, ardent, and prophetic side that radiated from her.

On 1 October 1829, two days before the wedding ceremony, Wilhelm was summoned to the home of Lea and Abraham to sign a prenuptial agreement whereby Fanny's inheritance would be put into a trust fund with an annual yield of five percent, and which would ensure their daughter a regular income.[14] She would also be entitled to decide what to do with the money without her husband's consent.

On the eve of the wedding the celebration at the Mendelssohn home was in the best bourgeois tradition – fine food and drink, and dancing until the small hours. As usual, Wilhelm sat drawing, and this time it was a pagan scene with a satyr in its center surrounded by naked dancing figures. Throughout the evening Fanny voiced her disappointment to him that Felix would not be at their wedding. When the engagement was formally announced she quickly wrote to Felix asking him to write a piece for organ that would be played at the ceremony. At the end of August, when he was in Wales, he informed her that he could already hear the work in his mind and was starting to put it down on paper. But a month later he was involved in a coach accident that left him with a seriously injured knee, which prevented him not only from completing the work, but also from attending the wedding in Berlin. At around nine in the evening Fanny was going out of her mind – not only would her beloved brother not be attending her wedding, the organ work that was to accompany her down the red-carpeted church aisle would not be played either. Wilhelm suggested that she compose a piece for the event herself, and so before the guests left the house she began jotting down ideas. Next morning, her wedding day, she wrote to Felix: "...Then, around 9 o'clock, Hensel suggested that I compose a piece, and I had the audacity to start to compose in the presence of all the guests. I finished at 12.30 and I don't think it's bad."[15] And she went on: "...your picture is next to me, and as I write your name again and almost see you in person before my very eyes, I cry, as you do deep inside, but I cry... I'm glad to have experienced it, and will be able to repeat the same thing to you tomorrow and in every moment of my life. And I don't believe I am doing Hensel an injustice through it."

At the ceremony held in a modest Lutheran church on 3 October 1829, Fanny walked down the aisle on her father's arm to the music of the Organ Prelude she had composed.[16] After the ceremony the couple moved into the small summerhouse in her parents' garden. Their life together was good, they loved one another, and they each respected the other's art. Hensel was an even-tempered man and held a liberal view of his new wife's musical career, while Fanny was happy with the freedom that enabled her to devote herself to playing and composing. They began their mornings with breakfast together, after which they would go into their respective studies, and in the evening they would share what they had done during the day.

On 6 March Fanny felt a new life stirring inside her, and the intimacy between her and Wilhelm deepened. This was one of the happiest periods of her life. The warm little house, with Wilhelm's paintings and drawings that filled the rooms, the English piano that stood in the center of the house at which she spent many hours every day, all filled her with joy. Not to mention Wilhelm's small, intimate gestures towards her, like the miniature he put into her journal of a slumbering baby enclosed by petals, and a winged faury hovering above. In the evenings a small circle of friends would gather in their house, and while Wilhelm worked on his portraits[17] the guests talked about events in France, the July Revolution, and argued vociferously. Wilhelm was an expert on the events of 1813-1814 instigated by Napoleon, and was not shy of voicing his conservative views that supported the monarchy. Fanny, on the other hand, held more liberal opinions, but she spoke only infrequently about politics in Berlin, or about what was going on in other parts of Germany. Her main interest was what went on in her own home.

Lobgesang (Hymn of Praise)

Fanny and Wilhelm's only son was born two months early on 16 June 1830, and they named him after his mother's favorite composers: Ludwig Felix Sebastian Hensel, and the family called him Sebastian. The premature birth, new motherhood, and concern for the premature baby preoccupied Fanny, and caused her to shift between days of depression and a dried-up fount of working, and bursts of creativity. The family came to her aid, and to raise her spirits they decided to convert what had been Abraham's study into a comfortable, fully accessorized studio for Wilhelm. Another room adjoining it was built for working with his students, who were an inseparable part of life in the Hensel home.

Together with Wilhelm's work at home, Fanny slowly recovered and gradually went back to her own study where she composed, played, and initiated new projects. First and foremost was the music salon that began with the intimate groups of friends that gathered on Sundays for conversation, light refreshments, and music. These events quickly became much sought after matinees for any self-respecting bourgeois Berliner, and Fanny was their heart and soul.

Over seven months, between June 1831 and January 1832, she composed four cantatas. She completed *Lobgesang* when her son was a year old, and wrote in the dedication: "To Felix Ludwig Sebastian Hensel on his first birthday, from Mother".[18] The structure of the cantata is similar to that of Bach's Christmas cantatas, but like other Baroque period composers Bach did not write cantatas as a personal testimony, and certainly not about a mother's love. On the other hand, for her work Fanny chose verses expressing her subject as a private woman, and mainly as a mother for whom the experience of giving birth was still fresh in her mind. "A woman when she is in travail hath sorrow, because her hour is come: but as soon as she is delivered of the child, she remembereth no more the anguish, for joy that a man is born into the world" (St. John 16:21). The first performance of the cantata in which the composer sang the leading role before an invited audience took place on 6 July 1831, Wilhelm's thirty-seventh birthday.[19]

Hiob

Fanny's personal womanly thanksgiving experience was cut short on 29 August 1831 with the outbreak of the cholera epidemic in Berlin. The city's authorities were unprepared for this event, there was no hospital capable of treating the many people taken ill, and even when the hospital that in the past had dealt with the smallpox epidemic was opened, it had only thirteen beds. Although the newspapers reported that the epidemic was less virulent than expected, it still affected 2,271 people and took 1,426 lives. Among the victims were friends and relatives of the Mendelssohn family such as Fanny's Aunt Yetta, philosopher Georg Friedrich Hegel, Peter Ulrich, a student of Wilhelm's and one of Fanny's close friends, Friedrich Zelter, Fanny and Felix's teacher, playwright Ludwig Robert and his wife Friederike, and the noted Jewish salonniere Rachel Varnhagen.

It was at this time that Fanny devoted herself to writing her *Hiob* cantata which she had begun in June, and for which she chose verses that had become more relevant than ever in view of the epidemic raging all around: "What is man, that thou shouldest magnify him? And that thou shouldest set thine heart upon him? And that thou shouldest visit him, and try him every moment?" And further: "Wherefore hidest thou thy face, and holdest me for thine enemy? Wilt thou break a leaf driven to and fro? And wilt thou pursue the dry stubble?" After two verses expressing despair and pondering Man's insignificance compared with the universe, she chose to conclude the cantata with a hymn of praise to the Almighty. The approaching Christmas holiday caused her and her family to feel they were lucky not to have been afflicted by the epidemic, and on 10 December 1831 the cantata had its first performance in their home in honor of Abraham Mendelssohn's birthday.

The epidemic was still raging, and in January Ulrike Peters, a noted soprano and close friend of Fanny's, fell ill. Once again Fanny turned to music and within a short time composed *Hero and Leander*, a dramatic scene she dedicated to her friend Ulrike's recovery. At the center of the narrative stand the mythological lovers – Hero, a priestess of the goddess Aphrodite who dwelled in a castle on the shore of the straits of Hellespont, and Leander, a young man from Abydos on the other side of the straits. Leander was in love with Hero, and each night would swim across the Hellespont to visit her, and she would light a beacon atop a tower to guide him. But on a stormy winter's night the waves swept Leander away, the wind extinguished Hero's beacon, and Leander drowned. In her grief Hero flung herself from the tower into the sea, killing herself. It was Wilhelm who wrote the text of Hero's monologue[20] and Fanny completed the orchestration of the scene in the course of January 1832. To their great sorrow, Fanny's friend Ulrike was unable to hear or perform the work. She died in February that year.

Northern Light

As the epidemic abated, life resumed its normal course. It was at this time that Lea came to the conclusion that her daughter Fanny's remarkable musical achievements – her lieder, piano pieces, and orchestrated works – were worthy of publication. But as a woman true to the values of the patriarchal society in which she lived, she requested the approval of her son Felix who was already a celebrated composer:

Permit me a question and a request. Shouldn't she publish a selection of lieder and piano pieces? For about a year she's been composing many excellent works, especially for the piano... That you haven't requested and encouraged her to do it – this alone holds her back. Wouldn't it therefore be appropriate for you to encourage her and help her find a publisher?[21]

Her composer son delayed his reply, and when it did come it was not at all encouraging. He contended that Fanny was not interested in either a career or the rights to her works. She is a woman, she runs her household, and does not think about publishing. Publishing her music would only interfere with her duties. He concluded by saying that he did not agree to the publication of his sister's works by any manner or means.

But Felix was wrong. Fanny, who had already composed more than 250 works, took no interest at all in running her household, in parties and fine clothes, or any other material pleasures. Her main interest was composing. Lea was also aware of this but did not dare oppose her son's opinion. Only Wilhelm felt that he did not need Felix's approval. He was sure that his wife's works were worthy of publication, and constantly urged her to have them published.

But Fanny was still not prepared to do so, for like other women artists down the centuries she too suffered from the "anxiety of authorship" syndrome.[22] Publishing a work meant revealing their most profound inner truth to the whole world, as though they were saying, "This is me, this is my work, and I present it to the whole world".

This fear led women artists to use pseudonyms they could hide behind (see the Prologue). Fanny, however, did not, but compared with Felix and other male artists in her milieu, she underestimated herself as a composer. Thus, for example, when she composed her *Lobgesang* cantata, and while she was working on *Hiob*, she wrote to her brother that her mind was full of ideas but she was unable to hold them down and consistently give them expression. "Therefore", she explained somewhat apologetically, "Lieder suit me best, in which, if need be, a pretty idea without much potential for development can suffice."

In his reply Felix affirmed that her creative talent was unsuited to composing liturgical music, which in his view was a monopoly controlled by male composers. Moreover, he criticized his sister's choice of texts and orchestration. "What the deuce made you think of setting your G horns so high?" he rebuked her, referring to the last part of the opening of *Lobgesang*.[23] And as we have seen in the Prologue, what seemed "incorrect" to Felix's ear in the nineteenth century sounds uniquely original to anyone listening to the cantata today. And the text? It is not a random choice, but precisely what Fanny wanted in it.

The Lemon Tree Is in Bloom

In early fall 1836 Fanny sent Felix some short character pieces for the piano, each of which expresses a specific emotion, some introvert and filled with expression, and others more extrovert and restless.[24] Her joy knew no bounds when he expressed his satisfaction, but as in the past she was self-effacing and presented herself as always needing approval. "I don't know exactly what Goethe means by demonic influence," she writes to him, "but this much is clear: if it does exist, you exert it over me. I believe that if you seriously suggested that I become a good mathematician, I wouldn't have any particular difficulty in doing so, and I could just as easily cease being a musician tomorrow if you thought I wasn't good enough at that any longer. Therefore treat me with great care".[25]

Despite this declaration it does not appear that Fanny ever considered stopping being a musician. Music was an inseparable part of her, and it sprang from within her in a constant flow. Paradoxically, despite the fear of publishing her works she constantly voiced her views in her extensive correspondence with Felix, in which she gave her professional opinion on composing in general and on his and her own works in particular, and also discussed personal issues that arose in matters pertaining to their lives and relationships with their parents, siblings, and their other relatives. Humor stands out in her letters, as does a deep (and critical) perception of her milieu. This was also the vein of the letters she wrote when she and Wilhelm were on their grand tour of Italy in 1839-1840.

At the end of August 1839 the Hensel family embarked on their tour of Italy, a country that had fired the imagination of the German bourgeoisie, a country linked with blossoming lemon trees, light and warmth, together with art treasures and a scintillating historical past. For Fanny it was an opportunity to get away from her sister-in-law Louise, who lived with them. Louise was a devout Catholic who purposely observed religious rituals, and criticized her brother's and sister-in-law's very active lifestyle. The Hensels traveled to Leipzig where they spent some time with Felix and his wife Cecile, and from there continued to Munich. Fanny enjoyed meeting the local artists that Wilhelm had met while in Rome, among them the talented pianist Delphine Hill-Handley (née von Schauroth) to whom Felix dedicated his *Piano Concerto in G minor*. Fanny and Delphine spent several enjoyable hours together before the Hensels went on their way toward the Alps, which they would cross on the way to Italy. Fanny was excited by the lakes and Milan; the water, the flora, and especially the exotic fruit – lemons, oranges, and figs – were indescribably romantic for her. But when they reached Verona and Padua she was shocked by the stench in the filthy streets, and the neglect she felt existed in the palazzos and museums as well. The mentality of Italy and the Italians was diametrically opposed to her Prussian education, but still, she enjoyed the sights she saw – the palazzos, churches, and museums of Venice and Florence with the works of the great Italian painters: the Florentines da Vinci, Michelangelo, Raphael, and Botticelli, and the Venetians Tintoretto, and Titian. In Rome the couple rented a four-room apartment on Via del Tritone, not far from Bernini's Triton Fountain and close to Casa Bartholdy, the home of Uncle Jakob. In Rome Fanny found the musical endeavor in the city to be of a considerably lower standard than that in Germany, the private concerts miserable, and the Vatican choir singers off-key.

The Hensels socialized with the German émigrés of their class who lived in the city. Fanny was also glad of the personal and professional encounters she had with the famous composers Gounod, Berlioz, and Massenet, among others, and she played in their homes. All of them were amazed by her intellect and musical talent, and the faith these eminent male musicians had in her strengthened her belief in the artist within her.

Das Jahr (The Year), January-December

In the first half of 1841, after their return from Italy, Fanny composed twelve character pieces for the piano, each representing a month of the year. The original music, which constitutes a challenge to pianists from the standpoints of expression and technique alike, was written by the composer on colored staff paper. Each season had its own color, an illustration by Wilhelm, and a short poem. The end product, which ultimately became the *Das Jahr* (The Year) cycle for piano, is unique, not only in the corpus of works that Fanny left behind, but also because the work is a milestone toward our understanding of nineteenth-century piano music.

On 13 December 1842 Lea Mendelssohn passed away. At the end of the mourning period the Hensels moved into the big house at Leipziger Strasse 3, and Fanny threw herself into running the house that was filled with the vibrant sounds of entertaining and renewed artistic endeavor. At the age of thirty-seven she was wholly devoted to renewing the Sunday concerts in her salon. Her musical works – choral and chamber music, and of course music for the piano – were presented in the music room, which could seat a hundred people. It was there that she spent many hours at the piano each day, and where on Friday afternoons she rehearsed with her choir which consisted of eight sopranos, four altos, and two tenors, and with the small private orchestra she formed. Thus she created a musical body that elevated the private milieu to the level of a prestigious, sought-after cultural institution. Even the Berliner Sing-Akademie – the internationally renowned music institution – was proud of Mrs. Hensel-Mendelssohn's important professional salon. Even though she sometimes complained about the coldness of the Berlin audience, every event she held in her salon played to a full house, with standing room only. On clear, warm summer days the Hensels opened the "garden hall", thus enabling the elegantly dressed audience the opportunity of enjoying the beautifully tended garden as well. And Felix, although not physically present, was there with his music. "It is impossible to describe the furor your lieder are creating here," Fanny wrote to him, "I play them everywhere, and a pair of ladies regularly fall into a dead faint nearby. Our little artistic circle, made up entirely of *fanatici parla* who love waltzes and Sebastian Bach, has, among other things, instructed me to kiss your hands in writing"[26]

The rehearsals and performances became her driving force, but it was as if Fanny felt that the sands of time were running out. "If only once I could have as many rehearsals as I wanted! I really believe I have talent for working out pieces and making the interpretation clear to people. But oh, the dilettantes!"

When she reached forty, for the first time in her life she placed herself as a professional entity vis-à-vis the amateur musicians and singers with whom she worked.

It was during this period that Fanny admitted to Felix that although she feared his opinion she was resolved to publish her works: "Since I know from the start that you won't like it, it's a bit awkward to get underway. So laugh at me or not, as you wish: I'm afraid of my brother at age 40, as I was of Father at age 14... In a word, I'm beginning to publish!" In almost the same breath she confessed she was angered by the fact that she was publishing her Opus 1 at such an advanced age, relative to that of her brother.[27]

Her deepening self-awareness coupled with the decision to break out and publish her work constituted a joyful part of 1847, the last year of her life. In early spring she wrote in her diary:

Yesterday the first breath of spring was in the air. It has been a long winter, with much frost and snow, universal dearth and distress, indeed a winter full of suffering. What have we done to deserve being among the few happy ones in the world? My inmost heart is at any rate full of thankfulness, and when in the morning after

*breakfasting with Wilhelm we each go to our own work,
with a pleasant day to look back upon, and another to
look forward to, I am quite overcome with my own
happiness.*[28]

Fanny Hensel died on Friday, 14 May 1847.

Postlude

What happened to the rest of the family following Fanny's
death?

Wilhelm sank into a state of deep grief that affected his
mind. Despite the commissions that flowed his way, he
could not manage to paint. Furthermore, his mental state did
not allow him to care for Sebastian, even though he lived for
fifteen more years after Fanny's death.

Fanny's sister Rebecka adopted Sebastian and raised him
until her own death of a stroke in 1858. Felix Mendelssohn
died on 4 November 1847, six months after his sister and
soulmate, and was buried beside her in Berlin.

Ten

A Shining Light:
Clara Josephine Wieck-Schumann
(1819-1896)

She was a particularly quiet child who did not start talking until she was four years old, and her father's concern was so great that he even thought she was deaf-mute. He would sit her down at the piano and play simple pieces for her. When she repeated the pieces precisely he knew for certain that she was not deaf. In the personal diary he opened for her, he wrote "I was born on 13 September 1819. My godparents were a notary named Streubel, a friend of my father; Madame Reichel, a friend of my mother; and Frau Cantorin Tromlitz of Plauen, the mother of my mother Mariane Tromlitz. My father kept a musical lending-library and carried on a small business in pianofortes... and beside this my mother practiced from one to two hours a day, I was chiefly left to the care of the maid, Johanna Strobel. She was not very fluent of speech, and it may well have been owing to this that I did not begin to pronounce even single words until I was between four and five years old, and up to that time understood as little as I spoke. But I had always been accustomed to hear a great deal of piano playing and my ear became more sensitive to musical sounds than to those of speech..."1

A Shining Light

Clara Josephine Wieck was born in Leipzig on 13 September 1819 to musician parents, the second child of Friedrich Wieck, a well known piano teacher and dealer in pianos, and Mariane Tromlitz, a soprano and pianist in her own right. When she was still in her mother's womb her father decided that the infant would grow up to be a great star. He named her Clara, which in German means "shining light".

But the light did not shine in their home. Little Clara adopted selective hearing. She heard the piano notes very clearly, but blocked her ears against the sounds of anger and squabbling that filled the Wieck house. Her parents quarreled a great deal, her father shouted a lot, and when things were not to his liking even beat his wife and children. Thus, for example, when her brother Alwin was practicing on his violin and played off-key, his father grabbed him by the hair and hurled him to the floor.

Before Clara reached the age of five her mother left her father, granting him custody of the children. Once the divorce became final, her mother married Adolph Bargiel, a piano teacher and good friend of the Wiecks, and moved to Berlin with him. Over the years Clara maintained contact with her mother, but it was her father who brought her up.

It was during this period that she began learning piano with her father, and her strict daily regimen included piano lessons twice a day, and another three hours of practice. When she learned to read and write, she was assigned another daily task of memorizing material through keeping a diary. To ensure that she learned everything her father thought she needed to know, he made her copy the letters he wrote to friends, his correspondence with concert impresarios, and all his business paperwork into diaries kept for this purpose. He, who had known poverty in his childhood, viewed it as his duty to teach her that music is not just show and fame, but also a business venture that must be properly managed, and that one must know how to conduct oneself in it.

As the years went by Clara grew into a piano virtuosa who earned a great deal of money and indirectly publicized her father's teaching methods.

She studied under the tutelage of the best teachers of composition, singing, violin, orchestration, counterpoint, and fugue. At the same time her father opened a music salon in their home that would provide a stage to demonstrate her talent before renowned artists, performers, music critics, and a large audience of friends and acquaintances.

He Took Her by Storm

On 31 March 1828, when she was eight, she played in the home of Dr. Ernst Carus, director of the mental hospital at Colditz Castle. This medieval castle gained notoriety during WWII as the "Escape Academy" when the Germans used it to incarcerate prisoners of war who were potential escapees, most of whom were Royal Air Force aircrew. There, in the home of Dr. Carus, Clara first met Robert Schumann, a law student and pianist. The eighteen-year-old Robert heard the little girl play, and was so amazed that he too wanted to study with Friedrich Wieck. After obtaining his mother's consent, he moved to Leipzig where he lived in the Wieck family home.

The presence of the young man, ten years her senior, brought joy and excitement into Clara's life. During the day each of them would practice in their own room and in the evening she and her brothers, Alwin and Gustav, went into Robert's room and played boisterously with him as if he were their age. He told them stories, dressed up as a ghost that frightened them, and hopped around with them. Clara laughed and enjoyed it more than anything she had previously experienced.

And she needed it, especially after her father married Clementine Fechner, a piano teacher twenty years his junior, who bore him three more children. Clara and her stepmother did not get on well, but Clementine was compelled to suffer the presence of her stepdaughter on all the journeys she and Wieck took, including their honeymoon.

On 20 October 1828 the nine-year-old Clara played at the Leipzig Gewandhaus, a celebrated concert hall on whose stage every musician aspired to perform, and where her mother Marianne had performed in the past.[2] The duet she played with Emily Reichwald, who was also one of Wieck's students, gained them critical acclaim from the audience and the newspapers alike. Immediately afterwards she appeared with her father before the nobles of the court of Dresden, capital of Saxony, which was a magnificent center of culture and the arts.

Wieck was fully aware that the concert in Dresden would bring in its wake invitations to the courts of Berlin and Vienna. And Clara did not disappoint him. She was diligent, possessed musical ability of the highest order, and the audiences responded to her with love and warmth.

At big concerts she played Themes and Variations of popular virtuoso composers who were loved by audiences, and she also performed her own works in the same genre. Even though it was shallow music aimed at audience taste in the view of her father and other musicians, from a commercial standpoint playing and composing such music was the right thing to do. But there were also those who took a skeptical view of the credibility of her work, as evidenced by a review that appeared in one of the music journals of the time: "From a woman? No; this time from a little girl who is yet to become a woman... yet there remains a question of how much of it was the child's own work and how much contributed by another. In any case we would have considered it better if this publication had not appeared. Not on account of the compositions... but for the child's own sake. What reasonable person wants to have school exercises printed, even if they turn out well?"[3]

Love of Beauty

Clara had high expectations of their visit to Paris. In that musical city they met the leading virtuosic composers of the time, headed by Friedrich Kalkbrenner, Henri Herz, Johann Pixis, and their colleagues.[4] These pianists impressed audiences with their spectacular performances at the center of which was dexterity , and in the first half of the nineteenth century they were better known and more successful than Mendelssohn and Schumann, earning four and five times more than them.

But as usual, the greater the expectation, the deeper the disappointment. For Clara, the Parisian piano virtuosity sounded flamboyant and superficial. She felt this way about Kalkbrenner, whose works she knew well, and even Chopin's pianism, about whom her father wrote: "a handsome fellow, but Paris has made him slovenly and careless in himself and in his art."[5]

Clara, however, possessed a deep and wide understanding of music, and from an early age learned how to direct it to the audience's taste and impress it, while at the same time preserving musical quality. She composed virtuosic music because it was what the audience demanded, but at the same time she assiduously worked on character pieces which years later would be viewed as part of her more adult and mature works. Two of these are her Opus 5 and Opus 6, which gained the critical acclaim of Robert Schumann in *Die Neue Zeitschrift für Musik* (The New Periodical for Music), which he edited.[6] Opus 5 embodies the union between the conscious and the subconscious in the formation of the composer's professional and personal identity. In this work Clara allows herself to soar to distant realms from both the standpoint of the aesthetic concept of music, and that of her emotional growth. In it the fantastic, the virtuosic, and the lyrical are reconciled, what was and what will be, Spanish folk music with German musical tradition, Clara's 'self' with the different, the other.[7] In Opus 6 she chose titles identified with other composers' genres, such the Mazurka and the

Polonaise, which was related to Chopin, or the Capriccio that was associated with Felix Mendelssohn.

On her return from Paris, Clara's relationship with Schumann – who was still living in their house – blossomed. During the day the two practiced in adjacent rooms, and quite naturally musical motifs flowed from one room into the other. These yielded works in which a resemblance can be found, and it is sometimes difficult to clearly state which of the two composers wrote which motif.[8] At other times of the day they played duets, took strolls, and enjoyed each other's company.

While Wieck was pleased with his daughter's professional progress, he was not enamored of the love blossoming between her and his adult pupil. Clara was the realization of his own unfulfilled artistic aspirations, and his possessiveness of her led him to tighten the ring of restrictions around her. He read every letter she wrote before it was posted, on their travels he shared her hotel room, and it was he who wrote her personal diary for her in which he expressed his own impressions, opinions, and criticism of her and their surroundings.

Between 1836 and 1837 Clara and Wieck went on a concert tour in Europe. On this occasion she obeyed her father and stopped writing to Robert, but one day her longing overcame her and she sent a message to her beloved through a friend. In reply Robert sent her a proposal of marriage, and since according to the law of Saxony every couple that wanted to marry had to obtain their parents' permission, Robert asked Wieck for his daughter's hand. Wieck refused, contending that the marriage would adversely affect his daughter's career as a pianist, just as it had done with three of her competitor colleagues who had given up their careers in favor of marriage.[9] Clara was persuaded that she should live for her art and the world for a few more years, and with her father departed on another concert tour. In Vienna she excited her audiences to such a degree that her name was perpetuated with a new confection, "Torte à la Wieck". Despite being a woman, her young age, and the fact that she was not a citizen of the Austro-Hungarian Empire, and even though she was not a Catholic, she was named *Königliche und Kaiserliche Kammervirtuosin* (Royal and Imperial Chamber Virtuosa), the Empire's highest musical honor.

Dreaming in the Dark

Side by side with her great success Clara secretly kept in contact with Robert. When Wieck discovered this he sent her to Paris on yet another concert tour. On this occasion he decided that she should go on her own, hoping in his heart of hearts that the tour would be a failure. Somewhat apprehensive, Clara reached the metropolis of the music world, but quickly regained her composure and started to put into practice everything she had learned over the years from her father. She stayed with friends, taught music, observed her practice regimen, organized concerts for herself, and met new people, some of whom became her close friends. One of them was composer-diva Pauline Viardot, who was also an accomplished pianist (see chapter Eleven). Clara trusted Pauline and to her revealed her cherished hope of marrying Robert when she turned eighteen, despite her father's outright opposition. Pauline reassured her, saying that the future would be brighter, and the retiring Clara was moved by the refreshing approach of the young Frenchwoman whose lust for life infected all around her.

The Paris newspaper reviews were filled with praise for the young composer-pianist from Leipzig, but in fact they proved to be a fly in the ointment. After hearing the rumors of her success, Wieck threatened to completely disown his daughter, but this time Clara did not take fright. She and Robert submitted a marriage request which, as expected, was held up until Wieck gave his approval. Robert sent her some money so she could come back from Paris, but on her return to her home she found that her father had locked her out. In her dismay she went to her mother in Berlin, while court hearings with her father and her intended husband were being held. Wieck stopped at nothing: he broke open his daughter's letterbox and quoted from the personal correspondence between her and Robert. He also accused Schumann of being "a mediocre composer, whose music is unclear and almost impossible to perform". Of Clara he said that she was unfit to be a wife and mother since she had been raised to be a pianist but had never learned to manage a household. Furthermore, he wrote to musicians, music critics, and managers all over Germany in the hope that they would support him in court. None of them, however, intended to spoil their relations with Schumann, who was the leading music critic of the time, by speaking out against him.

And Clara? Her compassion for her father in his weakness was stirred.

The court hearings ended with a decision in favor of the couple, and they were married on 12 September 1840, one day before Clara turned twenty-one. After the wedding she complied with her new husband's wishes, reducing her appearances and concert tours that demanded her prolonged absence from home. In their new-found free time the couple read the works of Shakespeare, Goethe, and Jean Paul, and also studied and analyzed in depth the music of Bach and Beethoven, which was not in Clara's repertoire before her marriage.[10] Despite her new husband's decree that she should forget her art and creative work and devote herself

entirely to him and their home, Clara was happy. As young
as she was, she viewed this as a great compliment, but she
soon realized that life with Robert demanded great and
painful concessions on her part. "My playing is getting all
behindhand, as is always the case when Robert is
composing. I cannot find one little hour in the day for
myself! If only I did not get so behind!"[11] At this point her
husband's composing was the top priority in their home. He
sequestered himself in his room for hours on end, working
on his first symphony, and when he emerged he was
enshrouded in silence.

In the course of thirteen years Clara had ten pregnancies,
which gave the couple eight children. In fact, throughout
their marriage she was either between one pregnancy and the
next, or between a miscarriage and the next pregnancy.
During this time she drifted between a constant desire for a
career of her own, and acceptance of her frequent
pregnancies with good grace. As a young girl she was sure
that she was ready to give up everything for her husband, but
as the years went by her frustration at being unable to
professionally fulfill herself increased. At a certain stage she
decided to follow her heart, and although pregnant women
did not usually appear in public, Clara continued appearing
on the concert stage even when her advanced pregnancy was
clearly visible. She left her children in the care of Robert's
brother Carl.

The Quiet Lotus Flower

She was welcomed with love and open arms wherever she
went, but together with her success was Robert's
deteriorating condition. He suffered from deep depression
and frequently collapsed. On their return from a concert tour
of Russia in 1844, Robert decided to devote all his time to

composing. He subsequently sold *Die Neue Zeitschrift für Musik* which was celebrating its tenth anniversary, and cut himself off from society. In August that year his plumbing the depths of his own soul and his hard work defeated him, and following yet another collapse the couple decided to move to Dresden. In the early 1840s the city, which in comparison to Leipzig had been considered musically provincial, was once again on the European cultural map. The new opera house, the Semperoper, staged operas by Wagner[12] who had been appointed Royal Kappelmeister in Dresden, and the who's who of the world of music came to see and hear them.

But life in the Schumann home was not at all glamorous. Five years in Dresden brought Clara five more children and fewer concerts. To boost the family finances she taught piano, and in every free moment, day and night, she composed her best works which included piano preludes and fugues, and her famous trio that was born during her pregnancy with their fourth child. She did not feel strong enough to undertake a concert tour, and since she spent many hours at home with Robert, together they studied the works of Johann Sebastian Bach and Luigi Cherubini. The outcome of their joint study was Clara's *Piano Trio in G minor*, op. 17. It was her most ambitious work which gained great acclaim and was frequently performed in the nineteenth century.

The Schumann family's Dresden period came to an end in May 1849 with the failed May uprising against the royal house. Some of the rebels barricaded themselves in the famous Lutheran Frauenkirche, among them Richard Wagner who at the time was the Royal Saxon Court Conductor. When the uprising was quelled, many of its leaders were executed, while others were imprisoned. An arrest warrant was issued for Wagner who was forced to flee to Switzerland, and for twelve years lived as a refugee far from his homeland. The violence all around them forced Robert and Clara, who was pregnant with their fifth child, to hastily leave the city and move to Düsseldorf. It was there in 1853 that the young Johannes Brahms came into their life. The man who introduced Brahms to the Schumanns was the violinist and composer Joseph Joachim who was already a renowned international artist. He chose the eighteen-year-old Brahms as his accompanist in his recitals, and as a gesture of gratitude introduced him to his close friends Clara and Robert. As we shall see, the relationship between Brahms and Clara was a very close one, but its intimate details remain an enigma which the two of them took to the grave.

The Pain of Parting

On 27 February 1854 Robert jumped into the River Rhine in a failed suicide attempt. He did not recover from his subsequent collapse and passed away two years later. Brahms, who was then twenty-one, came to the aid of Clara and her children. He traveled to Düsseldorf, stayed with them for a while, and took upon himself the running of the household. In addition to keeping an eye on income and expenditure, he helped to publish Robert's works and invested the money for Clara and the children.

For her part, Clara came to the realization that she was now the family's only breadwinner, and at the same time as she grieved for the loss of Robert she began planning a concert tour. As a sober, practical woman she was fully aware of the fact that people were raising eyebrows about her relationship with the young composer. She therefore jealously guarded her privacy and did not speak about it to anyone. It emerges from a letter she wrote to a friend that she admired Brahms as a composer, a pianist, and a close friend. "He came as a true friend, to share with me all my sorrow," she wrote, "he strengthened my heart as it was about to break, he lifted my thoughts, lightened, when it was possible, my spirits. In short, he was my friend in the fullest sense of the word."[13]

In their correspondence over the years Clara and Brahms discussed family matters, each other's career and those of other musicians, financial matters, and of course the music he regularly sent her for her professional opinion. Although music was an inseparable part of their relationship, the written dialogues between them are thought-provoking since they spoke of more personal subjects. Thus, for example, Clara wrote to him: "Yesterday and today I have at last succeeded in having a few hours alone, and now to my joy I know everything thoroughly. But I cannot summon up the courage to write to you in detail about them. All the same I will try to imagine that things are still as they were before, and that I can tell you all that my heart feels with complete confidence."[14] She destroyed most of the letters attesting to a relationship that went beyond pure friendship, but among those that survived there is one she wrote while she was in England: "How I would like to come! But would it be possible...? If Bargiel went, nobody could say anything, but it would be too noticeable if I, who have nothing to do there, came."[15]

In Your Eyes

In 1857 Clara moved to Berlin where she devoted herself to her piano career which enabled her to provide her family with a respectable living. She left the children with relatives while she planned a concert tour of Germany and beyond. Once more she was aided by the tools she had acquired and assimilated from her father, such as planning and organizing concerts, negotiating fees, overseeing expenses, and of course advertising and public relations. She was a one-woman institution, and as a result of her Prussian education possessed a high level of self-discipline and attention to detail.

Her attitude toward the music she played was no less meticulous. In an era of improvisation she insisted on focusing on the score and playing exactly what the composer had written. At the same time she was well aware of her audience's taste and the fact that performing virtuosic works led to a significant increase in her fees. She therefore chose works the audience loved, such as those by Kalkbrenner, Pixis, and Liszt, together with works whose artistic quality was beyond doubt, like those of Bach, Scarlatti, Beethoven, Schubert, Mendelssohn, and Chopin. She wrote piano arrangements for the works of close friends like Pauline Viardot, Joseph Joachim, and Johannes Brahms. But above all she took upon herself the performance of her beloved Robert's works, the only piano composer who did not perform his own works. At the same time she completed the editing of Schumann's works and prepared an annotated publication of his piano music.

At Pauline Viardot's urging, Clara bought a country house on the outskirts of Baden-Baden and moved there with her family and three pianos. For her, the place that was an artists' colony was an island of tranquility where she could devote herself to her work, entertaining, and to calmness. At her friend's salon she enjoyed the sound of the special organ that had been brought from Paris. The instrument, built to order for the Viardot family by Aristide Cavaillée-Coll (1811-1899), who was considered to be the master organ builder of the nineteenth century, aroused longing for the time when she and Brahms had played a similar instrument together. After an unofficial concert held in Pauline's salon, Clara wrote to him that while the organ sounded wonderful, Madame Viardot couldn't play the pedal keys. "Why couldn't I have such an organ?" she asked him, and added a wish, "And then when you came and played on it... what divine music that would be!"[16]

Aside from her wish, her words have a somewhat envious tone regarding Viardot's wealth. Pauline could buy whatever she wanted, from apartments and summer homes, through the purchase of valuable manuscripts such as that of Mozart's *Don Giovanni* (see Chapter Eleven), to instruments specially made for her by the best instrument builders. Both Clara and Viardot were born into musical families, had a brilliant career, and earned handsome fees. But Pauline was cosmopolitan in both character and personality, had a broad education, and was talented in many spheres including the piano, singing, and composing. Clara, on the other hand, despite her musical talent and the professional acclaim she gained, was in her soul a worker whose lot was hard labor. Thus, for example, before buying the country house in Baden-Baden she wrote in her diary that her life was unbearable, and that she constantly had to think about where to go to find refuge for herself and her work. Additionally, she frequently suffered rheumatic attacks while playing, and sometimes the pain was so severe that the physicians prescribed opium for her. She visited spas and underwent hydrotherapy and massage that were supposed to alleviate the pain, while she continued to perform.

In the course of the 1860s and 70s she performed in dozens of concerts in Europe, Russia, and the British Isles, where she was extremely popular.

Romance

She returned to Berlin in 1873, and from 1878 she lived in Frankfurt where she accepted the invitation of the Dr. Hoch Conservatory to become the first woman to teach there. The director of the institution, who had avoided employing women, explained her employment in a way that would be totally unacceptable today: "As for Madame Schumann, I count her as a man."[17] This was, of course, a somewhat left-handed compliment: Clara was a skilled musician with a career spanning many years, who worked full time, and earned handsome fees that enabled her to support her children, and later her grandchildren.

A concert series at the Leipzig Gewandhaus celebrated Clara Schumann's fifty-year career. The hall was decorated in green and gold, and oak branches and leaves symbolizing strength, daring, power, and longevity. The audience rose to its feet as she came onstage and showered the platform with flowers. And the program? It was devoted entirely to the works of Robert Schumann.

Her last public performance was on 12 March 1896 in Frankfurt, and the last work she played was Brahms' *Variations on a Theme by Haydn*, op. 56b.[18] She planned a summer vacation with Brahms, but in March she suffered a stroke. On her deathbed she asked her grandson Ferdinand to play Robert's *Romance in F sharp major*, op. 28, no. 2. [19] Afterwards her condition gradually deteriorated.

Clara Schumann died in Frankfurt on 10 May 1898. Brahms attended her funeral and passed away eleven months after her.

Eleven

The Queen of Drama:
Pauline Viardot-Garcia
(1821-1910)

Her stage charisma captivated many, among them the writer George Sand who had come to see Rossini's *The Barber of Seville*. Sand was exhausted after her frustrating journey with Chopin, and was seeking a rewarding artistic experience that would soothe her wounded soul. From the moment that Pauline set foot on the stage as Rosina, she took her breath away. She had never heard such a voice and not seen such a perfect performance. At the end of the evening she lost no time in declaring that Pauline Viardot was a seminal event in operatic history, and that it was she who would shatter the conventional wisdom holding that women are incapable of crossing the frontier of talent that was the sole domain of great male performers.

Paris-New York

Pauline Garcia came into the world in Paris on a clear July morning, the third child of Manuel Garcia, one of Europe's leading tenors of the time, and Joaquina, a teacher and opera singer of Spanish origin. She was lovingly welcomed by her thirteen-year-old sister Maria Felicitas and their sixteen-year-old brother Manuel. Her two older siblings were already singing in their father's opera company and were sure that their newborn sister would join them in due course. But their father had other plans for Pauline, and he was a man not to be crossed – Pauline would become a famous pianist.

Manuel Sr. was an accomplished musician, handsome and charming, intelligent and ambitious, but he was also a bellicose, and some say vulgar man, who brought up his children in an atmosphere of theater and music. A normal day in the Garcia family home began with breakfast, followed at nine o'clock by an hour of practice at the piano, and at ten a three-hour rehearsal with the opera company, and after lunch they would all go to a concert together. The late afternoon hours were devoted to meetings with leading musicians, theater personalities, and other celebrities who visited their home. The children had to attend all these meetings, their main task being to assimilate everything they heard, be it gossip or musical matters.

When she was four, Pauline went to New York with her family and her father's company, all of whom except her were to appear in Rossini's *The Barber of Seville*, the composer having written the role of Count Almaviva specially for her father. On the voyage all the members of the company were subject to a strict learning regime dictated by Manuel Sr., whereas Pauline, due both to her age and her special relationship with her father, was allowed concessions. Between rehearsals she and her father strolled on deck, and he took great pleasure in the amazement his little daughter aroused when she spoke to people they met in any one of four languages.

The company reached New York on 29 November 1825 and began performing at the New Theater (later the Park Theater) with *The Barber of Seville*, the first opera to be performed in Italian in the United States, and the emigrant audience, which included many Italians, gave the company a prolonged standing ovation. The applause swelled when Maria, the eldest sister who sang Rosina, came onstage. Pauline admired her beautiful sister who was thirteen years older than her, and heard people all around talking about her unique vocal technique.

Maria developed into a well-known figure who had prospective suitors flocking to the door of their home. This led to some serious quarrels with her father who was incensed by the fact that she was devoting more time to her relationships than to practicing her music. She came home one evening and announced that she had met a man who had won her heart, and that she intended to remain in New York and marry him. His name was Eugene Malibran, a French banker twenty years her senior who would be able to provide her with a good life. Her father was enraged, and had no intention of letting go of his leading star. He and Joaquina did their best to dissuade their daughter from her hasty decision, but to no avail – Maria was determined to follow her heart.

Two days before her eighteenth birthday Maria married the man whose name she would bear until her tragic death. After her marriage the family split up. Maria remained in the United States with her husband, and appeared in another opera season in which she sang in her fluent English, her brother Manuel returned to France, and Pauline went on to Mexico City with her parents and the opera company. At this point her father arranged a strict study program designed to advance her career as a pianist. To this end he hired the services of the organist Marcos Vega who came to their home to teach the five-year-old girl whose feet did not reach the floor when she sat at the keyboard.

But the political situation in Mexico was volatile, and Manuel swiftly decided to take his family back to Paris. He converted his money into gold, hired an armed escort, and the caravan set off. The family legend tells of a thirty-strong group, of which twenty were women and children that drove through the mountains in horse-drawn wagons. One of the wagons carried the family fortune in gold worth 600,000 francs, or 24,000 pounds sterling. On the way their escort changed sides, broke open the chests containing the gold, and fled with it. Joaquina wrapped Pauline in a thick plaid blanket, protected her with her body, and quieted her frightened questions. Another version of the story has it that before their escorts fled with their booty they ordered Manuel to sing and were so captivated by his voice that they returned some of the gold, and even escorted the wagon train as far as the coast.

On their return to Paris the Garcias were surprised to find that Maria was already there and living in a home of her own. Her supposedly wealthy husband had not provided her with the comfortable life she expected, and the operatic roles she was offered were not up to her high standard, not to mention the fees. She therefore decided to return to Paris despite Malibran's objections. There, in her hometown, her rise in the music firmament was meteoric. Large audiences flocked to the box offices to hear the unique voice of the beautiful singer who, as we shall see, would become a legend.

Meanwhile Pauline embarked on a strict regimen in which she studied composition under Anton Reicha, an eminent teacher at the Paris Conservatory, and piano with Franz Liszt, who at the age of sixteen was already a promising pianist. She greatly admired Liszt and impatiently awaited her lessons with him. In her eyes he was the embodiment of beauty and talent, and when he demonstrated to her how she should play, all she wanted was for time to stand still. Liszt, on the other hand, viewed her as the little daughter of Manuel and Joaquina, his mother Anna's close friend.

Pauline got the most out of her piano lessons, and by the time she was eight she was sitting in her father's studio accompanying his numerous students. From time to time she asked him to teach her to sing too, since he was always telling her that a professional pianist should be familiar with the secrets of correct and beautiful singing. However, because his schedule was overcrowded, he managed to do so only infrequently.

Crises

Life seemed promising, but one morning in early June 1832, Manuel contracted a respiratory illness that rapidly worsened, and after only a few days he passed away. For his wife and children his death was a devastating blow, but in the newspaper reports his passing was a minor event since the whole country was engrossed in the cholera epidemic which at the time of Manuel's death had claimed more than 18,000 lives, among them Prime Minister Casimir Pierre Perier.

Thenceforth Pauline's life changed from stem to stern. She and her mother moved into Maria's house, who was in any case helping to support them, to save on the upkeep of their big house. Pauline's education, which had been in her father's hands, now passed over to her mother, and she insisted that her young daughter concentrate on singing, not the piano. Many people in their circle wondered why the girl, who was a gifted pianist, was forced to become a reluctant singer, and the evil tongues tut-tutted, saying that her chances of becoming a good singer were small, for her father had died before she had managed to learn the theory of singing from him. But Joaquina, who was a teacher and opera singer in her own right, was determined, mainly because she viewed the change of direction as the right financial step to take. Viardot-Garcia would regret agreeing to this change until her dying day. Many years later she would tell friends that her parting from the piano broke her heart with the same force as her grief over her father's death.

Although she had bidden farewell to her dream of becoming a famous pianist, throughout her life she continued composing for the piano. From the day she moved into her sister's house she devoted herself to her singing studies and preparing for her first concert tour as a singer. Her mother was joined by two musicians who helped her with this task – Pauline's brother Manuel who was a successful teacher of singing at the Paris Conservatory, and Charles de Bériot, Maria's constant companion and a talented Belgian violinist known throughout Europe.

Prior to her tour Pauline worked from morning to night, and it was no coincidence that she was dubbed "the ant" by her family. She devoted many hours to vocal training, and in addition wrote piano accompaniment for de Bériot's violin etudes, music to the words of famous poets, music for fifteenth-century poems,[1] and short pieces for the piano, among them folk dances like the Tarantella and the Habanera which had taken their place in nineteenth-century artistic music.

Despite her young age she was attentive to the artistic winds blowing in her milieu, such as the French inclination toward nostalgia. She lived in an era in which the past was captivating, a captivation that became an obsession. Scenes from the past appeared everywhere in France, architects devoted all their time and energy to restoring the decorations of ancient churches and cathedrals to their former glory. The writer Gustave Flaubert viewed this as a totally new phenomenon, yet another of the century's enterprising inventions. "The historical sense was born yesterday," he wrote to a friend in 1860, "and it is perhaps one of the nineteenth century's finest accomplishments."

When Pauline was fourteen, Liszt, her teacher, shining example, and spiritual mentor for many years to come, left Paris. He went to Basel to be reunited with his love. Contessa Marie d'Agoult, the writer known also by her pen name, Daniel Stern. Pauline was left heartbroken, and some said that she would not agree to see him ever again. But young as she was, she was wise enough to recognize Liszt's qualities as an artist and teacher and remained his loyal friend for the rest of her life. In her eyes he was a sui generis and she ignored those who belittled him and thought of him as a composer of virtuosic popular music that presented the technical abilities of its performer. She could see the great artist in him, and for her, like many other artists in the 1830s, art was a religion and Liszt was its high priest in its sacred mission.

And as if she had not endured enough crises in her life, one morning in early June 1836 the family received terrible news from England: her sister Maria had died. She fell from her horse while out riding, was injured, refused to see a doctor, and insisted on going onstage that evening and singing. She died in Manchester as a result of cerebral complications a week after her injury, and was only twenty-eight. After her death Maria became a legend of talent and beauty that had been cut short before its time.

Expectations

After Maria's death there were expectations that the void she had left would be filled by a figure that would continue her legendary musical heritage. All eyes were on Pauline, and indeed, in the spring of 1838, accompanied by her mother and de Bériot, she embarked on her first concert tour of Germany and Italy, and also appeared in Paris. Her first performance in Paris was in the salon of Madame Caroline Joubert, the bastion of Parisian who's who. Madame Joubert was an extraordinary figure in the Parisian scene: although she was not particularly pretty and was diminutive of stature, every beautiful woman who stood next to her paled into insignificance. She charmed all her acquaintances, her conversational ability was outstanding as was her ability to listen and bring her friends closer. The greatest poets of the time confessed their loves and failures in life to her.

It was at the Joubert salon that Pauline met Alfred de Musset, a poet and great admirer of her sister Maria. He was amazed by the young girl's singing and even more so by her serious conversation, which was a great compliment for her.

In the cultural and literary monthly of January 1839 he wrote, "She sings as she breathes... she possesses that great secret of artists: before she expresses anything, she feels it. She does not listen to her voice, but to her heart!"[2]

The newspaper reviews, however, were divided, and the less flattering ones caused her deep sorrow. What upset her most was that they compared her with her sister, and focused on her looks rather than her art. They wrote that she was unattractive, that her mouth was too bloated or too big, that her upper lip was extraordinarily long. She was presented in caricatures published in the papers with an extremely long neck completely out of proportion to her body. And the recurring question was whether her looks would hinder her on the way to becoming a great opera singer.

George and Frédéric

It transpired that Pauline's stage charisma outshone all the criticism and she took her audiences by storm. This was also the case with George Sand who attended a performance of *The Barber of Seville*. Sand was exhausted after her frustrating journey with Chopin, and was seeking a rewarding artistic experience that would soothe her wounded soul. From the moment that Pauline set foot on the stage as Rosina, she took her breath away. She had never heard such a voice and not seen such a perfect performance. At the end of the evening she lost no time in declaring that Pauline Viardot was a seminal event in operatic history, and that it was she who would shatter the conventional wisdom holding that women are incapable of crossing the frontier of talent that was the sole domain of great male performers. That evening she made sure she was introduced to Pauline and took her under her wing right away.

George Sand was an illegitimate child who left home at the age of fourteen and went to live in Paris. She was drawn to mysticism and a life of abstinence, but her stay in a convent was mainly marked by the numerous uproars she caused. Following her father's death in a riding accident, her grandmother brought her to her country home in Nohant and raised her as the daughter of aristocrats. After her grandmother died she inherited the house and converted it into a retreat for intellectuals and artists seeking somewhere to write or ply their art. Pauline joined the list of composers like Chopin and Liszt, writer Antoine de Balzac, painter Eugéne Delacroix, and many others who were guests of France's most famous writer of the time.

Sand wore men's clothes, adopted a man's pen name, and was active on behalf of women's physical and intellectual freedom, yet she was captivated by the romantic dream of "There is only one happiness in this life, to love and be loved." She had a complex romantic relationship with Chopin who lived in her house and wrote some of his best work in the room she assigned him, far from the hubbub of her numerous other guests.

Pauline and Chopin struck up an acquaintanceship in Sand's house and became close friends, spending many days at the piano. He gave her professional advice on her playing, the vocal works she composed, and her adaptations of his mazurkas, while she taught him the secrets of Spanish music through which he came to a profound understanding of the human voice. Sand was usually present at their meetings since she enjoyed the company of the two who at the time were her closest friends, and also kept her place with Pauline who was seventeen years her junior. Pauline made sure that George was part of every major event in her life. When Alfred de Musset proposed to her it was Sand who persuaded her that he was not the right match for her. Immediately after this she introduced her to Louis Viardot, a respected art critic, publicist, director of the Paris Théâtre Italien, and twenty-one years Pauline's senior. Sand convinced her and her mother that the man was both wealthy and of high public standing, and that he could provide her with the security that was beyond the means of her younger suitors.[3]

Mlle. Garcia and Mme. Viardot

Pauline Garcia and Louis Viardot were married on 18 April 1840. The forty-year-old bridegroom worshipped the ground his new bride walked on, and decided to resign from his post at the theater and devote himself to advancing her career. This ambition, however, did not follow the line of the socialist journal he founded with Sand in 1841, which opposed the Napoleonic regime. As a result of the journal's content, the establishment withdrew its support of Pauline and she, like other artists who depended on establishment backing, was compelled to seek success away from Paris. Not only that, some of her colleagues at the Paris Opera did all they could to put a spoke in her wheel. Her fiercest rival was the Milanese soprano Giulia Grisi, an Italian aristocrat by virtue of her marriage to the renowned tenor Cavaliere Giovanni Matteo Mario. Grisi, who was ten years older than Pauline, and who sang the same arias as her, had no intention of allowing Viardot-Garcia to gain a foothold in the Paris Opera. Although Pauline's voice was not as clear and pure as Grisi's, the musician in her and her learning abilities foiled both Grisi and Rosina Stoltz, another prominent member of the company. Pauline was determined to succeed, and together with her husband Louis organized private recitals for herself in Paris. She appeared at the salon of Madame Récamier, one of the city's cultural institutions, at the royal salon of Louis XVIII, and at a charity concert for the flood victims in Lyon. Afterward she went to the London Opera and from there to music festivals in Gloucester. In her free time she sat at the piano and composed music based on folksongs from the Berry region, and adapted French folk and popular songs for concert performance.[4]

In December 1841 she gave birth to her daughter Louise Héritte-Viardot, who would grow up to become a singing teacher and composer. After recovering from the birth, Pauline and her husband embarked on a concert tour, leaving Louise with George Sand at Nohant. George was glad that Pauline viewed her as an anchor and Nohant as her home port, but her protégée's all too frequent travels soon became burdensome. Their relationship, replete with deep emotions, began as a mother-daughter relationship and went on to become one between two romantic muses. Sand spoke of what went on between them as a friendly fantasy. In one of her many letters to Pauline she wrote, "Queen of the world, you must tell me which day is mine... I am too jealous of the happiness I feel when I see you to require the presence of other than the elitists among your admirers. Answer with one word whether it will be next week or on Sunday that my poet's attic would be lit with four candles... If I had millions, I would spend them on that day to buy oriental carpets to place under your feet... I admire genius well enough, but when it is coupled with goodness, I prostrate myself before it."[5] Two years after their first meeting, Sand published Consuelo, a novel at the center of which is an eighteen-year-old opera singer, Pauline's doppelganger. Ugly, black-haired, large-mouthed, with beautiful eyes and white teeth, deep-bosomed and slim-hipped, with small feet, and lovely hands. Sand, for whom music was the most sublime art, saw Pauline as her Consuelo.

In Sand's eyes Pauline was the ideal artist, a high priestess of the arts. Although they were involved in each other's lives and loved one another, they also quarreled. Sand tried to guide and dominate her friend's life as she did with everybody close to her. But Pauline was focused on her music and channeled all her mental resources to the opera stage where every evening she rediscovered the mystery of dramatic passion. As a mid-nineteenth-century artist she wholeheartedly believed that drama is a projection of life, and therefore people's admiration and love were manifested through it.

Turgenev

And indeed, it was at the St. Petersburg Imperial Opera that drama brought her together with Ivan Turgenev, the man who would become the third side of the triangle consisting of Pauline, Louis, and him. Turgenev, a twenty-five-year-old writer at the beginning of his career, would in time become the first Russian writer to gain the recognition and fame that traversed frontiers and continents.

He wrote "Stay!" on the evening he first saw her on stage: "Stay! As I see thee now, abide forever in my memory! From thy lips the last inspired note has broken. No light, no flash is in thy eyes, they are dim, weighed down by the load of happiness, of the blissful sense of the beauty it has been thy glad lot to express... Stay! And let me share in thy immortality; shed into my soul the light of thy eternity!"[6]

Turgenev fell in love with Pauline and remained true to his love until the day he died. "And for you, I lie at your feet. By your beloved feet will I live and die. I kiss them for hours on end and remain forever your friend."[7] He followed her to Paris and wherever else she performed, not concealing his love for her, on the contrary, he shouted her name from the rooftops. "My God, how good you are, and how good I feel in confessing it to you. I beg you to give me your good and noble hands to kiss in devotion."[8]

Although he was a well-built man, he was as shy as a young boy. He had kindly eyes with a trace of melancholy in his expression, his hair was straight and as silvered as his beard. Their love was kindled and ignited a flame of creativity. In Paris he lived under the same roof as her and Louis, in three rooms they placed at his disposal on the top floor, lived at their expense for long periods, and on numerous occasions even had to borrow money from Louis. Louis treated him like an overgrown child, but they also had much in common like their love of literature, hunting, and talking politics. Turgenev never married and treated Louis and Pauline's four children as his own. The nature of their relationship has never been fully defined, but that said, Turgenev worshipped Pauline until the day he died, and viewed their relationship as an unofficial marriage. His play *A Month in the Country* reflects the extraordinary bond between them.

Château de Courtavenel

Turgenev's love, her successful concerts, and the publishing of the music she composed for voice and piano to de la Fontaine's fables, all made that year a particularly productive one for Pauline. Added to her list of successes was the purchase of a property, Château de Courtavenel. Louis found the property, which was up for auction, in Vaudoy-en-Brie, some six kilometers southeast of Paris. The chateau had more than thirty rooms, six turrets rising above it, natural springs around it, a bridge and a well, and gardens with roses, dahlias, geraniums, and ancient trees adorning its land. The chateau also had a courtyard with farm buildings, a vegetable garden, and extensive meadows. The surrounding area was wooded and dotted with small hamlets. Louis, who was taken by what his hunter's eyes could see, immediately wrote to Pauline who was on tour in St. Petersburg, and quickly received her enthusiastic agreement. Living on a country estate was extremely fashionable among members of their social class, and their dream of a place of their own was about to come true.

Their bid for the chateau was successful, and their joy was so great that they signed the deed knowing full well that the price was far higher than what they had planned to pay. On her return to Paris Pauline went to see the chateau right away, and her head spun at the sight. She ran from room to room like a little girl, and imagined how the house would look after it had been decorated to her taste. They spent every penny she had earned on the house, but they needed tens of thousands of francs more for renovations and furnishings. But this did not trouble Pauline. She was in love with the place and could not help comparing it with Sand's house in Nohant. She was happy and immersed herself in redecorating the spacious house: she began by choosing colors for the drapes, and went on to buy furniture and ornaments in Paris, England, and the surrounding villages. Louis, who was an art collector, found room for paintings in every corner of the house, and Pauline, who had a collection of expensive carpets and porcelain, bronze sculptures, crystal glass, and silver, scattered them throughout the picturesque chateau that was gradually taking on a new form. Its opening in July 1844 was attended by many guests, including the village priest, the elderly mayor, and neighbors from nearby estates who came to satisfy their curiosity.

Envy

George Sand was the only one to not share their happiness. She was worried that now they had a home of their own, which was not inferior to and perhaps even surpassed her own, the Viardots would no longer visit her at Nohant. She hastened to invite them to spend a summer holiday with her, but Pauline gracefully declined, saying that she was presently devoting all her time to redecorating the new house, so much so that she barely had time to practice. George was hurt, and revealed her envy by saying that Courtavenel could never be compared with Nohant, and that Pauline and Louis would be forced to sell it due to the great expense its maintenance would incur. That summer, Chopin, who was staying with her, received the news of his father's death, and was plunged into grief. His depression cast an even gloomier atmosphere on Nohant, and George feared that other guests would avoid coming.

By contrast, life in the Viardot chateau was serene. Pauline was enjoying her new home, and Louis, too, gradually took part in country life: in the morning he went into the garden to gather vegetables and collect eggs from the chicken coop, and afterward both he and Pauline put on work shoes and went out to pick plums. Now and then, Pauline, who needed time on her own, went walking by herself. Her favorite spot was a fifteen-minute walk from the house, and there, on a big rock beneath an elm, she would sit and drink in the magnificent landscape spread at her feet. At five p.m., when she heard the bell announcing that dinner would be served shortly, she started back along the path to the house.

Louis thought that country life could replace life in the opera, but Pauline could not live without the stage. Her ambition gave her no peace, and neither did the great expense demanded by the estate. She went back to performing at the opera and in private recitals, and sang wonderfully. The audiences rose to their feet calling for encores, but the Parisian critics were unkind to her, while praising – seemingly intentionally – her rival Giulia Grisi. After her return, the musicologist Henri Blaze de Bury, who in the past had lauded Viardot-Garcia, wrote that she did not meet her audience's expectations. He went on to describe her performance as "pathetic" and added that while her style was perhaps acceptable in literary salons, it was totally unsuited to the stage of the Theatre Italien.[9]

George Sand and Louis Viardot defended her valiantly, but the press had a field day with what they construed as her decline and fall as a singer.

St. Petersburg

Pauline, hurt and disappointed by the critics, left Paris with Louis and went to perform at the Vienna opera. At first she achieved great success, but on her return a year later she was treated to a very chilly welcome. Pauline's spirit was unbroken, and right away she began organizing a tour to St. Petersburg and Moscow where she was spoken of as a prodigy, and for good reason. Unlike other European women who spoke only their mother tongue, Pauline was fluent in six languages and comfortably communicated with the local people wherever she went. Furthermore, she was blessed with an exotic appearance which the European bourgeoisie associated with *le rêve espagnol*, the Spanish dream that was part of the orientalist trend, the magic of the Orient. Different landscapes, unfamiliar fragrances and colors, and the different appearance of people – especially women – captivated them, and in Western consciousness were associated with mysticism, and personal, creative, and sexual freedom. Mérimée and Bizet's *Carmen*, Flaubert's

Salammbô, Wilde and Strauss's *Salome*, and Gauguin's *Two Tahitian Women*, were but a small part of the romantic male dream in the mid-nineteenth century. Pauline, known as "La Garcia", met all the criteria: a Frenchwoman of Spanish origin, a Spanish woman who sang in Italian, German, and Russian as if born into those languages, she wrote operettas with libretti in French and Russian, and composed Spanish music in flamenco rhythm using vocal techniques reminiscent of strumming a guitar. She wrote music to the poems of Pushkin and Lermontov, and even translated them into French and German. One woman who was an entire orchestra of dialects, drama, and music, she reminded critics and audiences of beauty from another world: "She reminds us more of the terrible magnificence of the jungle rather than the civilized beauty and tame grace of the European world in which we live. In moments of her passionate performance, particularly when she opens that great mouth with its dazzlingly white teeth and smiles in such a cruelly sweet and gracefully snarling way, one would not be surprised if all of a sudden a giraffe, leopard or even a herd of elephant calves crossed the scene."[10]

Her profound awareness of drama, which among the opera singers of the time was quite unique, was what lay behind her great success. Drama was more important to her than all else, so when she sang Desdemona in *Otello*, for example, and the applause did not stop in the second act because the audience wanted her to sing again, she did not accede to their request so as not to intrude on the drama unfolding onstage. In Act Four she sang *The Willow Song* and *Ave Maria*, and once again did not accede to the audience's request for an encore, but continued in her role.

Spiritual Support

Even though she was one of the central musical figures in mid-nineteenth-century Paris, and despite her professional self-confidence, in every period of her life Pauline needed a man to provide her with spiritual support. Although she admired and respected Louis, he was neither the kind of intellectual nor creator she yearned for, while Turgenev, although a renowned writer, was too weak. She had literary colleagues she trusted, some of whom were wealthy admirers of stature, and there was also Sand who over the years had provided this support, but Pauline sought thrills. She met Ary Scheffer when Louis commissioned him to paint her portrait. After he introduced them, Louis asked the artist's opinion of her, to which Scheffer replied, "She is horribly ugly, but if I were to see her again, I think I would fall hopelessly in love with her."

Scheffer became her spiritual guide and mentor, a sort of father figure. She admired him and consulted him about everything, played at dinners he held, and published a volume of her works illustrated with his lithographs. It was in Scheffer's studio that she met Charles Dickens who was also there to sit for his portrait.

Pauline literally did not manage to put her house in order. Boxes littered the whole house and dirt piled up everywhere; even after eight years it looked as if its residents had only recently moved in and were to leave shortly.

But the disorder in her house bore no resemblance to the way in which she managed her social and professional life. Although Pauline was creative, instinctual, and unique, she was also deliberate and calculating. She did not stop at being one of the few lyric artists that drew the attention of composers, poets, and critics, nor at being one of the four women who influenced the arts in the second half of the nineteenth century.[11]

She preplanned her moves, and after Scheffer's death sought a new male figure that would enthuse her and be her spiritual guide. She found what she was looking for in Julius Rietz. They met in Leipzig in 1858 at the height of a particularly successful concert tour, when the press said that she was the greatest singer of her generation. Although Rietz was elderly and far distant from the realization of her romantic dreams, he was an extremely talented musician and an admired cellist, conductor, and composer. He worked with Mendelssohn on the revival of Bach's *St. Matthew Passion*, collated the works of Handel, Mozart, and Haydn, and was a colleague of Schumann who was resident conductor at the Leipzig Gewandhaus.

Rietz provided Pauline with the intellectual excitement and professional support she needed in Leipzig, and for a while after she left the city. When she went to England and Ireland they wrote to one another every day. During the day she performed on opera stages and enjoyed a social life, and in the evening she would sit in her room and write to Rietz, sometimes until the wee small hours. She called him "My teddy bear", and shared with him her experiences while on tour, and he wrote her about his thoughts and musical experiences. But after some time he tired of this intense writing, and the flow of his letters gradually tailed off. Pauline was hurt, stopped writing to him, and their relationship withered.

Don Juan

In the summer of 1855 all of Pauline's attention was given to the original manuscript, signed by Mozart, of his opera *Don Giovanni*. She had sung various roles in the opera for more than twenty years, and had come across the manuscript one day in London. It transpired that in 1800 this original manuscript had been sold by Constanze Mozart to Johann Anton André, a German composer and music publisher, and at the time one of the leading Mozart scholars. After his death in 1842, the manuscript was handed down to his daughter Augustina who was married to the Austrian piano maker Johann Streicher.[12] The Streichers offered to sell it to three libraries (the Imperial Library in Vienna, the Royal Library in Berlin, and the British Museum in London), but all three declined the offer. Pauline then purchased it in London for 180 pounds – money she raised through the sale of some of her diamonds – and her excitement knew no bounds, since for her the manuscript was sacred. She had it bound in eight volumes and stored in a specially-built thuya wood box, an aromatic wood that grew in the central Atlas Mountains. The box was finished in brass, with an escutcheon in the shape of an M on the lid, and an inscription in faux Latin lettering bearing the composer's date of birth and death.[13] She placed the box in a room next to what she called "my little organ room", which housed the instrument that had so captivated Clara Schumann, and which for Pauline was a sacred relic too. Only a chosen few were accorded the privilege of a close look at the manuscript, whereas others had to make do with observing it through a small glass panel in the lid of the box. Rossini, one of the lucky ones, knelt before the famed historical object, and Tchaikovsky claimed he felt that he was in the presence of divinity. The latter came to Pauline's house on a stormy, rainy day, and was charmed by the woman who, although no longer young, was still full of life and was pleasant, courteous, and warm. Pauline, who knew everything about everything, was fully aware of Tchaikovsky's longstanding love of Mozart, and two days later invited him to a festive dinner. That evening she led him into the shrine housing Mozart's manuscript. Tchaikovsky was beside himself at the sight of his favorite composer's original manuscript. "I saw the orchestra score of Mozart's Don Giovanni, written in his own hand!" he wrote. The autographed copy gave rise to a ritualistic discourse for many years, and was elevated to the status of a national monument when, in 1871, it was exhibited at the Exposition Universelle, the international exhibition marking France's recovery from the Franco-Prussian War. In 1887 the manuscript was on display at an event marking the 100th anniversary of the first performance of the opera in Prague. To mark the occasion Tchaikovsky orchestrated his Suite *Mozartiana*.

The Adviser

It was during this period that Pauline's reputation not only as a singer possessing extraordinary dramatic talent spread far afield, but also as a teacher and musical adviser to the leading composers of the time. The French composer Hector Berlioz, for example, who did not feel sufficiently skilled on the piano, was assisted by her in editing the final version of his opera *Les Troyens*, which later became a great success. On 20 April 1849 he wrote about her in *Journal des Débats*: "Madame Viardot... is one of the greatest artists in the history of music."

Baden-Baden

In 1863 Pauline Viardot-Garcia retired from the stage. Her voice had tired after performing difficult and demanding roles, including coloratura roles that were beyond her range. Writing to one of her students she cautioned her to protect her voice: "I wanted to sing everything and I ruined my voice," she wrote among other things. During this period,

Louis openly opposed Napoleon III, and Paris no longer suited them, so he and Pauline decided to move to Baden-Baden in Germany.

This small town, Europe's most fashionable resort, lay halfway between Paris and Vienna, and Italy and Russia, and was the meeting place of all the great writers, composers, and artists from France, Russia, Germany, and Austria. The King and Queen of Prussia wintered there, Johann Strauss, king of the Viennese waltz and composer of *Die Fledermaus*, and his orchestra gave daily open-air performance of his music, and scores of artists and thousands of visitors attended the numerous music festivals held in the town. Strauss was the main musical attraction. He was tempestuous, on edge, and electrifying, and under his baton the orchestra played in a manner second to none.

It was therefore not by chance that Viardot-Garcia, the cosmopolitan lyrical artist, made her home there. Her villa became an intellectual and romantic meeting place of the art world. There she admired, and basked in the admiration of poets, composers, and leaders; there she impressed her guests with her unique personality and conversation on music, singing, and improvisation, on the audience's acceptance of music, and on the virtuosity of Liszt, Chopin, Thalberg, and Kalkbrenner. On Thursdays she held professional concerts in her salon, and on Friday afternoons informal events were held – close friends and acquaintances played, sang, and mainly enjoyed themselves together. Their favorite form of amusement was the "portrait game" devised by Turgenev which was based on his drawing skills. Before the audience he would draw the profiles of divas, famous singers, and their common friends. From the moment the "portrait" was on paper he treated them as strangers, looked at them, studied their profile and learned about them with great interest, their habits, profession, their personal and cultural tastes – all from their appearance. Each participant had to conduct a similar study and record the results of his observations of the person he had chosen. The texts provided a fine opportunity to voice an opinion on the subjects of Turgenev's drawings, and thus Pauline detailed the attributes of the character she chose – a modest governess who worked for a large family: "Modest governess in a large family, has charge of several children whom she isn't managing to teach a thing – weak and timid character. She speaks too low – never looks you in the face – never loses patience. Lukewarm water, slightly sweetened. She's very boring – very honorable, very useless-silent. She hums little sentimental songs like a gnat, accompanying herself – all off-fingers atremble with fear, and never removing her foot from the pedal. She embroiders very nicely – and makes tea exactly according to ritual – is good at sums, but slow. A worthy girl whom people feel sorry for, she's such a bore." And Turgenev's response: "A young lady-companion, poor, sour, suspicious, ill natured, sly..."[14] One of the more active participants in the game was Camille Saint-Saëns who mimicked singers and famous operatic pieces to the laughter of the Viardot family's guests.

During the years she lived in Baden-Baden, Pauline was occupied with teaching and composing. She wrote more than fifty songs and five operas for the salon, and held concerts in her home which enabled her students to perform before an audience.[15] Even though the operas were small and she let her students sing them, they were written for far more advanced singers. On Thursday evenings, the who's who of the literary and cultural world came to hear the student-performers, as well as Pauline herself who often sang solo.

In 1870 the Viardots were forced to move to London as a result of the anti-French feeling that followed the Franco-Prussian War. Pauline's brother, who lived in England, helped her to establish a singing studio so that she could continue working. There she composed music for poems by Pushkin and Lermontov, and Turgenev helped her translate them into French and German. In 1864, 1869, and 1871, three volumes of her songs were published, and it was Turgenev – who had come into a large inheritance and was now an affluent man – who financed their publishing.

Parting

Napoleon's defeat spelled the end of the empire. Pauline and her family returned to Paris, where she ran a music salon until the death of her two life partners, Louis and Turgenev. Louis Viardot died in Paris on 5 May 1883, and Turgenev on 3 September the same year at his villa in Bougival. Saint-Saëns, who met her after the death of the two men, said that she was engulfed with deep sadness as a result of the void left by the two men who, as she told Clara Schumann, were "the oldest friends of this century".[16] But Pauline, who lived for another twenty-seven years after the death of her two men, was also a very practical woman. After Turgenev's death she was occupied with executing his will, in which he left her his entire estate. She was compelled to deal with those who contested the will and attempted to obtain a share of the estate, like the Russian literary establishment headed by the lyric poet Afanasy Fet who claimed that Turgenev was finally at rest in the place of his dreams, at the ruthless feet of Pauline Viardot. As a woman used to being in complete control, Pauline made sure that both history and her image were written and depicted as she dictated. To the Paris Conservatory she donated personal items of historical value which had belonged to Turgenev, his organ and a ring inscribed by Pushkin, as well as the *Don Giovanni* manuscript that was especially precious to her. Additionally, she made sure that the correspondence between herself and Turgenev that was kept in his Paris and Baden-Baden homes was destroyed. She consented to the publication of other letters.

Pauline kept herself fully occupied with musical and social activity until she was eighty-five. In the last years of her life her sight deteriorated, but she continued reading and writing and even worked on writing the history of the song in France. In the twilight of her years, her former student Mathilde de Nogueiras, whose father was the Portuguese consul in Paris, came to live with her.

Two days before departing this life, she said: "I have two days more to live," and in those two days she conducted imagined conversations with significant figures from her past. She died in her Paris home on Wednesday, 18 May 1910, leaving behind her four children, three grandsons, four granddaughters, and four great-grandchildren, the oldest of whom was ten when she died.

Twelve

Patriot Games:
Augusta Mary Anne Holmès
(1843-1903)

She fired the imagination and lives of many men. "We were all in love with her," wrote Camille Saint-Saëns, who ardently wooed her and even proposed marriage but was gently refused, "literary men, savants, painters, musicians, any one of us would have been proud to make her his wife."[1] The gossip about her ranged from speculation about her love affairs to feminist articles about her successes as a woman of her time. The French held her in high esteem, and named a square in Paris's 13th arrondissement after her – Place Augusta Holmès.

Dreams of Music

Augusta Holmes was born in Paris on 16 December 1847 to Captain Charles William Scott Dalkeith Holmes, a retired Irish army officer who fought in the Battle of Waterloo, and Mary Anne Shearer, a painter, poet, and professional rider of Scottish and Irish descent, and sixteen years younger than her husband. Her godfather was the French writer, poet, and playwright Alfred de Vigny, who was rumored to be her real father.

The Holmes' moved in society and were enthusiastic supporters of literary and artistic events, yet they took no interest in music. As a consequence, not only did they not encourage their daughter to develop her musical talent as a pianist, they stood in her way. Her mother repeatedly said that the painter produces paintings, the writer books, the musician a headache, and this became a source of tension and frustration between them.

Her mother died when Augusta was eleven, and it was her father who helped her realize her dream of becoming a musician and woman of the world. She learned to play the piano and the clarinet as well as voice training. At twelve she spoke French, English, Italian, and German fluently, and composed music for the works of contemporary poets, and for some of her own poems. She later wrote libretti for her own music and designed the scenery and costumes for her own productions.

Up to her early twenties she played and sang her compositions in her father's salon at 15 rue de l'Orangerie in Versailles where young people of her own age would gather, most of them painters and poets who shared a love of music. Augusta's multifaceted personality and distinctive voice enchanted her listeners, while men admired her and easily fell in love with her. One of the salon's habitués who was charmed by her was Henri Cazalis, a physician and symbolist poet, and a leading figure in the intellectual activity of Parisian salons.[2] Cazalis and his fellow poets, led by Stéphane Mallarmé, were influenced by Wagner's opera *Tannhäuser* that was playing in Paris, and subsequently they discussed the musicalization of lyric language, gestures and effects in singing, and the associations of color and resonance, but to no avail. The opera was performed three times in Paris in March 1861, and on each occasion was received with booing and catcalls. After the third performance it was taken off, and several months later the depressed Wagner left Paris, never to return. Augusta was filled with regret for she had fallen in love with the German composer's music, and as we shall see, his style was to greatly influence her own compositions.

Femme Fatale

The death of her godfather De Vigny in 1863 and of her father in 1869 left Augusta to fend for herself. Fortunately, the handsome inheritance left to her by Captain Holmes enabled her to enjoy financial independence and devote all of her time to furthering her career. In the salon of her home, which became a social and cultural institution, she held soirées, cultural evenings whose aim was to encourage the conservative audience to listen to new music, while promoting her own. The music, literature, fine wine, and her personal charm attracted numerous artists from all sections of the art world, including the well-known poet Stéphane Mallarmé, and the composers Charles Gounod, Vincent d'Indy, and Camille Saint-Saëns. After hearing her sing, d'Indy said that she had simply enchanted him, whereas Nikolai Rimsky-Korsakov, who was stunned by her appearance, preferred to relate to her plunging neckline.

After her father's death Augusta and some friends went to Munich to meet Wagner and see his opera *Das Rheingold*. Among the group were Catulle Mendès and his wife, the French poet Judith Gautier. Mendès, a French poet, playwright, author, and intellectual whose roots were in a Portuguese-Jewish family, was connected to a group of French poets that believed in and acted according to "Ars gratia artis", art for art's sake, in the positivist period that came after romanticism and preceded symbolism. Later, his wife Judith would become Wagner's secret lover and the inspiration for his opera *Parsifal*. A short time after this visit to Munich, Augusta announced that she was carrying Mendès' child. Their extramarital relationship would continue until 1895, during which time she bore him a son and three daughters.[3]

Winds of War

The Franco-Prussian War that broke out in 1870 dealt Augusta a devastating blow. Her close friend Henri Regnault came to one of her soirées and sang a moving song about death and tears. A few days later she received the sad news that he had been killed in battle. Her shock was accompanied by an upsurge of nationalist feeling that influenced not only her composing, but her other activities too. She became an active member of the *Société Nationale de Musique* whose aim was to protect the operas and concerts of French musicians, and widen the circles of their audiences in Paris and the provinces.

In 1871 she became a naturalized French citizen, and added the *grave* accent to the penultimate letter of her surname. It was in the 1870s that she moved from composing songs to composing music for symphonic poems and operas, ambitious large-scale works whose texts she wrote herself. Concomitant with her decision to gain recognition as a composer she became a pupil of César Franck, thus joining a respected elitist group. She was the only woman among them and also one of its oldest members. At the time, Franck, a charming and generous man who was a lodestone for numerous musical talents, was fifty-three. He was attracted to Augusta who was the most eccentric of his pupils and, paradoxically, the least documented of them. Franck's wife Felicité, who had been married to him for over thirty years, was quick to realize that her husband harbored strong feelings for his young and talented pupil. It was during this period (1878-9) that Franck wrote his Piano Quintet in F minor which, much to the surprise of critics and pupils alike, was different from all his other works. It was passionate, with a particularly erotic tone. Felicité did not attend its premiere, and some say that she also boycotted its later performances. For her part, Augusta remained in contact with Franck until his death, and attended his funeral.

It was in Franck's circle that Augusta became more profoundly conscious of Richard Wagner's music which was to influence her own work. Wagner's predilection for mythological subjects, the connection between poetry, music, and orchestration also dominated her songs, and became an integral part of her composition. But the post-Franco-Prussian War Parisian audience was contemptuous of the German composer's music, and did not connect with the transformation undergone by orchestral music all over the world. On 15 January 1877 the *Andante Pastorale* from Holmès' symphony *Orlando Furioso* was performed at the Théâtre du Chatelet. The work, based on an epic romance by the Italian poet Ludovico Ariosto, reflected both Augusta's studies under Franck and her admiration of Wagner. To the astonishment of conductor Édouard Colonne, a specialist in the music of Berlioz and other eminent nineteenth-century composers, the audience rose to its feet during the performance and greeted it with boos and whistles.

Augusta's critics contended that her orchestration contained far too many dramatic effects, and that she lacked an original tone of her own. Furthermore, the fact that she was a woman and mother of four who managed to keep to a demanding schedule led the critics to label her a masculine woman, an image that did not trouble her in the least and even served her purposes. She said of herself that she had a man's soul in a woman's body, and explained that she had been raised by her father who, in her words, was "a rough old soldier".[4] Perhaps it was this roughness that she spoke of that constituted her unique style which combined French music with the German instrumental style: between dynamism, clarity, the logical presentation of musical themes on the one hand, and a huge orchestra with a leading role for the brass section and for fanfares associated with a masculine-military image on the other.

Competitions

Holmès, who was determined to succeed, realized that in order to gain the greatest public exposure she would have to take part in competitions. The prestigious Prix de Rome awarded by the French government in conjunction with the *Académie Royale de Peinture et de Sculpture*, was closed to women at the time, but others were open to her. In 1879 she entered her program symphony *Lutèce*, a title derived from the Roman name of Paris, in the Prix de la ville Paris competition. The work dealt with death, grief, and the pain of the loss of soldiers' lives, together with a hymn of praise to the patriotic heroes who must do the Hiob for their country until salvation comes. The text is dramatic and does not shy away from graphic descriptions like blood flowing on the ground, and calls for vengeance and killing.

The work, whose unifying element is love of country, was awarded second place. A year later she entered the same competition with her symphonic poem *Les Argonautes*, which emphasizes the sacrifice of romantic love for more sublime ideals. The panel of judges included the composers Camille Saint-Saëns, Jules Massenet, and César Franck, and the conductors Edouard Colonne and Charles Lamoureux, who unanimously awarded the prize to Holmés' work. However, the officials on the panel who knew nothing at all about music, decided to award the prize to Victor-Alphonse Duvernoy who competed against her, and Augusta had to make do with a consolation prize.

Paradoxically, even Saint-Saëns who intended to give a positive opinion on the work related to the fact that she was a woman with a certain astonishment. "Women are curious when they seriously attend to art," he wrote. "Above all they seem preoccupied with making us forget they are women, of showing an overwhelming virility, without dreaming an instant that it is this preoccupation that reveals the woman."[5]

She explicitly expressed her awareness of being a creative woman in a hegemonic society thus: "Do not believe... that the artistic career is more accessible to my sex. This is a grave error. The steps are infinitely more difficult, and the good fellowship, which helps so many artists, is in a way

Love of the Siren

shut out from a woman who has the good – or the ill – luck to be born a musician."[6]

Ode Triomphale

Yet on her professional path Augusta was undeterred by gender discrimination. Although she had initially used the male pseudonym Hermann Zenta to surmount the gender barrier, at this point in her career she used her own name and continued to seek ways and means of gaining recognition that was as wide as possible. Like other composers in the Third Republic, she too was conscious of patriotic images, and during the 1890s composed works connected with her dual French and Irish heritage. *Irlande*, *Pologne*, *Ludus pro Patria*, and *Ode Triomphale* are but a small part of her orchestral works in which a warm, familiar, popular tone is expressed in the form of brass fanfares.

In 1888 the French government announced a prize to be awarded for a grand cantata to be performed at the Paris Exposition the following year. Augusta entered *Ode Triomphale*, a cantata on French cultural life that she wrote for thirteen choruses and 1,200 musicians. Each of the performing ensembles represented a different element of French culture, such as wine growers, farmers, soldiers, workers, and artists. She also designed the sets and costumes, and oversaw each and every ensemble. The entire production cost 300,000 Francs, the equivalent of 37,000 Euros today. At the end of the premiere the audience lifted her into a small carriage and drove her through the city streets. The fact that she specified in her performance instructions that all the singers must be white and blond did not worry the masses in the least. Moreover, the composer who emphasized that the importance of France's women lay in their privilege of bearing sons for the French army, became a national icon. Was this an authentic belief or simply a ploy to give the masses what they wanted to hear? Whatever the case, Augusta's reputation, who became known as "La Grande Holmès", preceded her throughout France and even beyond its borders. In May 1890, her *Hymne à la Paix*, a work she composed to further peace between France and Italy, was performed at the Dante and Beatrice Festival in Florence. The work was warmly received, and at the end of the concert the audience threw roses at the composer's feet, shouting "Vive la France". She would display her impressions of Italy in her symphonic suite *Au Pays Bleu*, the work which marks the end of her most successful period.

La Montagne Noire

The fame of Augusta Holmès ended in the mid-1890s. Her opera *La Montagne Noire* (The Black Mountain), her last great work, was staged in Paris in 1895 and was taken off after only eleven performances. The expectation of the work becoming a great success came to naught, yet the composer refused to listen to those who advised her to cut parts of it and end it with a ballet so as not to overburden the audience. Charles Holman Black, a writer with *The London Musical Courier*, suggested that the negative criticism of the opera could have had a lot to do with the fact that it was composed by a woman.[7]

That year was one of the hardest in her life. Catulle Mendès left her, and a few months later her son Raphael died. The inheritance left by her father dwindled, and she was forced to move into a small apartment where she taught and continued composing. During this period she espoused the Catholic faith but was never a devout believer. In the last eight years of her life she composed another forty songs.

Augusta Holmès died in Paris on 23 January 1905. *The New York Times* announced the death of the composer best known for the songs she composed, "but her orchestral works are quite unknown to music lovers in this city."[8]

Thirteen

Pastorale to Childhood:
Cécile Louise Stephanie Chaminade
(1857-1944)

When Cécile Chaminade played for her teacher a fugue purported to be her own work, the teacher said it was full of blunders and rebuked her for not listening to what he told her. "I beg your pardon, *maitre*," she replied, closing the score on the piano, "but I have made a mistake. The fugue is not mine – it is one of Bach's." The teacher, Marie Gabriel

Augustin Savard, whose attitude toward her compositional aspirations was usually patronizing, gradually and skillfully turned his criticisms into praise.

The Chateau

She was born in Paris to musical parents. Her mother was a pianist and singer, and her father – who managed the Paris branch of Gresham Ltd., the British underwriters – was also a violinist. Cécile was the third of the couple's six children, two of whom died in their childhood. The Chaminade's salon regularly hosted artists from various spheres. The family summered at their chateau in Périgord, an area drowning in pastoral scenery in which prehistoric art rubs shoulders with medieval sites, and which is renowned for its pâté de foie gras and Bergerac and Monbazillac wines. In the mid-1860s her father purchased a chateau in Le Vésinet, a quiet town with parks and lakes to the west of Paris, which would later be the composer's own home. Her autocratic father Hippolyte thought that studies at the Paris Conservatory were inappropriate for a young woman of her standing, therefore he hired the services of tutors who taught at that august institution to instruct her at their home.

At the beginning of her career she composed piano miniatures, including Mazurkas and Etudes. Once she felt surer of her compositional abilities, she wrote two Piano Trios which from a professional standpoint were so good that they were played daily in the Conservatory's classrooms, and also at concerts in Brussels, Geneva, and Lyon. Cécile viewed music as a profession and she intended to publish each piece she composed. Every day she spent many hours working, and aside from composing new pieces she adapted her own works and those of others from one medium to another, from song to piano and to trio.[1] And they were indeed published. In the early 1880s she began composing symphonic works. In a review of the performance of one such work, the reviewer posed the question: Did the audience realize that the symphony, which reveals an extraordinary talent for orchestration, was written by a young lady?[2]

The young woman began performing regularly in chamber concerts, often with Martin Pierre Joseph Marsick, a Belgian violinist, composer, and teacher, and even tried her hand at writing an opera. On 23 February 1882 she conducted *La Sévillane*, a one-act musical drama, performed in her parents' home. Invitations were sent to music critics and other respected guests, including the composer Ambroise Thomas, director of the Paris Conservatory. The opera is centered around a female protagonist from Andalusia, a character that was part of the obsessive preoccupation of artists – including composers – with the characters of exotic women embodying otherness, in contrast with the figure of the Parisian bourgeois woman of the time. Bizet's *Carmen* is a fine example of this. She is a black-eyed, raven-haired gypsy who enchants every man around her, but more than anything else she is assertive and declares herself free to do whatever she wants, mainly to love whoever she wants, the way she wants. Cécile attended the premiere of *Carmen* in 1875 and totally sympathized with Bizet's bitterness after the composer was roundly castigated by the establishment as a result of the opera. She knew Bizet who lived nearby, and recalled how he had applauded her and called her "My young Mozart" when she played her works for him. He suggested to her parents that they give her an intensive musical education. She would later write an essay on the way he had been treated and called her opera *La Sévillane*, a title embodying the roots of his *Carmen*, which tragically became a huge hit only after his death. And perhaps it was not by chance that Cécile's opera never became a proper operatic production. Bizet's experience of rejection at the premiere of his opera engendered grave concern in her. However, her opera did not completely disappear. The public liked it, and arrangements of parts of it were performed at numerous private concerts.

Her father's death in 1887 gravely affected the family's financial situation. The money he left was imprudently invested and the remaining property was divided among the family. Cécile realized that she would have to work even harder to provide for her mother and herself. In order to write additional works and increase the frequency of her performances she abandoned large-scale symphonic works for smaller forms, mainly songs and solo pieces for the piano. She performed in numerous recitals, playing her own music that included arrangements of her large-scale works, one of which, *Konzertstück*, in a version for two pianos, was particularly popular. *Le Monde Artistique* published in Paris wrote: "The new work... is written with a rare assurance; without being absolutely original, it's never ordinary; the orchestration is varied, but a bit heavy-handed. Despite this fault, which experience will correct, the work is extremely interesting. It has varied rhythm and is never sentimental. If its sonorities were occasionally less brutal it would recall L'España of Emmanuel Chabrier."[3]

Reviews of her works were generally mixed, and often touched upon the fact that she was a woman composer. One reviewer noted in *La Semaine Artistique* that many women are engaged in composing, but their education in the sphere is sadly lacking, yet on the other hand, a review of her musical drama stressed that she is one of the more successful ones. Compared with Augusta Holmès, her large-scale works are filled with energy and power, yet she is far more "feminine". This comparison with Holmès is not a random one since both were considered leading composers in France during the same period, albeit their temperaments, musical demeanor, and works, were entirely different. Holmès was active in the various salons and mingled with leading mainstream male figures. By contrast, Cécile preferred the privacy of her home and the company of her mother, family, and close friends.

Romance Without Words

The 1890s were years of intensive concert tours. As a woman working for a living she knew full well that composing, performing, and sales go hand in hand. She composed new works for the recitals she arranged for herself, and her performances boosted sales. She appeared both in Western and Eastern Europe, the Balkans, as well as the United States, where she performed in Chicago and Philadelphia. Yet perversely it was in her hometown, Paris, that she did not gain appropriate attention. On the other hand, the English audience loved her, and journals like *The London Magazine* and *Madam* reviewed her successful concerts in London, Sussex, and Surrey. Furthermore, Queen Victoria, who admired her music, invited her to Windsor, and Cécile dedicated one of her songs to the Queen's daughter, Princess Beatrice.

In July 1901 Cécile married Louis-Mathieu Carbonel, a music publisher twenty years her senior. She met him when her mother, an old friend of his, asked him to accompany her daughter on her concert tour of Eastern Europe. The union was not one of love nor physical attraction, but a platonic relationship throughout, with each living in their own home, she at Le Vésinet and her husband in Marseilles. Her mother's anger – and that of the whole family – increased when Louis fell ill with a lung disease and Cécile nursed him until he died in 1907. After the event her family would say that she sacrificed years of her professional life to care for her husband. Why, then, did she enter into this marriage in the first place? The reason is unclear, and she took the secret with her to the grave.

She did, however, have some gender insights as a consequence of her marriage. A year after her husband's death she said that a woman must make a choice between marriage and art since she can not have both at the same time. For male artists, everything is arranged and accepted. The man marries and right away goes back to his art, whereas his wife takes care of him, the home, and later, the children. The expectations of a woman, on the other hand, are that she function within the conventions of a patriarchal society, and therefore marriage destroys her art.

Cécile usually worked at night in the villa by the sea she purchased in Tamaris-sur-Mer in the south of France, where she drew inspiration for the works she had in mind. While she did not like working under pressure, she never once forgot her objective – to make a living from her music. Once a work was ready in her mind, she wrote the score quickly, and then put it aside for a while. After some time she reexamined it, and only then sent it to a publisher.

She composed over four hundred works, the vast majority of which are piano miniatures, and songs with piano accompaniment. Her compositional style is romantic with emphasis on a beautiful, engaging melody, and accompaniment based on clear tonality, a point of departure, a brief development, and a return "home". The exotic titles she used, like *Romance Without Words*, *Arabesque*, *Oriental Serenade*, and *La Sévillane* were a genre trend much like Fanny and Felix Mendelssohn's *Songs Without Words*, and clearly evident in them is the Spanish influence characteristic of French composers of the period. The most famous of the latter were Bizet and his *Carmen*, Chabrier's *España*, and Debussy's *Iberia*, but more than anything these titles took the audiences to places far distant from their everyday life.

Pastorale to Childhood

In the United States her most popular work was *Pas des écharpes* (Without Scarfs), whereas in England her *Automne* (Autumn) won her an award by selling 21,000 copies in three years. The miniatures she wrote were typical of composers of her generation who were also pianists. Every now and then she composed in the musical idiom of earlier periods, pieces such as *3 Danses Anciennes* for piano, or *Toccata*, a work for keyboard in seventeenth-century style, pieces which demanded very high piano skills. And there were also two albums for children, *Album des Efants*, Books 1 and 2, and a work entitled *My Childhood*.

Cécile's popularity soared all over Europe, the Balkans, and especially in the United States where some two hundred Chaminade Clubs were opened. At one of them in Brooklyn, which she visited in 1898, she discovered an acrostic named after her and which was their motto:[4]

C   Concentrated and Concerted Effort

H   Harmony of Spirit and Work

A   Artistic Ideals

M   Musical Merit Maintained

I   Inspiration

N   Notes

A   Ardor and Aspiration

D   Devotion to Duty

E   Earnest Endeavor

Even existing institutions changed their name to hers, weeklies and monthlies were filled with pieces about her, and adulation of her was similar to that accorded to rock stars. She herself wrote several articles in which she interpreted her own music, and even opined that classical music such as that of Brahms, Beethoven, Schumann, and Fauré was far too heavy and serious for people who are not professional musicians. Her works were aimed at a mixed audience of professionals and music lovers, adults and students of varying levels of skill. The fact that it was possible to learn to play one of her pieces in a short time was especially appealing to women busy with running a home and raising children, and it was Cécile who enabled them to move into the creative world for a while.

Like the music she composed, her concerts were also light and entertaining and filled a void that traditional classical music was unable to fill. Her pieces were mainly loved by virtue of their French character, captivating melodies, and their style which depicted images, moods, or the seasons.

Her appearance and the tranquil atmosphere that surrounded her were no less magnetic than the art she brought with her. Her pleasant and buoyant character, coupled with the fact that her audiences comprised mainly women admirers, led the critics to label her work "salon music", or in other words, music that was neither sufficiently sophisticated nor serious.[5] After a performance at Carnegie Hall the critics wrote that while her works were feminine and elegant, they were shallow. One even went so far as to say that while women would one day have the vote, they would never be able to compose a work of any value.

Cécile felt that it was the ignorance of these critics that pigeonholed her work as "salon music". In the 1 November 1908 issue of *The Washington Post* she wrote that women composers needed special conditions to both write and preserve their work. Her words sprang from her understanding of her own social and personal situation, as well as that of her women colleagues: "I do not believe that the few women who have achieved greatness in creative work are the exception, but I think that life has been hard on women; it has not given them opportunity; it has not made them convincing...Woman has not been considered a working force in the world and the work that her sex and conditions impose upon her has not been so adjusted as to give her a little fuller scope for the development of her best self. She has been handicapped, and only the few, through force of circumstances or inherent strength, have been able to get the better of that handicap."[6]

Despite this, Cécile was awarded numerous medals and prizes for her musical accomplishments. Whereas her works for piano are considered a minor repertoire, they brought great joy to both pianists and audiences throughout her life and to the present day. Her musical syntax is indeed traditional and perhaps even conservative since its roots are in the aesthetics of her first years of study. As we have seen, her father did not allow her to attend the Paris Conservatory and therefore she was unable to study under the tutelage of the great teachers, and neither did she have the contacts that might have helped her in the future. She was a lone wolf who functioned on the periphery, and as a woman found it difficult to break into the circle of musical life in Paris. Yet her works were published far more than those of any other woman composer of her generation, and her genius is clearly evident in the fact that she composed for pianists of only average ability.

Parting

Between 1901 and 1914, against the backdrop of World War One and despite her deteriorating health, Chaminade made several important recordings, most of which are works for the piano. In 1913 she was awarded the French *Légion d'Honneur*, the first woman composer to win this prestigious award. In 1925 she sold Le Vésinet and moved to a villa near Toulon. Her left leg was in a bad condition and she suffered chronic pain. In 1936 she moved again, this time to Monte Carlo, where her left foot was amputated as a result of bone decalcification, yet despite her disability she refused to use a wheelchair. On 23 April 1942 she wrote to Irving Schwerke, a musician and internationally-known music critic with whom she was on friendly terms: "I see that you haven't been forgetting your musical friends and they're deeply grateful. Not to be forgotten, to live in the heart and memory of those who understand you—that is the supreme consolation for an artist. Thanks to all who remember…"[7]

In the last years of her life she was cared for by her niece Antoinette Lorel, who also promoted her aunt's music after her death.

Cécile Chaminade died on 13 April 1944 in Monte Carlo.

Fourteen

The March of the Women:
Dame Ethel Smyth
(1858-1944)

In 1912, in the course of a women's suffrage demonstration, Ethel Smyth smashed a window for which act she was sentenced to two months in Holloway Prison. From the window of her cell, brandishing a toothbrush, she conducted her fellow suffragettes as they marched in the quadrangle singing *The March of the Women*, which she had composed a year earlier and which became the anthem of the British suffrage movement.

Fantasio

She was born on 23 April 1858 in Sidcup in the London borough of Bexley, the fourth of the eight children of Nina Struth, her French-born mother, and Major-General John Hall Smyth. As the daughter of an upper-middle class family she was educated in the arts, learned foreign languages, and was skilled in painting and playing the piano. When she was twelve she heard her new governess, who had studied music at the Leipzig Conservatory, playing Beethoven. Ethel was enchanted, and made up her mind that she, too, wanted to be a composer.

Although her mother backed her decision, her father was shocked. As far as he was concerned, the thought of his daughter studying composition was tantamount to working as a prostitute, and he ordered her to put a stop to her music studies instantly. Ethel responded by shutting herself in her room and boycotting all family activities, including attending church on Sundays. Her father eventually gave in, and when she was nineteen he agreed to her going to study at the Leipzig Conservatory, which at the time was thought to be the best in Europe. He also made sure that he met the family with whom she was to live, and conditioned her studies on her returning home for the summer holidays every year.

The Leipzig Conservatory was founded by Felix Mendelssohn on 2 April 1843. At the time women were accepted only for vocal, piano, or harp studies, but in the 1870s they were accepted for regular orchestration and composition studies too. Her studies at the conservatory were a great disappointment for Ethel: she thought the composition lessons were a farce, while in the other lessons she was bored and felt she was not fulfilling her potential. At the end of her first year she left the conservatory and began studying composition privately with Heinrich von Herzogenberg, a composer who founded the *Leipzig Bach-Verein* (Bach Society) and was also its president. His wife Elisabeth, known as Liesel, joined in the lessons. While composing Bach-style chorales and practicing the composition of canons and fugues, an intimate friendship blossomed between the two women.

It was in Leipzig that Ethel met some eminent composers, among them Johannes Brahms, Pyotr Ilyich Tchaikovsky, Edvard Grieg, and the renowned violinist Joseph Joachim. When Herzogenberg introduced her to his close friend Brahms, she realized that they had been talking about her when the famous composer looked at her and said, "So this is the young lady who writes sonatas and doesn't know counterpoint!" In the wake of this scathing remark she began studying Berlioz's *Treatise on Orchestration* on her own, and practiced the orchestral color that would later be manifested in her works.

In the course of that year she kept to a strict study regimen, and in the summer went home where she had time to engage in her favorite sports – golf, cycling, riding, foxhunting, and mountaineering. In 1882, after five arduous years of study, Ethel went to Florence where she met Julia, Liesel Herzogenberg's sister, and her husband, Henry Brewster. Brewster, an American writer and philosopher who grew up in Europe, was a handsome and outspoken man, and he and his wife held very unusual views on marital relations, views which until Ethel's arrival were solely theoretical. But from the moment she came into their life she and Henry felt that their souls met in a parallel universe, and that what linked them was something far beyond time and place.

The three of them spoke quite openly about their feelings, and to Ethel's surprise Julia encouraged her and her husband to take their relationship to the physical level. Alarmed, Ethel decided to end her relationship with the Brewsters and left Florence. In 1890, Henry Brewster was at London's Crystal Palace to listen to Ethel's Serenade in D, and five years later, after Julia's death, he and Ethel renewed their relationship which lasted until his death. It was a close and unique relationship during which he proposed, she declined, and each of them lived in their own home. Ethel continued living in England and Henry in Italy, but since both of them were cosmopolitans who traveled frequently, they met in different places in Europe. Between their meetings they corresponded regularly, and although their relationship continued this did not stop Ethel's relationships with women, and Henry acquiesced. According to Ethel, Henry was never jealous of her other relationships, and like her he believed that every love affair enriched the other friendships.

In her old age and after Henry's death she would write that he was a very significant part of her life, not only on the personal level.

Der Wald (The Forest)

It was in the mid-1880s that Ethel began making her way as a composer. She wrote piano and chamber music, and like her violin sonata, her string quintet was performed at the Leipzig Gewandhaus, the former in 1883 and the latter in 1887. The German audience liked her works, which at the time were influenced by the Brahms tradition.[1] Towards the end of the decade, in 1889, she entered the English arena with the help of her close friend Empress Eugénie, the widow of Napoleon III. They had met in 1883, when the Empress donated to the municipality of Marseilles the impressive palace her husband had built for her in the southwestern part of the old port, and she moved to live not far from Ethel.[2]

Ethel also became friendly with influential figures in the British musical establishment, such as the composer Arthur Sullivan, and conductor August Manns who conducted her *Serenade* and the overture *Antony and Cleopatra* at the Crystal Palace. During this period she also met artist and patron of the arts Lady Pauline Trevelyan, a devout Catholic, and their friendship was a catalyst in Ethel's religious awakening. She subsequently wrote her *Mass in D*, her first large-scale work in which her dramatic abilities are manifested. Clearly evident in this grandiose work is her compositional self-assurance. Following its performance by the Royal Choral Society at the Royal Albert Hall, the newspaper reviews acclaimed the composer, albeit between the lines there was some surprise at the fact that a woman had composed a work of such magnitude. Was this the reason why the *Mass* was performed in 1893 and then disappeared until 1924?

Ethel continued energetically writing music, and the conductor Hermann Levi, a close friend from her Leipzig days, advised her to turn to opera. But England had no operatic tradition, and consequently no opera house, no orchestra suitable for large-scale productions, and no experienced singers. The audience demanded more rapid and lighter output than a serious opera, and so from the mid-nineteenth century to the mid-twentieth, England was inundated with opera and operettas written by foreign composers. In 1869, Carl Rosa and his wife Euphrosyne founded the Parepa Rosa English Opera Company in New

York, the precursor of the Carl Rosa Opera Company, and in the 1880s it commissioned works by composers such as Arthur Goring Thomas and Alexander Mackenzie, but by the 1890s it was financially unfeasible to stage them. Ticket prices were reasonable and the operas were performed in English, but the Covent Garden auditorium was less than full since the English audience preferred the works of Wagner and Mozart.

Smyth harbored hopes of a serious establishment-supported English opera house. She came out in opposition to short-term productions that were performed once and then taken off for a while and then revived, and proposed models for the establishment of a body that would be responsible for consolidating the genre. In 1920 she published a six-part series on English opera. "Mont Blanc and Mount Everest do not spring out of flat plains", she wrote in one of them, and went on to describe how opera should be supported so that audiences would want to hear it.[3] She herself was addicted to the genre for thirty years, and experienced firsthand the difficulties involved in producing an opera and selling it to the audience. An example of this is her third opera, *The Wreckers*, whose French libretto was written by Henry Brewster.

The opera's story is based on the folklore of Cornwall, a county in southwestern England situated on a peninsula, which accords it a national dimension. A small fishing village on a Sunday, and the villagers are enjoying a drink at the inn on their way to chapel when Pascoe, the local preacher, chastises them saying that drink is the reason why the Lord had stopped sending them ships to plunder (a common practice in that part of the world). Lawrence the lighthouse keeper has another explanation for the absence of ships: he has seen beacons burning on the cliffs and is certain that somebody is warning the ships of the danger of piracy. The villagers vow to find the traitor in their midst, and as usual in opera, in the village where life is frequently violent and merciless, a story of love and betrayal unfolds which ends in death. The lovers, Pascoe's wife Thirza, and the young fisherman Mark, die in a cave chained in each other's arms as the tide rises around them.

Smyth scoured Europe for five years trying to sell her opera to impresarios in the French-speaking countries, but in vain. Despite the fact that its libretto was in French, the opera was eventually performed in English and German translations. Its premiere was in Leipzig's Neue Theater on 11 November 1906. The work was considered difficult to perform, and Smyth's friend Mabel Dodge, an American-born patron of the arts who wanted to help her, hired the His Majesty's Theatre for six performances, and persuaded Thomas Beecham to conduct. But the match between Smyth and Beecham was not a success. He regularly arrived late for rehearsals, which enraged her. Furthermore, in her view he maltreated the singers by not giving them enough time to rest their voices. Beecham, on the other hand, contended that the opera was performed so infrequently because there was no English female singer able to give full expression to the original and extraordinary character of Thirza, and not only that, the tenor role of Mark was also difficult.

The March of the Women

In 1910 Smyth met Emmeline Pankhurst,[4] the leader of the British suffragette movement, and was enthralled by her speeches. The two women were both fifty-two, but vastly different in character and appearance: Emmeline was delicate and wore lace, whereas Ethel liked tweed and had a cigar clamped in her teeth. Their relationship led Smyth to abandon her music for two years and devote herself to the fight for women's suffrage. She was part of the suffragette demonstrations in 1912, smashed a window, and was sentenced to two months in Holloway Prison together with other members of the movement, including Mrs. Pankhurst. In her autobiography she wrote that they were in adjacent cells, and during exercise periods in the quadrangle and on various other occasions, the wardresses let them spend more time together than was officially allowed. In the course of her incarceration Smyth organized athletic competitions in the quadrangle, and even made sure that the ribbons used were in the suffragette movement colors (purple, white, and green). She also composed a women's anthem whose music is based on a folksong from the Abruzzo region in central Italy, a region she visited with Henry Brewster.[5] From the window of her cell, brandishing a toothbrush, she conducted her fellow suffragettes as they marched in the quadrangle singing *The March of the Women*.

Smyth also wrote articles and essays in which she demanded equal rights for women. Among her detractors were those who held that her composing lacked direction since it was spread over far too many spheres not directly connected with music. But her professional life and other activities cannot be separated, nor can the fact be ignored that she was an interdisciplinary entity that paid no heed to personal or societal stereotypes. On her release from prison she composed the two concluding movements of the string quintet she had begun writing ten years earlier. During this period she also traveled to Egypt where she crossed the desert in a camel-drawn caravan and there, in a palace outside Cairo she composed her opera *The Boatswain's Mate*, the only one of her operas with a feminist storyline. Twenty years later she would describe this trip in her book, *Beecham and Pharaoh*.

Philosophical Dialogues

Smyth rubbed shoulders with the who's who of Europe, and despite her success she felt she was a victim of gender discrimination. She vented her frustration in an essay, *Female Pipings in Eden*, in which she writes about the inner circles of the political forces exerted on composers and their works in general, and the difficulties experienced by women composers in particular. At the same time she continued her fight to have her operas produced in England, giving lectures, writing letters to newspaper editors, having her music broadcast on the radio and voicing her opinions, and also writing a schema for a national opera house in England.

From her fifty-fifth year Ethel's hearing began deteriorating until she became completely deaf. Just before losing her hearing she managed to write four more large-scale works,[6] one of which, *The Prison*, is based on the philosophical dialogues of Henry Brewster, originally published by him as *The Prison: A Dialogue*.

In 1910 she was awarded an honorary Doctorate of Music from Durham University, and thenceforth signed herself "Dr. Ethel Smyth". Additionally, in 1922 she was made a Dame Commander of the British Empire, and in 1926 was awarded an honorary doctorate from Oxford University, and yet another from the University of St. Andrews in 1928. To mark her seventy-fifth birthday numerous concerts were held which were supported by leading musicians, and she herself did not cease her efforts to have her music performed even though she was already a sick woman and confined to her home in Woking. But Smyth was also active in spheres outside music. By 1940 she had written ten books, each of which was partly autobiographical. The audience felt it knew Dame Ethel Smyth through her memoirs, and wanted to hear the music she had composed to deepen their knowledge of her.

Although she strove not to introduce music into her writings, it was clear that in her view her music did not gain the appreciation it deserved.

In 1933 she wrote in her diary: "It's too late to be something".

She died in her cottage in Woking after a short illness. In the eulogies delivered after her passing it was said that no other woman left behind her such masterworks as her Mass and operas.

Fifteen

Birdsong:
Amy Marcy Cheney Beach
(1867-1944)

"Help me steal from the birds," the poet asked her, and the eleven-year-old girl's eyes lit up. He gave her a pencil and paper and she sat next to him behind a stone, rapidly writing down the songs of the different birds. By the end of the morning she had transcribed some twenty songs. For years afterward Amy Cheney continued transcribing the birdsongs

Love of the Siren

she heard, and introduced them into some of her works. She would keep that first morning experience she had with poet and professor of English literature Edward Steele in San Francisco as a happy memory for years.

New Hampshire

She was born on 5 September 1867 in Henniker, New Hampshire, the only daughter of Charles Abbott Cheney and Clara Imogene Cheney, who were one of the state's highly respected families. Her mother was an amateur pianist and singer who imparted the secrets of music to her daughter when Amy was still a baby. By the time she was a year old little Amy could hum forty tunes accurately, and always in the key in which she first heard them. Before she was two she was improvising alto lines to the tunes her mother sang in soprano. At three she could read, and at four composed her first piano pieces; a little later she was playing them, adding four-voice harmonies.[1] When she was seven she gave her first public recitals, playing works by Handel, Beethoven, Chopin, and some of her own compositions. In her teens she was performing in recitals and was considered a pianist of the first order, but the most significant event in her life thus far was her first appearance with the Boston Symphony Orchestra in 1883 when she was only sixteen. Two years later the family moved to Boston where she studied the various subjects of music with leading teachers of the time, among them famous performers and professors from academic institutions.

But Amy did not stop at the impressive list of teachers that her parents placed at her disposal, and just as she had taught herself to read at age four, she taught herself to orchestrate works and compose in a number of voices. She would later study under the tutelage of some famous performers including the concert pianist Ernest Parabo, and Carl Baermann, who was a pupil of Liszt.

After moving to Boston, Amy married Dr. Henry Harris Aubrey Beach who was twenty-four years older than her. He was a physician and surgeon and also an anatomy lecturer at the Harvard School of Medicine, as well as being an amateur singer, pianist, poet, and painter. Amazed by his wife's abilities, he thought that formal training was likely to spoil her originality. In his unassailable opinion she should concentrate on composing and stop performing in concerts. She duly acceded, concentrated on composing, and limited her public performances to one recital a year whose proceeds went to charity. As a married woman and in accordance with the social mores of the time, she signed her works under her new name, Mrs. H.H.A. Beach.

Puritan Boston abounded with music and musicians of all levels, from beginners and amateurs to brilliant professional performers. The piano was the instrument of choice in almost every home, and music was an inseparable part of family and social gatherings on Sunday afternoons, at dinners, and of course in the public arena at concerts and the theater. At the time this was her comfort zone and she would later write that this happy period would never return. She loved life as she loved people, and her positive thinking and innate generosity caused those around her to connect with their own good qualities. Aside from a prodigious memory she also possessed some impressive intellectual attributes, had a wide range of spheres of interest, spoke German and French, and was interested in science and philosophy. But her greatest loves were composing and her professional piano performances, and she was determined to become famous and gain professional recognition and audience acclaim. She believed that internal and external order were part and parcel of the creative process, whereas disorder disrupts a person's creativity. Accordingly – and although she did not bother with household chores, and some say she never cooked a meal in her life – she started her day by tidying her studio and its surrounds.

For Her the Jasmine Buds Unfold

Amy's musical output yielded fruit with the performance of her *Mass in E flat major* in 1892, her first large-scale work that premiered in Boston which both gained her royalties and placed her firmly on the list of recognized American composers. On 1 May 1893 her *Festival Jubilate* written for the dedication of the Women's Building at Chicago's Columbian Exposition was performed. The prestigious exposition marked the 400th anniversary of Christopher Columbus's discovery of the New World, and America's great cities, including Washington and New York vied for the privilege of hosting the composer, but Chicago won. Aside from composing, Beach was involved in the search for the typical and unique American sound. As in most nineteenth-century European countries, in North America, too, a national consciousness was being formed, and in its wake the need to nurture mindfulness of the country's cultural heritage. The influence of national consciousness was also manifested in the music of the time. Composers employed folk songs and dances from their countries of origin, and incorporated them into their works, and works like Sibelius' *Finlandia* and Dvořák's *Slavonic Dances* were part of a declaration of nationalism and patriotism. The year Amy's work was performed for the dedication of the Women's Building in Chicago, an article about it was published in *The Boston Herald*. Its writer, Henry (Harry) Thacker Burleigh, related that while visiting the National Conservatory of Music in New York he had heard Czech composer Antonin Dvořák recommend that American composers should seek musical material in their own country's popular music, such as slave songs and songs connected with tilling the soil. Burleigh, himself a composer, arranger, and professional baritone, was thought to be the first black composer to incorporate black music into its classical sister. Amy read what Dvořák had said and was incensed. She wrote a response to the paper in which she argued that the blacks' melodies were not typical of the entire American nation. For example, she wrote, people like her who were born on the east coast were influenced to a greater degree by old English, Scottish, and Irish songs which were part of their musical and literary heritage. Three years later The Boston Symphony Orchestra performed her *Gaelic Symphony*, the first symphonic work to be written by a female American composer, whose four central themes are based on Irish-Gaelic songs.

Years later, when she was asked if there was an American school of composition, she replied that there was an American spirit. But, she said, qualifying her reply, it is based on the diverse development of different people, each of which are seeking their path in it, espousing what is right for them. She herself embraced the melodies she particularly liked, not only because of ethnic preference. She owed her popularity to the patriotic anthem *A Hymn of Freedom* which she set to words by Frank Lebby Stanton, a newspaper columnist for *The Atlanta Constitution*, and which was performed all over the United States.

Like other romantics of her time, Amy's writing also stemmed from literature. In the Late Romantic style that typified her music in the 1880s, her sensitivity to the language and lyricism of the melody is manifested.

Forget-me-not

In June 1910 Henry Beach passed away. Amy had no time to mourn his passing since her mother, too, was ill at the time and she devoted herself to her care. Medicines, doctors, and treatments all cost large sums, money she did not readily have. And since it was Henry who managed their financial affairs, Amy was now compelled to learn how it was done. One practical step was to approach her publisher and ask him to try and sell her works so that she could meet her current high expenses. He offered her an advance, which she declined. Then he suggested hiring the services of an impresario to arrange her concert tours, but she decided that her mother was too ill to be left on her own.[2]

It was only after her mother's death that for the first time Amy was the only woman in her life, but oddly, now that she was free she sought meaning in her life and felt a fierce need for deep inner work. She found what she was looking for in the Episcopalian Church. She joined the church at which the funerals of her husband and father had been held and she herself had been baptized, and now she took religious instruction and became more devout than before. But her longed-for peace was still over the horizon.

Hymn of Freedom

On her forty-fourth birthday she boarded a ship and sailed to Europe, determined to convince the European audience of her professional ability. She based herself in Munich, apparently due to her close friendship with Marcella Craft. Craft, an American soprano and prima donna at the Royal Opera House in Munich, met Amy when she was studying in Boston and specializing in performing her songs. A close friendship was forged between them which provided Amy, among other things, with an entrée into German musical life.[3]

Beach's social contacts blossomed, due both to her friend and her own music, but first and foremost by virtue of her positive personality, welcoming smile, and her ability to form warm relationships with those around her. She was invited to clubs where women's music was performed; she appeared in recitals in various cities, accompanying herself on the piano; and she played her own sonatas and chamber music. Now was the time to change her name: no longer Mrs. Henry Beach, but the composer Amy Beach, which was what she wrote for "Profession" on her Republican Party registration form in 1916.

Her main problem was finding a conductor to perform her large-scale orchestral works, since women's music had no place in masterworks, unlike the music of male composers which was part of the musical canon. This problem was solved when she met Theodore Spiering, an American violinist and conductor with a brilliant international career behind him, who came to Germany to conduct the Berlin Philharmonic Orchestra in the 1913-1914 concert season. He had a great affection for American composers, especially women composers, and he decided to perform her orchestral works. Her symphony was played wonderfully as were movements from her piano concerto. Much to her surprise the reviews were favorable. The critics spoke of a Brahms-like style, but definitely not a copy of it. Ferdinand Pfohl saw in her a virtuosa pianist with a spark of genius, and another critic wrote that Amy Beach is a leading American composer. They spoke of her piano technique that was not completely clean, but perfect from the standpoint of musical expression. Others found that she possessed a good technique but it lacked magic. She herself wrote that prewar

Germany was skeptical about women composers, and that her friends had warned her about cold audiences and hostile critics. But the audience took to her works, and despite her plans to remain in Europe for only a year, Amy stayed there for three.

Separation

With the threat of imminent war, Amy left Germany on the last train that the American government arranged for its citizens. Before she left she parted from her friend Marcella Craft – who also left Munich – with the song *Separation* set to John Stoddard's words:

> *Who knows if we shall meet again?*
> *Behind each parting lurks a fear;*
> *We smile to hide the haunting pain,*
> *The rising tear.*[4]

She returned to the United States in 1913, on the eve of World War One, and voiced her pro-German views in the American press. Although she declared that she was committed to music and not to militaristic Germany, she defended the Kaiser, claiming that he was not seeking war. Quite naturally, Boston was her home base and for two years she was committed to dozens of concerts arranged by her impresario, to women's dinners, and recitals that filled her schedule.

Despite her busy schedule she was overcome with profound loneliness. In the second decade of the twentieth century Boston no longer reflected either her or her spirit, and her colleagues from the New England school were not sparing in their criticism of her. Some accused her of "Brahmsism" while others viewed her as continuing the Late European Romanticism of Rachmaninoff and Tchaikovsky. The intentional eclecticism in her works which reflected the different periods of her life, and the various musical schools of thought during those periods, were interpreted as a lack of originality.

Amy decided to move to New York, where she set up home in a Fifth Avenue hotel. She began to attend services at St. Bartholomew's Episcopal Church on 50th Street, between Park Avenue and Madison, where she met David McKinley Williams, a talented organist and composer. He was twenty years her junior and preferred male company, yet a strong friendship was forged between them. When she attended church she always made sure she sat on the left of one of the back rows so she could see Williams at the organ.[5]

Her works reflected the controversial discourse in the United States about women who tried their hand at the art of composing music. A 1905 performance of her *Gaelic Symphony* in Philadelphia drew mixed reviews. One critic contended that she was a genius, while another wrote that it was a woman's symphony and therefore not good enough. A third reviewer claimed it was difficult for him to imagine the open-faced, energetic, little lady as a composer and pianist. But the biggest storm was stirred up by the conductor of the New York Symphony Orchestra, Walter Damrosch, when he declared that the most sublime beauty is given to the world by the masters. According to him, women are incapable of creating such beauty since their works are like bubbles of froth lacking weight and depth, and even more so when compared with the masterworks of male composers.[6] Pianist and music critic Emily Bauer countered this with an article in which she quoted German critics who proved that Beach's symphony meets all the "male" criteria noted by Damrosch.

Te Deum

Between 1913 and 1930 Amy spent the winters on concert tours, with her summers devoted to composing at the MacDowell Colony in Peterborough, New Hampshire. This secluded farm, which was purchased in 1896 by Marian MacDowell and her composer-husband Edward to enable him to work in quiet surroundings, became after his death, and in accordance with his request, a retreat to which artists were invited to work in ideal conditions.[7] Amy went to the colony in the 1920s to connect with her inner voice and recover from two grievous losses: the death of her Aunt Ethel, and the untimely passing of her close friend Arthur Hyde, the St. Bartholomew's Church organist who she first met in Boston.

Every morning after breakfasting together, the artists retired to their rooms. Amy would sequester herself for hours on end in her studio at the concert piano or the rococo desk. In the short breaks she took she went out onto the verandah and enjoyed the wide expanses and surrounding greenery, and at noontime she found a lunch basket outside her door. The evening meal was served in the dining room, and afterwards the artists sat in groups either talking or enjoying a game of table tennis or billiards.

All the works she wrote from 1921 onward were formulated at the MacDowell Colony, at least in draft form. It was there, too, that she searched for innovative artistic solutions in the wake of the modernist movement in the arts. In Rome, to which she came on a European concert tour, she completed her *String Quartet, op. 89,* which represents a turning point in her style – she moves away from traditional tonal harmony, and employs dissonances.

Ironically, the Wall Street Crash of 1929 benefited Amy's work, since many musicians as well as audiences were seeking material from the past, and her *Gaelic Symphony*, which in the 1920s had been forgotten, was given a new lease on life. Beach spoke about a career as an inseparable part of women's lives, and contended that every woman must remove obstacles she encounters in order to give her spirit space and time. Paradoxically, even though when she was younger she had accepted her husband's dictum to discontinue her formal studies lest she lose her originality, she testified about herself that as a woman she had never felt inferior. America, she argued, offers equal opportunity to young women and men, and the main question is how women choose to divide their time, and how much of it they devote to their art. She herself produced the lion's share of her works when she was a married woman, was an autodidact, and learned through her musical work.

Amy did not only talk, she also acted. She exploited her network of contacts in the United States and Europe to help young women artists to advance their careers. She was involved in professional organizations and was the first president of the Society of American Women Composers. In New York she had a studio on the 11th floor of a 24-story building overlooking the Hudson River. The building, which was exclusively for women residents, housed hundreds of women engaged in various professions who enjoyed both social and professional relations.

Amy's health deteriorated in the 1940s. In June 1941 she announced that her strength was failing, but nevertheless she composed several more short pieces. Numerous friends visited her at home or took her to concerts or the theater. In the course of 1941 she stopped going to church whenever her works were to be played, and she spent the summer of that year in Centerville on Cape Cod, but returned to New York in the fall. At the MacDowell Colony's annual meeting in

December, playwright Esther Bates reported that she had spoken with the composer, who was sitting in bed wearing a pink jacket, surrounded by roses and Christmas cards, and in a clear voice had sent her love to them all.

She died of heart disease on 27 December 1944. The funeral service took place at St. Bartholomew's, the church so dear to her heart. The coffin covered with white flowers stood in the aisle, David Williams played an organ prelude, and the choir followed the coffin in procession singing a hymn.

After her cremation, her friends took the urn containing her ashes from New York to Boston, where it was buried in the Forest Hills Cemetery next to the graves of Henry Beach and her parents.[8]

Sixteen

Miraculous and Fragile:
Lili Boulanger
(1893-1918)

When she was twenty-three Lili Boulanger was informed by her doctors that she had only two years to live. She was undismayed and filled with ambitious creativity. She completed works that lay unfinished on her desk, and even began writing new ones. On the days she was well enough she worked unremittingly, and when she was bedridden she dictated her works to her sister Nadia.

Femme fragile

Marie-Juliette Olga Lili Boulanger was born into a musical family that resided in Paris's ninth arrondissement. The arrondissement was home to famous composers and a center of attraction for those who came to the city for a prolonged stay. Her parents' home abounded with musical activity, and self-discipline in general and professional discipline in particular were a supreme value. "Everyone at [our] home played," wrote her sister Nadia who was six years older than her, "and music was the center of the universe." Her father, Ernest Boulanger, a composer of operas, conductor, and voice teacher, met her mother, Raissa Myshetskaya, when she was his student at the Paris Conservatory, and they fell in love and married. Grandfather Boulanger, too, was a famous cellist, and Grandmother Juliette – whose name Lili and Nadia bore – was a singer.

When Lili was born her father who was already seventy-eight years old, adjured Nadia to protect her younger sister as if she were her own child.[1] And with good reason. When she was two Lili contracted pneumonia that so weakened her immune system that she constantly suffered from a variety of chronic illnesses. In her adulthood the thin, dreamy-eyed girl was dubbed a "femme fragile".

When she was five she accompanied Nadia to her lessons at the conservatory. A short time later she too began learning music theory and the organ, and she also sang and played the piano, violin, and harp. According to Nadia, her father's death when Lili was only six was the catalyst of her little sister's desire to express herself in music. But at the time opinions were divided on whether it was appropriate for a woman to take up music as a profession.

When she was eleven the family holidayed at Honnecourt-sur-Escaut near Gargenville, where the composer, teacher, organist, and one of the most brilliant pianists of his generation, Raoul Pugno, lived. In order to be close to the man who became a central figure in their lives, and Nadia's professional life in particular, the Boulangers rented a house opposite his and maintained a close friendship with Pugno and his daughter. Between his many concert tours of Europe and the United States, Pugno would return home to teach, entertain, and play concerti and works for two pianos with Saint-Saëns and Nadia. Lili was witness to her sister's great love for the gifted musician who was an inveterate womanizer and frequently broke her heart. The girls' mother Raissa, for whom her daughters' advancement and position in society were of paramount importance, held festive dinners in their home to which she invited leading composers and performers, and also held concerts there. On 4 February 1905, for example, a concert was held in which Nadia and her teacher, Louis Vierne, took part. This was a fine opportunity to show off their new organ to the leading musicians of Paris.

At sixteen Lili announced her intention of becoming a composer – an unusual choice for a young girl, even if her name *was* Boulanger. In 1910 she began studying intensively, progressing at meteoric speed. She learned voice training as well as the violin, piano, and harp, and was considered to be a musical genius of her time. Studies at the Paris Conservatory were based on practice prior to writing for the lyric theater, and voice lessons focused on the nineteenth-century repertoire which was the institution's bread and butter. But separation between the sexes was almost complete in theoretical and practical studies alike. The curricula were both separate and different, and the repertoire required from women was less demanding.

Prix de Rome

Success in music studies was measured, inter alia, by participation in competitions and winning awards. At age sixteen Lili announced her intention of winning the prestigious Prix de Rome. The prize was awarded by the French government in conjunction with the *Académie Royale de Peinture et de Sculpture* to French artists in the fields of music, painting, architecture, sculpture, and engraving. Winning it was the dream of every French artist under the age of thirty, since it gave the winner five years of study free of financial worries. The happy winner received an annual bursary of 3,000 francs over the five-year period, and signed an agreement whereby he or she undertook to spend the first two years at the Villa de Medici in Rome, and the third in Germany. In 1903 the prize committee announced the opening of the competition to women, and in 1911 it was won by the French sculptress and illustrator Lucienne Heuvelmans. Inspired by Heuvelmans' success, Lili entered her *Faust et Hélène* cantata, and on 5 July 1913, seven weeks before her twentieth birthday, she became the first woman musician to win the prize.

A happy band of some twenty friends came to see Lili and her mother off when they left Paris for Rome. The two reached Nice the following day where they stayed with Miki Piré, a close family friend. It was there that Lili first encountered *Tristesses*, a collection of poems by the French poet Francis Jammes, some of which he set to music and will be discussed later. She reached Rome on 19 March 1913, but that day the taxi drivers were on strike so she was late arriving at the Villa de Medici, which greatly angered the director, Albert Besnard. Not only that, he complained about the young composer being accompanied by her mother, but still, Lili was happy. Winning the prize was her great ambition and she enjoyed the publicity she gained as a successful composer and a pretty woman possessing personal charm.

Lucky Number

Lili loved wordplay and numerology. The fact that she was awarded the Prix de Rome in 1913 strengthened her belief in the mystical power of the number thirteen. Her name had thirteen letters, and the initials with which she signed her works – LB – conjured up the image of that number. The biblical texts she chose to set to music are Psalms 130, 131, and 137. In her *Faust et Hélène* cantata, which she entered for the Prix de Rome, there are thirteen bars of basso ostinato depicting the shadow of the victims of the Trojan War, and in addition she selected thirteen poems from Jammes' *Tristesses* which she set to music and entitled *Clairières dans le Ciel* (Forest Clearings in the Sky). This is her longest work which describes the different moods that surface in a young woman's memory in the wake of an emotional relationship that ended in enforced separation. It premiered in Paris on 8 March 1918, a week before her death. Nadia Boulanger related that Lili's emotional reaction to Jammes' poems was most profound. She identified with the young woman who appears in the poem without a name, and is only referred to by the pronoun "elle". For Lili this was yet another sign, since the letter L appears in her initials.[2] In this work, which she composed in December 1913 before leaving for the Villa de Medici, and up to November 1914, the numbers twelve and thirteen appear as symbolic numbers. A thirteen-tone interval, and use of the first and third notes of the scale are only a part of the symbolism she created in her music.

It is widely assumed that this song cycle was inspired by Lili's relationship with David Devriès, the great tenor who was an old Boulanger family friend, and eleven years her senior. On 13 December Devriès sang the role of Faust in the premiere of *Faust et Hélène*, the cantata that won the Prix de Rome. Lili, wearing a velvet dress, accompanied him on the piano, and at the end of the performance they stood onstage to prolonged applause.

In the spring of 1914 while she was in Rome, she dedicated two songs from the *Clairières dans le Ciel* cycle to Devriès, one of which describes a lonely man immersed in memories of his lost love, and in his hand her medallion.

August 1914 saw the outbreak of World War One and Lili and Nadia volunteered for charity work for French soldiers. They were members of the Franco-American Committee which aided not only enlisted men but also their families, and they also edited a newspaper published by the committee. They dealt with thousands of requests for help, among them some that required sensitivity and discretion, such as one on behalf of Nadia's former teacher, Louis Vierne, who had lost his sight, or a request for help for composers like Erik Satie and Camille Saint-Saëns who had fallen on hard times.

The Beginning of the End

When she was twenty-three Lili was given the awful news that she had only two years to live. But instead of losing hope she embarked on the most artistically productive period of her life, completing unfinished works and starting on others, including the opera *La Princesse Maleine* which remained unfinished. A year later, in 1917, her health deteriorated but that did not stop her dictating her final work, *Pie Jesu*, to Nadia. During the German bombardment of Paris, Lili was bedbound in her country home in the fishing village of Mézy-sur-Seine, knowing her days were numbered. Nadia nursed her devotedly, and when she had to leave for work, their friend Miki Piré sat at Lili's bedside. On 8 March 1918 Lili's *Clairières dans le Ciel* had its first performance that was attended by Piré.

Only twenty-four years old, she died a week later. At her request she was buried in the velvet dress she wore for the performance of *Faust et Hélène* in November 1913.

Postlude

A few months after her beloved sister's death, Nadia stopped composing and decided to devote her life to conducting and teaching. She was one of the first women conductors and a brilliant organist, best remembered for her unique method of teaching composition. Among her students were some famous names such as Aaron Copland, Thea Musgrave, Astor Piazolla, and Philip Glass, who became known as the "Boulangerie". We owe our awareness of Lili Boulanger's works to Nadia who performed them and made sure they were published.

Nadia died in 1979 and like her sister was buried in the Montmartre Cemetery in Paris.

Seventeen

A Tropical Afternoon:
Florence Beatrice Price
(1887-1953)

She was a well-known figure in her hometown. She had a music studio where she taught piano and was professionally engaged in composing. But despite her impressive résumé she was not accepted for membership in the Arkansas State Music Teachers Association because she was black.

Mississippi River Suite

Florence Beatrice Price was born in Little Rock, Arkansas, on 9 April 1887. Her father, James Smith, was the only dentist in town, and her mother was a teacher who also played the piano. Her mother taught her to play and she gave her first recital when she was only eleven.

She was later accepted for the New England Conservatory of Music in Boston, no mean accomplishment for a black woman. Boston was the same puritan city where Amy Beach had begun her career, the Boston where the piano was the instrument of choice at Sunday afternoon social gatherings, the Boston of public concerts. Founded in 1867, the conservatory was one of the first institutions of its kind to accept African-American women students.

After completing her studies and receiving her diploma as a piano teacher and organist, Price returned to Arkansas where she taught music, but at the same time she was infected by the composing bug. Three years later she moved to Atlanta, Georgia, where she was appointed head of Clark University's music department. There, too, she found no inner peace since she was not doing exactly what she thought she *should* be doing – composing music. In 1912, after two years in the post, she decided to go back to Little Rock. On her return she met Thomas Price, a successful lawyer. They married, moved into a small, modest house, and a year later purchased a more spacious home in a middle-class black neighborhood.

At the time Little Rock was a comfortable place to live for middle-class black people. People like Price and her husband, who both had academic degrees, were considered aristocrats and were expected to be community leaders. And indeed, Florence served as president and director of the Little

Rock Music Society, and Thomas was the legal adviser of the Mosaic Templars, an international organization devoted to the preservation of black culture, and which today is a cultural center and museum celebrating African-American history. The Prices had two daughters, and a son who died in infancy. After her son Tommy was born Florence composed a somewhat melancholic and nostalgic piece called *To My Little Son* set to words by the American poet Julia Johnson Davis:

> *In your face I sometimes see*
> *shadowings of the man to be.*
> *And eager dream of what my son shall be*
> *in twenty years and one.*
> *When you are to manhood grown*
> *And all your manhood ways are known,*
> *then shall I wistful try to trace*
> *the child you once were in your face.*

Dance of the Cotton Blossoms

Price established a music studio, taught piano, and composed short pieces. But despite her professional experience she was not accepted for membership in the Arkansas State Music Teachers Association.

Life between blacks and whites took a dramatic turn in 1919, when black sharecroppers began suspecting that white landowners were deliberately undervaluing the cotton grown by blacks. It was against this backdrop that a union for the protection of black sharecroppers' rights was formed, which started the racism snowball rolling. On 30 September some white Missourian officials opened fire on a union meeting, and in the ensuing exchange of fire two whites were killed. The rumor of the shooting incident spread like wildfire, and within a short time hundreds of armed whites appeared on the scene seeking revenge. They torched black homes and businesses. In response to the rioting, armed federal troops opened fire on the blacks trying to protect their property and their lives. Two hundred African-Americans were killed, among them sixty-seven children, hundreds were arrested, and scores were charged with incitement to riot and held in the basements of the city's public schools. Thomas Price was the defense counsel of twelve black men charged with murder who were subsequently found guilty and sentenced to death.

In the wake of the unrest in the city, the Prices began thinking about relocating, and in 1927 they moved to Chicago. It was there that opportunities for professional development were opened for Florence, and within a short time she consolidated her standing as a teacher, pianist, and organist. A year later the prestigious Schirmer Music publishers decided to publish her work, *At the Cotton Gin*. The gin, invented by Massachusetts-born industrialist Eli Whitney Jr., a machine for separating cotton seeds from the bolls, was to turn cotton growing into a profitable industry, but it is a safe assumption that Whitney did not imagine that it would accelerate the spread of slavery in the United States. Florence composed numerous short pieces for the piano which combined a Romantic-European style with sounds of black soul music, and rhythms from African heritage, like the Juba dance. The audience received her warmly, which ran completely counter to what was happening in her personal life, which during those years was in crisis.

Following the Wall Street Crash of 1929 and the global economic crisis, Thomas found himself in dire financial straits and the family, which until then had lived a comfortable life, began to feel what poverty meant. Florence decided to take action. She mustered all her talent as an organist and improviser, and started working as an accompanist to silent movies. On The Stroll, the popular name of the theater district's State Street, she was one of the few women organists, and her musical talent stood out. She played any score put in front of her and improvised in a way that impressed her listeners.

Thomas, on the other hand, became irate and irritable and vented his frustration by abusing his wife. Relations between them became impossible until he left her in 1930, and a few months later Florence filed for divorce. She obtained the decree on 19 January 1931 and was given custody of their two daughters, but at the same time her financial situation became direr. With nowhere to live, she and her daughters moved from one friend's house to another. The three of them eventually moved in temporarily with Margaret Bonds, a former pupil of Florence's who had become a piano teacher, composer, orchestrator, and organist in her own right. To make ends meet Florence wrote music for silent movies and sold works for the piano. In addition she composed pop music under the pseudonym "Veejay".

For a while it seemed that the composer had turned her life as an independent woman around, but only a month after her divorce was finalized she married a man thirteen years her senior. Her second marriage also failed and the couple divorced after three years.

From that point on nothing stopped Florence on her way to the top. She was determined to gain recognition and continued to enter her works in competitions to win awards. Her efforts yielded fruit in 1932 when she won four prizes, including a first prize for a symphony. That same significant year her student Margaret Bonds also won a prize.

In the course of the competition in which she won first prize, Florence became acquainted with the conductor Frederick Stock, who became her close friend and mentor. At the Chicago World's Fair that was held a few months later, the

Chicago Symphony Orchestra under the baton of Stock played her symphony. Originally called *Negro Symphony*, this title was replaced by a more neutral one, *Symphony in E minor*. With its performance Price would be immortalized as the first African-American woman composer whose large-scale work was performed by this august orchestra.

The Moon Bridge

1933 was a particularly fruitful year. Encouraged by Stock, Florence began working on a piano concerto, and dedicated it to her friend and patroness Helen Armstrong Andrews. At the concerto's premiere on 24 June 1934 held to mark the commencement of the sixty-seventh class of the Chicago Musical College, Price was at the piano, and the orchestra of the college at which she studied composition and orchestration, accompanied her. The program also included movements from Beethoven's Piano Concerto no. 3, excerpts from Weber's opera *Der Freischütz*, and Eduard Lalo's *Spanish Symphony*, but the Price concerto was the evening's great success. Praise was heaped upon the work and its performance by Chicago's *The Musical Leader*, and a long article on Price and her work appeared in *The Chicago Tribune*. Her patroness wrote a moving letter in which she thanked Florence for the dedication and praised the work, stressing how wonderful it was that a woman could compose music of such a high standard.

Florence's reputation as a composer gained impetus and bookings flowed in from all over. She was invited to conduct her concerto at the Century of Progress Exposition Negro pageant, *O Sing a New Song*, a celebration of African-American music, dance and drama. The who's who of the African-American art world took part in the event, including conductor and songwriter Noble Sissle of Broadway fame, who was also one of its organizers.

Two months later, on 30 August, Price performed her concerto again, this time in an arrangement for two pianos at an event held by the National Association of Negro Musicians in Pittsburg. She played the solo version at one piano, while at the other sat her former pupil, the black composer-pianist Margaret Bonds who rendered the orchestral version. On this occasion too, Florence gained critical acclaim. J. Fred Lissfelt, music critic of the *Pittsburg Sun Press*, wrote that her style revealed a characteristic voice. He added that there is real American music and Florence Price is speaking a language she knows. From this standpoint she embodied what Dvořák had seen as a composer of "American music". In his view a combination of slave songs and Negro music connected with tilling the soil within artistic music was American music. But Price's work verifies what Amy Beach before her had believed – that the American spirit is a combination of the origins of each and every one within the classical heritage. Therefore for Florence, who was born in Little Rock, it was indeed Negro music, whereas for Amy who hailed from New England, it was the ancient Scottish and Irish songs.

On Friday 12 October 1934 Price's concerto was performed by the Woman's Symphony Orchestra of Chicago, an event that marked the start of her long association with this important orchestra. The orchestra was founded in 1925 by three women musicians: clarinetist Lillian Poenisch, flautist Adeline Schmidt, and cellist Lois Bichel. Like all the other members of the orchestra, each of them played in various ensembles. At first they were unable to find a suitable conductor, so the Berlin-born violinist and composer Richard Czerwonky was appointed temporarily. The orchestra numbered some sixty-five musicians, all women, except for a few men who played instruments for which women musicians could not be found, like the brass. Its early programs were similar to those of other orchestras, but it was the only orchestra in the United States whose program included subscription concerts. Six highly successful concerts were held under Czerwonky's baton, and after the third, music critic René Devries wrote: "[The Woman's Symphony Orchestra of Chicago] will, no doubt, play a great part in years to come in the musical success not only of this city, but also of the Middle West. Many changes will have to take place, however, before the orchestra is placed on a safe basis. Symphony orchestras are not run without backing, and at the present time the Woman's Symphony Orchestra needs a good angel – one or more backers who will have faith in these excellent women musicians, who so well deserve support."[1] Two concerts were held on the Friday when Florence's concerto was performed, one in the afternoon and the other in the evening. Both were broadcast on the radio and were reported in the *Women in Music* journal. The program included Amy Beach's *Gaelic Symphony*, *Concert Piece* by Cecile Chaminade, and the one act opera *A Legend of Spain* by the Philadelphia-born composer and philanthropist Eleanor Everest Freer. But yet again it was Price's concerto that stole the show. People spoke of her melodies that sprang from popular Negro idioms alongside the symphonic treatment, the role of the piano, and the unique form of the one-movement concerto, unlike the traditional three movements of the classic (and Romantic) concerto.

These years were kind to Price, both from the standpoint of her professional development as well as socially. Her circle of friends widened, and she heard her music performed in public. In March 1935 she made history by becoming the first African-American woman accepted for membership in the Chicago Club of Women Organists.

My Soul's Been Anchored in the Lord

The artistic songs and her arrangements of soul music were special favorites of leading professional singers. The repertoire of Marian Anderson, for example, contained more than fifty of Price's songs, some of which were dedicated to her. But the most dramatic concert that went down in history took place on the steps of Washington's Lincoln Memorial on Easter Sunday, 9 April 1939. This unique event was arranged by First Lady Eleanor Roosevelt and Secretary of the Interior Harold L. Ickes after the Daughters of the American Revolution refused to allow Anderson to sing in Constitution Hall because she was an African-American. After a moving rendering of the American national anthem, the singer sang Price's *My Soul's Been Anchored in the Lord*.

She maintained her standing in the black community with her involvement in black musicians' organizations, and gained headlines in the community's leading newspapers, while at the same time continuing to record achievements as a composer. But despite her success, her insecurity as a career woman was constantly evident. In a 1936 interview she gave to *The Chicago Defender* she was asked if she was satisfied with her work, and replied:

> *I am deeply thankful for progress, but satisfaction – no, not satisfaction. I am never quite satisfied with what I write. I don't think creators are ever quite satisfied with their work. You see there is always an ideal toward which we strive, and ideals, as you know, are elusive. Being of spiritual essence they escape our human hands, but lead us on, and I trust upward, in a search that ends. I believe*

only at the feet of God, the One Creator, and source of all inspiration.[2]

In another newspaper interview in 1940 given after a performance of her Symphony no. 3, she told the interviewer how she had been recalled to the stage again and again, and how the women in the audience, all of them white, had stood, drawing the rest of the audience after them. But, she added, qualifying her success, she wasn't very good at pushing herself into the public's consciousness. According to her, this calls for self-confidence and aggressiveness, qualities mainly attributed to the male gender. The paradox here is in the fact that despite her shyness and lack of aggressiveness, Price *did* actively promote herself, but her inner feelings told her that she had not achieved what she thought she should have. Aside from being black, she knew that from a gender standpoint the world of music viewed her works through a stereotypical filter. It was therefore doubly important for her that her large-scale works gain recognition. Price did not forget her origins for one moment, and together with her success was active in the National Association of Negro Musicians in Chicago, where her works were performed together with series of church concerts. She later became the first black woman to join the Illinois Federation of Music Clubs and the Chicago Club of Women Organists. All of these organizations lauded her works and performed them. The entire corpus of her work totals more than three hundred works, from piano exercises published in a prestigious series by Oxford University Press, through chamber music and music for radio, to large-scale works like symphonies and concerti.

Her great achievement crossed the Atlantic, and Price gained popularity in Europe too. And as usually happens in these cases, with her national and international recognition came sudden popularity in her hometown. In late 1934 she received a challenging invitation to give a recital at Dunbar High School. The Alumni Association of Philander Smith College in Little Rock sponsored her return to Arkansas, billing her as "the noted musician of Chicago". But Florence declined. She had no desire to return to the racist South, but in the end her sense of commitment to the community prevailed, and she recanted. The concert, held on 19 February 1935, was a resounding success and the papers were filled with reports about the audience that filled the hall, and how they were enthralled by the playing of the composer-pianist who was one of their own.

Florence Price died in Chicago on 3 June 1953, while planning another tour of Europe. Eleven years later, in 1964, a Chicago elementary school adopted her name as its own in recognition of her legacy.

Eighteen

The Maestra and Les Six:
Germaine Tailleferre
(1891-1983)

She was born at the end of the nineteenth century as Marcelle Germaine Taillefesse, the youngest of five children. The family lived in Saint-Maur-des-Fossés – today's Parc St. Maur, a Parisian middle-class neighborhood – in a private house with a chicken coop. Her parents' marriage was not a happy one. Her mother, Marie-Desirée, was an amateur pianist who began teaching her daughter to play when she was four. Learning the piano caused Germaine great happiness, and to thank her mother for her efforts she would kiss her hands. By the time she was five she was playing pieces she had heard, short pieces she wrote herself, and even began composing an opera based on a children's story, but did not complete it.

Her mother encouraged her talented daughter to diligently pursue her music studies, but her father, on the other hand, opposed this and refused to pay for her tuition. A contentious man, he was the cause of a harsh atmosphere at home. Marie-Desirée, however, was determined, and when her daughter was twelve she enrolled her at the Paris Conservatory. On her mother's instructions Germaine would surreptitiously slip out of the house to her studies, thus keeping her father in dark about them. Later, as a consequence of her father's animosity, she changed her name to Tailleferre.

Les Six in Paris

At the conservatory Germaine was an outstanding student and won numerous awards for her achievements. She paid her part of the tuition fees by giving lessons to younger students. It was during these years that she composed her first significant work, *Premières Prouesses* (First Feats) for piano duet. In addition, she was enchanted by the sound of the harp and composed short pieces for the students of Mme. Tardieu who taught the instrument.

It was at the conservatory that the musical young woman met the composers Darius Milhaud, Georges Auric, and Arthur Honegger, who were to become her close friends and colleagues. Together with Louis Durey and Francis Poulenc, and encouraged by Erik Satie, they founded "Les nouveaux jeunes", the new young [composers], and later, in 1918, they became *Les Six*, which is how history remembers them. Although not homogeneous from the standpoint of musical style, their motto was the creation of new French music which, as opposed to the German-Romantic tradition, was characterized by simplicity and unpretentiousness.[1] As we can see, Germaine was the only woman and was dubbed "the smile of The Six". In 1920 they published *L'Album des Six*, a suite of six solo piano pieces, and this was the only work in which all the members of the group participated. Germaine's contribution to the album is a Pastorale, a genre whose immediate association is shepherds tending their flocks in an idyllic world, which she dedicated to Milhaud.

Café de la Rotonde

During World War One the conservatory was almost emptied of students and teachers alike, but Tailleferre continued to attend her composition classes which were now held only once a week. The group's meetings were moved to Milhaud's apartment in rue Gaillard, Montmartre, and on Saturdays they would meet for dinner at Café Delmas that was on the building's second floor. During those years Tailleferre studied the music of Schoenberg and Ravel while continuing to compose and orchestrate in accordance with her own perception whereby if the listener was unable to immediately identify with the musical style on hearing the first notes, the work lacked the desired artistry.

Germaine left Paris in 1917 and went to Brittany with her mother and sister, and from there to Barcelona and Biarritz. On her return to Paris a few months later she rented an apartment in rue Notre Dame des Champs in Montparnasse. Her afternoons were spent by the fire in her apartment with Coco, her fox terrier, curled up at her feet. It was there that she felt safe and secure working on her unique needlepoint tapestries, one of which was exhibited in a Montparnasse gallery in 1932.

Although her talent was beyond doubt, her professional soul-searching was hard for her. She suffered from stage fright, so it was clear that she would never become a concert pianist. But she still needed a way of making a living for both herself and her mother. She was given unexpected encouragement on one of her visits to the neighborhood Café de la Rotonde immortalized by Picasso in 1901. The café was a meeting place for the artists of the time, and it was there that she met Modigliani who gave her some cubist sketches he did on paper napkins, and also Picasso who convinced her to go back to composing with ideas filled with the new wind that was blowing.

The change came when she played *Jeux de Plein Air* for two pianos at the home of pianist Marcelle Meyer. Its style, which on the one hand has naivety and ambivalence on the other, captivated Erik Satie who was there. At the end of the performance he went over to Germaine to find out who had composed the piece. On hearing her reply he kissed her and called her "my musical daughter".[2]

Although she was one of *Les Six*, Tailleferre zealously guarded her artistic and spiritual independence. She wrote music for films, radio and opera, chamber music and songs, and in the 1960s she even engaged in electronic music. In her works she employed genres from before her time, including six volumes of ancient songs. She also composed in the style of Ravel and Fauré, but her master was Johann Sebastian Bach, a large lithograph of whom hung over her piano.

For Germaine the 1920s were years in which she flourished. Russian producer Sergei Diaghilev commissioned her to write music for a ballet, and thus she broadened her professional activity while at the same time forming some important associations. Thus, for example, Princess Winnaretta Singer de Polignac, the source of whose wealth was the Singer sewing machine family as well as her second marriage to Prince Edmond de Polignac, heard her ballet music and commissioned her to write a piano concerto. Herself a professional pianist and organist, the princess was a supporter of young musicians like Debussy, Stravinsky, and Nadia Boulanger. Her music salon was one of the most important and sought-after in Paris of the 1920s and 30s, and the concerto that Tailleferre composed for her was a great success.[3]

It was during those years that Germaine became friendly with the Russian composer Igor Stravinsky, and they spent time together at Gabrielle "Coco" Chanel's villa in Garches. Tailleferre arranged Stravinsky's *The Rite of Spring* for two pianos, and the arrangement, which won popular acclaim at Princess de Polignac's salon, was recorded with her at one piano and Stravinsky at the other. The two had a very close relationship until she ended it for unknown reasons in the 1930s.

Six chansons françaises

As well as being musically talented, Tailleferre also moved in society and possessed the ability of forming relationships with the right people, which helped her to navigate her career. In early 1925 she went to the United States where she performed her piano concerto at Carnegie Hall. This tour was facilitated by the eminent conductor Leopold Stokowski, founder of the New York City Symphony Orchestra who also conducted the music of Walt Disney's *Fantasia*, in which he also appeared. She was also helped by her friend, film casting director Marion Dougherty.

She returned to Manhattan in the spring of that year and was invited to a party where she met Ralph Barton, an American caricaturist who worked for *The New Yorker* and was recently divorced from his third wife. After the party he drove her back to her hotel and that same evening proposed to her.

They were married in Connecticut and settled in Manhattan in a house that became a pilgrimage site for friends and celebrities alike, including the English novelist W. Somerset Maugham, American writer and playwright Sinclair Lewis, and actress Loretta Young. At one of their music evenings she met George Gershwin and following their meeting she wrote an arrangement for two pianos of his *Rhapsody in Blue*. In 1926 she was working with the Boston Symphony Orchestra, and at one of the rehearsals she met Charlie Chaplin. Chaplin was enthralled by the way she worked with the musicians and commissioned her to write the score for his film *The Circus*.[4]

But while Germaine was busy forming contacts with the wealthy and influential, her husband was consumed with envy by the attention being lavished on her. He was particularly disgusted when he was frequently referred to as "Mr. Tailleferre". He tried to dissuade her from composing, and they went to Paris where they bought a fine house on rue Nicolo near Bois de Boulogne. The house was actually an impressive palace which drew much attention, particularly from *Vogue*, which published photographs of it in its "House and Garden" series.

In the course of their years together Ralph's mental state gradually deteriorated and he abused his wife. When she was pregnant he told her he was going to shoot her, but insisted that the bullet would not kill her. She fled in panic, he pursued her, and in the end he indeed shot her. She consequently miscarried and while still in hospital she received a luxuriant bouquet from him. He managed to deceive the nurses who cared for her and who were suitably impressed by their wonderful relationship.

She and Ralph never saw each other again. The thirty-nine-year-old Barton went back to Manhattan, and a short time later shot himself in his luxurious Fifth Avenue penthouse. He left a letter of apology and money for his housekeeper, and admitted to what Germaine had suspected all along – that he was in love with his ex wife, movie actress Carlotta Monterey until his dying day. It was after this series of tragic events that she wrote *Six Chansons Françaises* to words that reflect disillusionment with love and which mock the loyalty and mutuality that go with marriage.

Germaine's financial situation during those years was as bad as it could be. Her works were commissioned, but the commissions were usually very short term. The speed at which she wrote was dictated by financial necessity, and it affected both the profundity of the work and her deep professional insecurity. In every interview she gave she related to her own music as being of a lower standard than that of her contemporaries.

After her mother's death she remarried, this time to a French lawyer, Jean Lageat, with whom she had her only daughter Françoise, in 1931. They settled down in Grasse on the French Riviera, and it seemed that finally life was good and promising for her, but then Jean contracted tuberculosis and began drinking and acting violently towards her. He would spill ink over her music sheets and call her up to the second floor for no reason. They left Grasse after a short time and went to Switzerland where Jean underwent treatment, and

Germaine stopped writing music. As in her childhood and first marriage, in her second marriage, too, she was a victim of physical and emotional abuse. Her well of creativity dried up and she concentrated all her energy on her life's mission – Françoise's education.

With the German invasion of France in 1942 and the subsequent shortage of both food and music paper, she and her daughter went to Marseilles and from there to Spain and Portugal, until they eventually boarded the *SS Serpa Pinto* that took them to America. Although Jean held a diplomatic post in Washington where he remained throughout the war, Germaine settled in Philadelphia where she enrolled Françoise as a music student at Swarthmore College. However, life in Philadelphia was not kind to her. She felt foreign and alone, did not manage to learn English, and was consequently dependent on her daughter in both her everyday life and for the purpose of working.

Grasse

Mother and daughter returned to Grasse in the spring of 1946. Their house, which during the war served as a German communications center, had been occupied by senior officers who destroyed her manuscripts, and the place had been heavily vandalized. Many of her friends, including Jewish pianist François Lang, had been taken to the south of France and from there to Auschwitz, where they perished.

Germaine's second marriage also ran aground and in 1955, after discovering that her husband had a mistress, she divorced him and bought a small house in Saint-Tropez in the south of France. The sun, golden sands, and the sea inspired her and finally gave her mental respite. It was there that she took care of her granddaughter Elivre when the child's mother was away, and painted seascapes and sailboats. She particularly loved paintings which employed a technique that created an optical illusion together with realistic elements.

On several occasions during those years she was visited by one of *Les Six*, François Poulenc, and in the living room an armchair known as "Poupoul's chair" was set aside for him. She only heard of his death in January 1963 from a journalist seeking an interview. The news left her bereft and grieving, and in its wake she composed *L'adieu du Cavalier* (the Knight's Farewell) to a poem by Apollinaire. Following Poulenc's death she was unable to listen to his music or play her own.

In the 1960s, like many other artists she joined the French Communist Party but was not actively involved in it, and later, with Russia's invasion of Afghanistan she left the Party. In 1976 she accepted the post of accompanist for a children's dance class at the *École Alsacienne*, a private school in Paris. The children adored her both by virtue of her pianistic skills and fame, and the fact that her name appeared in the French dictionary. Germaine became a close friend of the school's principal and his wife, and they played her works at concerts they held. Teaching sustained her vitality, and she continued composing until close to her death, dined every day in a Vietnamese restaurant near her home where they served the dumplings she so loved, drank coffee, and met with friends and young students. She was a well-known figure in the town, and the corner patisserie sold a "Gateau Taileferre".[5]

At the age of ninety-one she was hospitalized and said that if she could not write music she would prefer to die. The last of *Les Six*, she died in Paris on 7 November 1983, and was buried in the family plot in Quincy-Voisins near Meaux Cathedral. Her grave does not bear her name, and only a small plaque with a sculpted rose made by her pupils and friends from the *École Aalsacienne* indicates her last resting place. The plaque bears the words "Our Master".

Nineteen

The First Israeli Woman Composer: Verdina Shlonsky (1905-1990)

Verdina Shlonsky, the extremely talented, prizewinning pianist and composer who also painted and wrote poetry, spurred Marc Chagall to say of her, "You aren't the flower of this land".[1]

She was born on 22 January 1905 in Yekaterinoslav, Ukraine, to a religiously traditional, Zionistic, educated, and affluent family. She was the youngest child born to her father Tuvia, a Hasid and amateur violinist, and her mother Zipporah, an amateur singer, who named her Rosa. Shlonsky was considered a child prodigy who began playing the piano when she was five. When she was eighteen the family emigrated to Palestine but she remained in Europe to continue her musical development. In this period of her life she studied under the tutelage of Artur Schnabel and Egon Petri at Berlin's Hochschule für Musik. While Schnabel was impressed with her pianistic talent, he also encouraged her to engage in composition, and she took up the challenge and later studied in Paris with Nadia Boulanger, Max Deutsch, and Edgard Varese.

After a while her sister Ida returned to Berlin and the two sisters met two brothers from Russia. The two couples married but divorced after a short time. Rosa visited her parents in Palestine, and in the 1930s stayed there for a prolonged period, and then went back to Paris. In World War Two she escaped to London where she worked as a seamstress for Marks & Spencer, and also as a pianist in a Piccadilly café.

She decided to immigrate to Palestine in 1944, but was disappointed to discover that she was unable to become part of local musical life. Her works were not performed and she could not find a position appropriate to her talents. Her brother, the poet Abraham Shlonsky, was a well-known figure whose place in local society was assured, whereas she felt like a fish out of water both as far as her character was concerned and from a musical standpoint too.[2] She set her brother's poems to music and he translated her articles from

Russian, but she contended that although she understood him, he had never understood her.

Deep inside she remained a European. She maintained close ties with French avant-garde artists, and for nearly forty years wrote in Hebrew about the artists she had met, including the Austrian composer Hanns Eisler, French composer Olivier Messiaen, and painter Pablo Picasso. She had met Arnold Schoenberg in 1933 when he was working on his opera *Moses und Aron* and trying to found an institute for Hebrew music. Thirty-three years later she would describe her meeting with Schoenberg, who converted to Lutheranism in 1898 and returned to Judaism after the Holocaust, in an article entitled "Arnold Schoenberg returns to Judaism".[3]

Verdina spoke Russian, joked in French, corresponded in German and English, but even after many years in Israel her Hebrew was basic in the extreme. As a result she was thought of as an outsider more interested in the international than the national. The founding fathers of artistic music in Israel struggled with the constraints of the Hebrew language, and did everything they could to sound "Israeli", which in itself was a problematic concept in an emigrant country that embraced different cultures and was in a state of constant flux. There were some who incorporated music of an Eastern European religious tone, including Hasidic melodies and Yiddish songs, whereas others turned to biblical sources, and yet others for whom the Arabic, the Eastern, sounded local. In the end all of them sought a collective idiom that would reflect the "Israeli". Verdina did not connect with attempts to reflect "Israeliness" in music, and this had an adverse effect on her popularity. She claimed that in the Diaspora there was concern about assimilation, and therefore people preserved Jewish music, but in Israel Jewish identity could be preserved without the shield of religion. Therefore it had to be fashioned as impartial artistic music.

As we have seen, her popularity was badly affected but that was not the case with her professionalism. Her String Quartet, written in 1948, gained her Hungary's Bartok prize, and following this award came an article by the weekly *Haolam Hazeh* music critic, Dr. Emil Feuerstein, who wrote, among other things:

> *The woman who is a genius is nothing but a man... The woman who becomes a true and independent artist divests herself of her femininity. This is the price she must pay... Woman's genius is in the area of love, but the qualities necessary for every genius, such as perseverance, maximal ability to concentrate, monotony in the good sense of the word – these are not her lot... They lack prolonged inspiration, the patient soul, the ability to think things through... to the end. The strength that is needed for the bitter struggle with the idea of a composition entails a difficult technical problem... They lack the sense of architecture, the sense of musical construction and even the sense of form is not given to woman in most cases... It is harder for her to submit to rules... He then goes on to note that "we have a rare phenomenon in the Land of Israel. We have a woman composer!"[4]*

Sadly, Verdina Shlonsky did not meet with success in Israel. In an interview she gave to composer Oded Assaf she said that she asks herself what sort of a person she is and why she writes music, but that the search for an "Israeli" style seems to be hysteria and a power struggle like those in a political party. Yet she still sought her own unique voice, not only as "Verdina the composer" but as "Verdina the composer who lives in Palestine". For her part, the Hebrew song was the voice of Palestine with all its existential implications, and the Jewish song must be transformed accordingly. For her, Zionism was rooted in the fact that she lived in Israel and used Hebrew texts in her compositions. She composed music for more than one hundred songs set to the words of various poets, including Guillaume Apollinaire, Shalom Shabazi, Shin Shalom, Abraham Shlonsky, and Nelly Sachs. Her *Hebrew Poem*, op. 1, was composed in 1932 in memory of her father. She wrote the music first and only afterward her brother Abraham wrote the words. This work won her a prize awarded in Paris to women in the liberal professions, and a year later it was published as part of a cycle of six songs entitled *Images Palestiniennes*, with words by Abraham Shlonsky. Abraham also wrote the words for Verdina's cantata *Hodaya* (Thanksgiving) composed in 1946 and first performed at the Israel Festival twenty years later. Her *Symphony No. 1* which she composed in 1935 and her *Piano Concerto* that she wrote between 1942 and 1944 were also first performed some twenty years after they were written.

In 1973, when she was sixty-eight, she was awarded the Association of Composers, Authors, and Publishers of Music in Israel (ACUM) prize, and in 1984 the Association gave her a lifetime achievement award.

"Verdina Shlonsky did not succeed in integrating into the musical establishment in Israel," Haggai Hitron writes, "neither before the founding of the state nor after. Her works saw performance only many years after they were written, and neither was she offered remunerative or fitting positions. She earned her living mostly as a piano teacher, and among her students were Ido Abrabaya, Benjamin Perl, and Yehudit Cohen. She was and remained an outsider and died alone and impoverished in 1990." In that same article in

Haaretz, composer Oded Assaf said: "She was avant-garde before anyone else here was. Her works are certainly just as good as other nonsense that does get played. She deserves homage as a pioneer of the avant-garde in Israel."[5]

Verdina Shlonsky died in Tel Aviv on 20 February 1990 aged eighty-five.

Twenty

Points, Lines, and Zigzags:
Sofia Gubaidulina
(b. 1931)

One of the expressions of hospitality in the culture in which Sofia Gubaidulina grew up was silence. A guest in the family home was welcomed, a meal was shared with him, and then silence reigned at the table until conversation slowly began.[1]

She was born in Christopol to a family with Tatar roots – a Turkish-speaking ethnic group from eastern Asia that in the thirteenth century intermarried with Mongols and in the fourteenth century became Sunni Muslims. Her grandfather was a *mullah*, her father an engineer, her mother a teacher, and she – the youngest of three sisters – was in charge of the day to day running of the household.

From an early age she dreamed of becoming a composer, and at the sight of every shooting star she prayed that her dream would come true and that God would show her the way. One of the family's neighbors was an accomplished accordionist, and Sofia, enchanted by his music, listened attentively and danced to it. Almost seventy years later her Concerto for Bayan and Large Orchestra, *Under the Sign of Scorpio*, would have its first performance. Another neighbor whose daughter was a piano teacher saw the talented young girl, and on her recommendation Sofia and her sisters began playing. When she was seven a picture of her and her sisters appeared in a Tatar newspaper, and by the time she was nine she performed with them in a concert at a Bach festival held in the music gymnasium auditorium.

Her acceptance into the Music School for Gifted Children was a natural step. Sofia studied there in the afternoons, and for her the place was something of a religious shrine. At a time when the USSR was generally atheistic, and Stalin's secret police – the precursor of the KGB – cast terror and closely followed anyone who observed their religion, Sofia had experiences that influenced both her life and her work. One summer, which the family spent in a mountain village, she noticed a simple icon of Christ. As she knelt and murmured a prayer she heard music inside her, and felt she was having a mystical experience. Many years later she would say that all things sublime are first revealed to her through music.

Jetzt immer Schnee (Now Always Snow)

Germany invaded Russia when Sofia was ten. Refugees fled eastward, and the family kitchen became a humanitarian project for them and also for six women and children who lived in their home. At the end of the war Sofia contracted malaria, and her condition deteriorated to such an extent that her mother swore to have her baptized if she recovered. After two months in hospital she made a full recovery and returned home. In the meantime her mother had forgotten the oath she had sworn in her distress, but Sofia made sure it was upheld. She insisted on attending church and being baptized. She and her mother went to a church on the lower Volga, but found only a drunken priest who was no help. They continued to the next church along the road, but it was closed for renovations. While her mother was prepared to give up, Sofia did not. The religious and mystical feelings she had were already a part of her.

Fairytale Poem

In 1946 Sofia began her studies at the Kazan Music Academy. She completed the usual four-year program in only three, and would say in retrospect that the effort was too great for her. Later, when parents brought their young children to her to learn composition, she would ask them to leave the children alone until they were older. In her view, children need different experiences on which they can base the burden called "creativity and composition".

Although composition was a part of her during her studies at the Academy, deep inside Sofia wavered between performing and composing. She felt that when she concentrated on composing she was neglecting the piano, and vice versa. Since she loved performing and did not suffer from stage fright, there were times when she was determined to focus solely on her piano studies. It was in this period of her life that she fell in love with Shostakovich's *Piano Trio*, and years later would meet the composer who was to influence her life and work.

She left Kazan for Moscow where she studied under the tutelage of Nikolai Peiko at the city's famed conservatory. She began her piano practice each morning with a long walk in the countryside, which for her was an inseparable part of her work. It was there, with the earth beneath her feet that the seeds of ideas germinated within her. When she felt ready to start her day's work, she made her way the conservatory's practice rooms. She did this in the early hours of the morning when there was nobody around – just her and the piano – and thus she sat playing every day in total isolation, completely at one with the work.

When she was twenty-two she met Mark Alyexandrovich Liando, a geologist who was also something of a poet. Liando was captivated by the young Tatar woman and also by the fact that she had studied composition, and they started spending time together. They saw German films, went to the theater and concerts, and talked about music and literature, and the difference between what the papers wrote and life itself. They were married three months before her twenty-fifth birthday.

The Garden of Joy and Sorrow

With the help of her teacher Peiko, who supported and encouraged her, she forged contacts with a circle of composers and performers she had previously not met. They would gather on Fridays, and it was in one of these meetings that she came to the home of Vissarion Yakovlevich Shebalin, who was considered to represent soft modernism and was Shostakovich's admired teacher. In the first two hours of the evening they played works by Prokofiev and Shostakovich, and then enjoyed the food and drink prepared by the lady of the house who was known as the perfect hostess. Sofia greatly enjoyed this cultural experience as well as spending time in the company of famous people who included, among others, two of Shostakovich's sisters and the neo-Romantic composer Georgy Sviridov.

In the year in which she sat her final examinations at the conservatory she met Shostakovich, who became her role model as a musician, for his way of thinking and his human behavior. Hundreds of students flocked to the composer's door to show him their works and seek his advice, and he welcomed them all, listened, and counseled as if the person standing before him was the only person in the world. Sofia went to his apartment accompanied by her teacher in the spring of 1959. Shostakovich listened to her attentively, made some comments, and praised her music. He was well aware of the prevailing opinion that her work was "incorrect", and encouraged her to continue."Be yourself. Don't be afraid to be yourself. My wish for you is that you should continue on your own, *incorrect* way,"[2] he told her. Years later she would attest that in difficult times, when experiencing failure or harsh criticism, she would recall these words which gave her the strength to carry on.

For her final examinations at the conservatory which took place at the end of that summer, she submitted the symphony she had composed as her degree thesis. The auditorium was filled to capacity; on the stage were the eighty musicians of the Moscow Philharmonic Orchestra which played the successful works of the graduates, including Sofia's symphony. It was given a high grade together with some criticism of its melodies which were composed of small ideas instead of a single, long and beautiful one.

And the Roses Wither

In early November 1959, after sitting her final examination, Sofia gave birth to her daughter Nadia. It was a particularly harsh winter, Mark was away on long geological expeditions, and Sofia and the baby were left on their own. The apartment had one stove, a rented piano, and a shelf on which there was a Bible and several other books proscribed by the Soviet authorities. The yards were deep in mud and she had to fetch water from across the street. In the evening, when the fire in the stove died out and little Nadia cried, the young mother sat at the piano and played Beethoven sonatas until the baby fell asleep.

During those months she was consumed with fear because her spring of composing had dried up, and the feeling that she would no longer be able to write music cast her into a depression that led her to the brink of suicide. Her life and Mark's were led on separate paths, and their relationship gradually collapsed. In the spring of 1960 Sofia reached the decision to end their marriage. She and Mark divorced, Nadia was left in the care of Sofia's parents in Kazan, and she went back to Moscow.

In 1965 she married her second husband, Nikolai (Kolya) Bokov, a revolutionist intellectual and opponent of the Soviet regime. Sofia began composing film music, which in the first years of their marriage brought in enough money to allow her to compose more complex works, and also to deepen her knowledge of the compositional methods of her predecessors in the field. The Bokov home was a sort of

Western salon to which numerous young people were drawn every evening where they drank a lot and discussed poetry. Russian poet Gennady Aygi whose poems were not published in Soviet Russia, was a frequent visitor and related that Sofia was very quiet on those evenings, and often left the crowded room for a quieter one. She asked Aygi to leave her some of his poems, and she composed *Roses*, a cycle of five songs for soprano and piano, set to the texts of five of Aygi's poems. In this work she proved that poetry and music shared equal rights, and that one was not superior to the other.

Among the visitors to their home was an attractive but somewhat odd young woman. She and Kolya would withdraw from the rowdy group in the living room and sit talking in the kitchen for hours on end as if there were nobody else around them, in a way that to an onlooker seemed very intimate. This went on until one evening Sofia blew up and informed her husband that it was all over between them. She was extremely agitated and Aygi, who was present that evening, tried to pacify her, but in vain. Sofia and Kolya were divorced in 1972.

Night in Memphis

Sofia's release from her marriage coincided with her release from the influence of her teacher, Nikolai Peiko. She matured as a composer and tried various techniques, using different languages including the serial, electronic, and mathematical. From her standpoint the "golden section" was the perfect form. She made a living writing film and theatre music, her name became known and her works aroused much curiosity. Her belief in the power of art to form a connection with the transcendental deepened, and the personal transformation she underwent led her to a radical conclusion. Instead of writing music for the theatre and ballet and symphonies, she decided to compose miniatures – small musical forms that would enable her deeper inner reflection. She, who loved broad canvas music like that of Shostakovich, now sought to convey her artistic messages in a whisper, or in her own words, "to be a filter, not a generator."[3]

From this standpoint Sofia underwent a process that was diametrically opposite to that undergone by other women composers like Clara Schumann and Fanny Mendelssohn. They began their careers as composers of small pieces for the piano and songs, and only at a later stage of their professional maturation composed large-scale works like Clara's Piano Concerto and Fanny's cantatas.

One of the means employed by Gubaidulina to express depth and stillness in her work was sound, and a good example of this is her choice of instruments such as the double bass and harp whose sound she muted. It was at this time that she felt she was finally doing what she loved, and expressing her musical reactions to events occurring around her. In 1968, for example, the year of the Prague Spring, she was among the intelligentsia who looked forward to a more humane communist future. But in August that year when the Soviet tanks rolled into Prague, her hopes, and those of her friends, were shattered. She composed two cantatas dealing with existential problems: the first, *Night in Memphis*, a rational work that was only performed in Moscow twenty-one years after it was written, deals with the pain of living in a world in which death is a chronicle foretold. The libretto, which is based on inscriptions on ancient Egyptian tombs, she arranged in seven movements expressing the distinction between the world of the day and the world of the night, the world of humans and that of the gods. The sound of the trumpets is muted, and the flattened notes of flutes are heard over the strings when the human soul turns to the night and speaks of its loneliness on the way to death: "O night, give me peace".

The second cantata, *Rubaiyat*, engages in a dialogue with God. The libretto, comprised of texts from translated Persian poetry (including texts by poet, philosopher, and mathematician Omar Khayyam, and Sufi poet Hafiz) speaks of the pain and suffering of human life. The leading role is for a male voice (baritone) that shifts between nine different vocal techniques until in the end the human soul reaches acceptance and tranquility:

> *Be not frightened by the fleeting nature of this world.*
> *Sit quietly in a corner and be content!*
> *Focus your mind on the playfulness of fate.*[4]

Points, Lines, and Zigzags

From a professional viewpoint, Gubaidulina's compositional style, which can be defined as a combination of post-Shostakovich and Alfred Schnittke, is a union of dramatic and spiritualistic. Her music is at times improvisational and at others arranged in accordance with ancient principles. The common thread in this varied style is her constant search for the sublime. She herself defines her style as "religio", as the connection between the self and the transcendental, and she believes in the power of art to change humankind. She was influenced by composers like Bach and Anton Webern, by Carl Jung's psychology, by Nikolai Alexandrovich Berdyaev, the philosopher-theologian whose texts were proscribed in Soviet Russia, but she managed to obtain and study them. Like Berdyaev, she too believed in the freedom of the spirit and the individual freedom of the creator which enable him or her to use materials taken from the reality, mold them, and translate them into action. If in the eighteenth century tonality was the unifying element in a musical work, for Gubaidulina it is tempo – through it she attains oneness with the sublime. Her musical narrative is open and somewhat coarse, and it contains contrasts symbolizing the polarity between darkness and light, between the human and the divine.

In the mid-1970s Sofia began a long-term relationship with pianist-conductor Piotr Meshchaninov who specialized in contemporary Russian music. They began living together and married in the summer of 1991. When she started traveling to the West in the mid-1980s Gubaidulina was surprised to discover not only that women composers had founded organizations and festivals, but also publications in which the music was exclusively by women. She had never seen anything like it in Soviet Russia. The figures of strong women were well known in Russian history and culture, and Sofia had never experienced suppression or exclusion because she was a woman. But she did experience censorship and attacks on her music, which was considered to be too spiritual, over-emotional, and went beyond what could be reasonably expected. However, Gubaidulina's insights on feminine nature should be emphasized, insights which draw a distinction between herself and her male colleagues. Each new idea she discovers or learns, the composer says, deprives her of vast resources of energy. Although she is able to work through entire nights in order to submit a work on time, her physical powers are rapidly depleted.[5]

In the Shadow of the Tree

In 1980 Sofia made her big breakthrough in the West with her *Offertorium* concerto for violin and orchestra, a virtuosic work based on a J.S. Bach theme. She wrote it for the Jewish-Latvian violinist and conductor Gidon Kramer.

It was during this period that she began taking an interest in the prophetic, visionary texts of three writers: poet T.S. Eliot; Marina Tsvetaeva, one of the leading poets in the Sliver Age of Russian poetry; and Chuvash-Russian poet Gennady Aygi. The four quartets comprising *Hommage à T.S. Eliot* engage with the concept of time, including cyclic time. Four seasons of the year, the four Christian concepts of Divinity (the Father, the Son, the Holy Spirit, and the Virgin Mary), the four periods in Man's life (childhood, youth, adulthood, and old age), and the four dimensions of existence (past, present, future, and eternity), all interplay in this seven-movement work.

In 1991 Sofia chose to emigrate to Germany. For her, the first decade as a citizen of the Western world was something of a late artistic rebirth. She examined different ways of working with material, and sought her own unique language. In the course of her numerous journeys she went to Japan to study under the tutelage of Kazue Sawai, a koto player specializing in contemporary music and free improvisation. In the wake of these encounters she composed *In the Shadow of the Tree*, a work in which one instrumentalist plays three solos on koto, bass koto, and chang.

Sofia has been awarded numerous prizes and honors, among them Japan's Praemium Imperiale, the Polar Music Prize in Sweden, The Koussevitzky International Record Award, Composer of the Vienna Festival of Modern Music, the Living Composer Prize of the Cannes Classical Awards, and various other awards for her works that have been performed the world over.

Sofia Gubaidulina has kept her promise to make music her life, and continues to do so to this day.

Epilogue

The canon in Western culture was indeed a male one, but today the book of that canon is closed and the rules of the game have changed. The disappearance of the "great composers" culture is taking place concurrently with women taking their place in Western society. And even though women composers represent half of humankind, the gap between men and women in the world's artistic music industry is still wide. In England, for example, in the PRS for Music Foundation, an association comprised of composers and performers, only fourteen percent of its members in 2011 were women. At the 2006 BBC Promenade Concerts, "The Proms", not a single work by a woman composer was submitted for selection, whereas in 2008 117 works were submitted, only six of which were by women composers.[220] In the United States only three of the 1,530 works performed in the 1995 concert season by twenty-one orchestras were written by women. In Israel, too, there are more than one hundred active women composers, some of whom are members of the Israeli Women Composers Forum, while others prefer not to join a gender group of this kind. But how many of us have heard of Verdina Shlonsky or Yardena Alotin who lived and worked in this country? And how many people have heard of Hagar Kadima, Tsippi Fleischer, Deganit Elkayam, Avia Kopelman and many others who live among us, and for whom composing is both a vocation and a career?

Therefore, raising the veil that has hidden women's musical endeavor over a period of more than eight hundred years – as in these twenty monographs – not only brings them to center stage but also, to some extent, does them historical justice. Knowing their life stories and the creative processes of each of them in the period and place in which they lived is a first step in an attempt to understand how regime systems related to gender ones. Thus, extending knowledge of unfamiliar talents enables a more accurate evaluation of the role of women creators in history.

Furthermore, on the day when practice books include the works of women composers, and in concert halls both in Israel and throughout the world the works of women composers past and present are performed as part of an annual program, and not on a separate evening devoted to their works, we shall then know that a reconstruction of the musical and historical discourse is taking place, and that change is indeed here. And if this book opens a door to further study, to learning about and examining the lives and works of women composers past and present, then I am content.

Notes

Prologue

[1] Showalter, 1989, 76.
[2] Woolf, 2004, 56.
[3] Hensel, 1884, vol. 1, 82.
[4] Tuchman, 1995, 50-51.
[5] Shahar, 1990, 344-345.
[6] Trobairitz (female troubadour), trouvères, jongleurs, minstrels, meistersingers, cantigas d'amour (male) and cantigas d'amigo (female) are the various names by which troupes of singers were known in different countries.
[7] Bowers & Tick, 1987, 46-47.
[8] Briscoe, 1987, vol. 1, 18.
[9] The founding group of "Concerto delle donne" consisted of its founder, Laura Peverara (1550-1601), Anna Guarini (1503-1598), and Livia d'Arco (1565-1611).
[10] The music of "Concerto delle donne" permeated through *musica secreta, musica reservata,* and *musica privata.* The only remaining written publication from this group is one of madrigals for solo soprano, two sopranos, and three sopranos, written for them by Luzzasco Luzzaschi.
[11] In the main, women were not given the opportunity to develop their talent to the high standard that would satisfy their patrons, and the vast majority did not obtain positions that would enable them to be leaders of musical life in the various courts. They therefore lived in the hope that they would be chosen for a leading musical role in one court or another
[12] Peacock, 1988, 19
[13] Rosand, 1978, 279.
[14] Ibid, 274
[15] Ashton, 1997, 201
[16] Reich, 1985. 292.
[17] Ibid, 228-229.
[18] Ibid, 135.

[19] Citron, 1987, 209.
[20] Hensel, Vol. 1, 117.
[21] Jung, 1963, 23, 78-79
[22] Firestone, 1979.
[23] Sadie, & Samuel, 1994
[24] Fauser, 1998, 89
[25] . Rockwood, 2002, 58
[26] Kurtz, 2007, 65.
[27] Aisling, http://www.unigraz.at/muwi3www/SysMus08/
index2Datein/Content/Proceedings_SysMus08_Kenny_Aisl
ing.pdf
[28] Ibid., 2
[29] Ibid
[30] Ibid
[31] Ibid

Chapter One

[1] Tuchman, 50-51.
[2] Silvas, 1998, 149-150.
[3] A sibyl in Greek and Roman mythology is a priestess possessing prophetic attributes.
[4] Beer, 1992, 121.
[5] Fox, 1985, 334.
[6] Sacks, in Maddocks, 2001,63.
[7] Singer, ibid., 64.
[8] Hozeski, 1994, 24-25.
[9] Newman, 1985, 171.
[10] Baird & Ehrman, 1998, vol. 1, 144.
[11] Ibid., 27.
[12] Maddocks, 164.

Chapter Two

[1] Nagler, 1976, 116.
[2] Cusick, 2009, 33.
[3] Ibid., 47.
[4] Ibid., 48.
[5] Ibid., 90-91.
[6] Ibid.

[7]   Kirkendale, 1992, 318. The book contains two sonatas, four madrigals, one aria, three arias allegro, five motets, and ten canzonettas.

[8]   The libretto was written by Ferdinando Saracinelli.

[9]   Cusick, 192-193.

Chapter Three

[1]   Rosand, 1978, 279.

[2]   Magner, http://barbarastrozzi.blogspot.co.il/

[3]   Glixon, 1999, 138. The dates of birth of the three children appear in documents of San Sepulcro monastery, which Isabella and Laura joined.

[4]   The three volumes of Opus 2 were dedicated to Ferdinand III, Holy Roman Emperor.

[5]   This is the *stile nuovo* developed by the Florence Camerata, a recitative accompanied by figured bass. Some of the cantatas appear in two important collections which demonstrate this style: one is Florentine composer Giulio Caccini's "Le nueve musiche" published in 1602, and other by Jacopo Peri, "Le varie musiche", published in 1609.

[6]   *G'locchi Superbi* (Proud Eyes), op. 2, no. 20.

[7]   *La Riamata da chi Amava* (The former lover's revival of love), op. 2, no. 18.

Chapter Four

[1]   Her first husband was in charge of hunting in the House of Orleans whose dukes were considered important in the royal court.

[2]   Carol-Bates, 1982, 62.

[3]   In contrast with Italian opera, Lully's innovation was the introduction of dances, with the minuet among the numerous ones he was the first to compose and introduce. To this he added a recitative filled with expression which faithfully followed the lines of the French language, brilliant string orchestration, and an overture that became known as "the French overture" (a slow introduction in a marked "dotted rhythm", followed by a lively movement in imitative style).

[4] Neuls-Bates, 63.

[5] The work contains unmeasured preludes.

[6] Rosow, 2000, 1024.

[7] Jerold, 2003, 150-151.http://www.jstor.org/stable/40374475

[8] In that year de La Guerre published six sonatas for violin and harpsichord, and two suites which could also be played on the violin. The works, written in the Couperin le Grand style reflect the Italian influence on French society in the early eighteenth century. The first Italian sonatas published in Paris in 1701 were those of Arcangelo Corelli, but in the introduction to his sonatas Couperin states that the first Italian sonatas appeared in the city in 1693.

[9] Buckley, 2011, 23.

Chapter Five

[1] Pietro Antonio Trapassi (1698-1782) adopted the pseudonym Pietro Metastasio.

[2] In her music she makes much use of Baroque-like embellishments and presto passages in which she demonstrated her mastery of the instrument.

[3] One of the most notable examples is the Concerto for Harpsichord in E Major, which she completed when she was twenty-eight.

[4] The hammers of the pianoforte were covered with leather (unlike those of the modern piano which are felt-covered), which enables softer contact and a better response from the instrument. Its strings are thin, similar to those of the harpsichord. Its structure is far lighter and enables holding and muting a note. The sound obtained from all this is somewhat soft, delicate, and transparent.

[5] Giovanni Battista Martini (1706-1784) was a composer, theoretician, music researcher, and an avid collector of musical literature whose collection reached some seventeen thousand volumes. On his death the collection was transferred to the empire's library in Vienna.

[6] Godt, 2010, 20.

[7] Franz Anton Mesmer (1734-1815) gained fame due to his theory on magnetic forces that exist in humans and the

universe, and which could cure numerous ailments. This theory, which at the time met stiff resistance, was dubbed "mesmerism" and later led to the use of hypnosis in modern psychotherapy.

8   Godt, ibid., 137-138.

9   Charles Burney's (1726-1814) writings are historically no less important than the documents of professional researchers, and they express the special relationship he enjoyed with figures such as Gluck, Hasse, Carl Philipp Emanuel Bach, Galuppi, Padre Martini, Farinelli, Metastasio, Rosso, Klopstock, and others. His book, *A General History of Music from the Earliest Ages to the Present Period* was published in four volumes, the last of which was published in 1789.

10   Kelly, 1826, vol. 1, 249-250; Godt, ibid., 197-198. Michael Kelly was an Irish tenor and actor known for viewing life from a comic standpoint. He was born in Dublin and died in London where he was the manager and musical director of the Drury Lane Theatre. From 1783 to 1786 he lived in Vienna where he played leading roles in operas by Cimarosa, Paisiello, and Mozart. In his *Reminiscences* he wrote about Mozart and other figures in the context of the European music of the time.

11   Godt, ibid., 3-4.

Chapter Six

1   Pincherle, 1938, 301.

2   Ibid., 302.

3   The correspondence between Maddalena and Tartini (in Charles Burney's English translation 3http://petrucci.mus.auth.gr/imginks/usimg/0/08/IMSLP606 07-PMLP124143-Letter from Tartini. 1779.pdf http://conquest.imsip.info/files/imginks/usimg/8/80/IMSLP 178942-PMLP124143-tartini-letter.pdf

4   Harpsichord adaptation by Tommaso Giordano.

5   Arnold & Baldauf-Berdes, 2002, 100.

6   Composer-violinist Giovanni Battista Viotti (1755-1824) was a member of the Turin court orchestra who went to

Paris and in 1782 gained great popularity after his first performance. Most of his works are for violin, of which twenty-nine are concerti that are considered to have influenced the style of composition and playing of this specific instrument

7   Arnold & Baldauf-Berdes, 99.

8   Ibid., 115. Six string quartets, six string trios, six violin duets, six concertos for violin, a violin sonata in A, and a string trio in B flat.

Chapter Seven

1 De Valera, 2003, 54.

2   Her later works were also published by Casa Ricordi of Milan.

3   John Field (1782-1837), an Irish composer and pianist, studied in Dublin and later studied under Muzio Clementi who was considered the father of piano virtuosity. Field, who composed more than eighteen nocturnes at a time when the genre was largely unknown, is credited with originating the piano nocturne.

4   *Le Murmure*, Nocturne for piano in A flat major.

5   Nocturne for piano in B lat major.

6   Kijas, 2010, 111.

7   Ibid., 79-80.

8   Ibid., 125.

Chapter Eight

1   His works are still on show in the Louvre, the Musée des Beaux-Arts in Rouen, the Musée des Beaux-Arts in Troyes, and the Musée des Beaux-Arts in Angres.

2   She later studied under famous teachers such as the young Ignaz Mosecheles who at the time performed in concerts, and also with Johann Hummel, who would have considerable influence on her teaching and composition.

3   Aristide Farrenc, 1794-1865.

4   Louise and Aristide resided at no. 22. Chopin, who came to Paris five years later, in 1830, lived at first at no. 27.

5   One of his best known publishing enterprises, which at the time was something of a "scoop", was two versions of Beethoven's opera "Fidelio", adapted for piano with French and Italian libretti.

6   *Piano Quintet No. 1 in A minor*, op. 30, was composed in 1839, and Piano Quintet no. 2 in E major, op. 31 in 1840.

7   *Les Italiennes*, Theme and Variations on Three Bellini Cavatinas, op. 14, (1835).

8   Air Russe Varié, opus 17.

9   Robert Schumann, *Neue Zeitschrift für Musik*, vol. 5 (1836), in Friedland, 1971, 263.

10   Ibid.

11   Among the works she composed during this period were violin sonatas, a cello sonata, a sextet for piano and woodwinds in C minor, a nonet in E minor for string quartet and wind quintet, op. 38 (flute, oboe, clarinet, French horn, bassoon, violin, viola, cello, and double bass), and a trio for flute, cello, and piano in E minor, op. 45.

12   Josef Joachim (1831-1907), a violinist of Jewish extraction who also engaged in conducting and composition. He gained fame as a virtuoso performer of the works of composers such as Bach and Beethoven, which comprised the main part of his repertoire. In Weimar he played first violin in an orchestra conducted by Franz Lizst. Additionally, he was director of the Berlin Royal Academy of Music, and founded a noted string quartet. Joachim was a close friend of Brahms, and also advised him on composing for the violin. The violin concerti of Schumann, Bruck, Brahms, and Dvořák were written for and dedicated to him.

13   Other recipients of the prize after her were Gabriel Fauré and César Franck.

14   The anthology includes complete scores and a biography of each composer. A separate part discusses ornamentation.

Chapter Nine

1   Felix sent to the publishers six Lieder with piano accompaniment (op. 8), and a Trio for Piano, Violin, and Cello (op. 11), which were published in 1850.

[2] Tillard, 1992, 35.

[3] Hertz, 1988, 218-219.

[4] Ibid., 148.

[5] Todd, 2010, 27.

[6] Hensel, 1884, vol. 1, 82

[7] Todd, 67.

[8] Mercer-Taylor, 2000, 66 (sorry☹)

[9] Todd., 68.

[10] The three songs by Fanny that appear in Felix's op. 8 are: *Das Heimweh* (Yearning for Home, librettist, Friederike Robert); *Italien* (librettist, Franz Grillparzer); and *Suleika und Hatem* (librettist, Wolfgang von Goethe). The three that appear in Felix's op. 9 are: *Sehnsucht* (Longing, librettist, Johann Gustav Droysen); *Verlust* (Loss, librettist, Heinrich Heine); and *Die Nonne* (The Nun, librettist, Ludwig Uhland).

[11] Hensel, 84.

[12] Ibid., 117.

[13] Tillard, 163.

[14] Her inheritance was worth 19,000 thalers (one thaler was equivalent to forty-eight schillings).

[15] Citron, 1987, 91.

[16] *Prelude for Organ in F major*, H-U in the list of works by Fanny Hensel-Mendelssohn.

[17] More than a thousand of these drawings were gathered into forty-seven albums by Fanny and Wilhelm's son, Sebastian.

[18] Hensel, vol. 1, 251-253.

[19] Todd, 153.

[20] From the standpoint of its poetic concept, Hensel's work is reminiscent of Schiller's 1801 Ballad of the same name.

[21] Unpublished letter, GB VI 44, in Citron, xli.

[22] Citron, 1993, 54.

[23] Sirota, 1981, 64.

[24] Todd, 211. For example, no. 9, [Largo con espressione] in E minor and no. 8, [Allegro moderato] in B major, are both introverted, whereas no. 7, [Allegro agitato] in G minor, and no. 4.[Allegro con brio] in F minor, are both extrovert.

[25] Citron, 1987, 209.

²⁶ Ibid., 144.

²⁷ Ibid., 353.

²⁸ Ibid.

Chapter Ten

¹ Chissell, 1983, 1.

² The Leipzig Gewandhaus is a concert hall situated on Augustusplatz and was inaugurated in 1743. It is home to Germany's oldest public orchestra which has an impressive musical tradition.

³ Iris, 2 (June 17), 1831, 96, in Reich, 1985, 232-233.

⁴ Friedrich Kalkbrenner (1785-1849) was a virtuoso pianist, composer, teacher, and piano maker. Henri Herz (1803-1888) was a pianist of German extraction who for most of his life worked in England and France. Johann Pixis (1788-1874) was a piano virtuoso of Jewish origin born in Vienna and who lived in France.

⁵ Litzmann, 1927, vol.1, 40; Mazuz, 25.

⁶ *Die Neue Zeitschrift für Musik* was founded in 1834 by Robert Schumann, who was also its editor. It appeared twice weekly.

⁷ Mazuz, 64.

⁸ Mazuz, 36. Among the themes noted by Mazuz in this context are the theme from Clara's *Romance Varié*, op. 3, and the theme from Robert Schumann's *Impromptus*, op. 5.

⁹ The three in question were the pianist and composer of French origin, Anna Caroline Oury (née de Belleville, 1808-1880); Marie Pleyel (1811-1875), a brilliant piano vitruosa who was admired throughout Europe, with many comparing her to Liszt; and Leopoldine Blahetka (1809-1885), a composer and pianist born in Vienna.

¹⁰ Mazuz, 124.

¹¹ Ibid.; Nauhaus, 1993, 44.

¹² Rienzi, der Letzte der Tribunen in October 1842, and Der Fliegende *Holländer* in January 1843.

¹³ Gerig, 1974, 218.

¹⁴ Litzmann, vol. I, 91.

¹⁵ Reich, 1985, 176.

16 Owen, 2007, 19.

17 Reich, 1999, 95.

18 Originally written for two pianos and later arranged for orchestra.

19 Robert Schumann, Romance in F sharp major, op. 28, No. 2.

Chapter Eleven

1 Waddington and Žekulin, 2011. 22, 62. http.//dspace.ucalgary.ca/bitstream/1880/48502/3/viardot.ca talogue.201. 1 pdf.

2 Kendall-Davies, 2004. vol. 1, 49.

3 Ibid., 83-84.

4 Including songs from collections, such as Chants et Chansons de la France and Chansons nationales et populaires de la France.

5 Azoury, 1999, 152.

6 Retrieved from http://www.online-literature.com/turgenev/2707.

7 Knowles, 1983, 41.

8 Ibid., 14, 29.

9 Steen, 2007, 93.

10 Fizlyon, 1964, 231.

11 The other three were the German Princess Helene von Racowitza, George Sand, and Letizia Bonaparte.

12 Everist, 2001-2, 167.

13 Ibid., 168-169.

14 Fitzlyon, , 123.

15 The libretti of her first three operas, *Trop de Femmes* (1867), *L'Ogre* (1868), and *Le Dernier Sorcier* (1869) were written by Turgenev. She wrote the libretti of the last two, *Le Conte de Fées* (1879) and *Cendrillon* (1904) herself.

16 Steen, 421.

Chapter Twelve

1 Rockwood, 2002, 5.

2 Henri Cazalis (1840-1909) wrote under the pen names of Jean Caselli and Jean Lahor.

3   The three girls, Huguette, Claudine, and Helyonne, are the subject of Renoir's painting, *The Daughters of Catulle Mendès,* which is housed in The Metropolitan Museum of Art, New York.

4   Theeman, 1983, 16.

5   Pasler, 2007, 213.

6   Leung-Wolf, 1996, 302.

7   Rockwood, 60.

8   The New York Times, 23.1.1905.

Chapter Thirteen

1   Her first chamber work to be published was the Piano Trio No. 1 in G minor, op. 11. It would be followed by her Piano Trio No. 2 in A minor, op. 34, and Capriccio for Piano and Violin, op. 18.

2   Citron, 1988, 6.

3   Ibid., 138,

4   Ibid., 15.

5   Ibid., 24.

6   Ibid., 19.

Chapter Fourteen

1   String Quintet in E, Op. 1, and Sonata for violin and piano in A minor, Op. 7.

2   In the early twentieth century the palace was converted into a medical school, and today is a venue for official events.

3   Kertesz, 2001, 75.

4   Emmeline Pankhurst (née Goulden, 1858-1928), a fighter for women's rights also founded a movement of women writers. Before she died she managed to hear that women had been granted to right to vote. A statue of Pankhurst is located in Victoria Park Gardens, Westminster.

5   The anthem's words were written by the actress, playwright, journalist, and fellow suffragette, Cecily Hamilton (1872-1952).

6   As well as *The Prison* cantata, the three works mentioned are *Fete Galante, Andante Cordiale*, and *Concerto for Violin and Horn in A. Fete galante*, a painting genre

popular in France in the early eighteenth century, at the center of which are richly-dressed figures in a pastoral setting. Jean-Antoine Watteau (1684-1721) was a leading exponent of this genre.

Chapter Fifteen

[1] Block, 1998, 4.
[2] Ibid., 177.
[3] Ibid., 180.
[4] Ibid., 292.
[5] Ibid., 218.
[6] *Walter Damrosch Scrapbooks,* vol. 1, 1881-1927, NN-L. "Woman Has Achieved Little in Musical Spheres", Block, 201.
[7] Block, 222-225; Falconer-Sakeld, 2005, 449-450.
[8] Block, 295.

Chapter Sixteen

[1] Potter, 1999. 536.
[2] Dopp, 1994, 560.

Chapter Seventeen

[1] Brown, 1993, The Woman's Symphony Orchestra of Chicago and Florence B. Price's Piano Concerto in one movement, 189.
[2] Price, Symphonies Nos. 1 & 3, xxxiv.

Chapter Eighteen

[1] As well as Tailleferre, *Les Six* were Arthur Honneger (1892-1955), Georges Auric (1899-1983), Louis Durey (1888-1979), Darius Milhaud (1892-1974), and Francis Poulenc (1899-1963).
[2] Shapiro, 1994, 5.
[3] Ibid., 10; Brooks, 1993, 425.
[4] Shapiro, 4, 12.
[5] Ibid., 27.

Chapter Nineteen

[1] Hitron, Haggai, "You are not a flower of this land".*Haaretz* literary supplement, 24.6.2007.
[2] Hirshberg, 93-94.
[3] Seter, 8, fn. 19.
[4] Aouizerate-Levin, Jenny, in Hitron, *Haaretz*, 2007.
[5] Hitron, 2007.

Chapter Twenty

[1] Kurtz, 2007, 15.
[2] Ibid.,45.
[3] Ibid., 69.
[4] Ibid., 81.
[5] Ibid., 65.

Epilogue

[1] Maddocks, Fiona, *The Guardian*, 13.3.2011

Bibliography

Prologue

Aisling, Kenny. "Integration or Isolation? Considering Implications of the Designation Woman Composer." http://www.unigraz.at/muwi3www/SysMus08/index 2Dateien/Content/Proceedings_SysMus08/SysMus0 8_Kenny_Aisling.pdf

Ashton, Rosemary. *George Eliot: A Life* . London: Penguin Books, 1997.

Bowers, Jane & Judith Tick (eds.) *Women Making Music: The Western Art Tradition, 1150-1950*. Urbana and Chicago: University of Illinois, 1987.

Citron, Marcia J. The Letters of Fanny Hensel to Félix Mendelssohn by Fanny Mendelssohn Hensel, Felix Mendelssohn-Bartholdy. Hillsdale, New York: Pendragon Press, 1987.

Fauser, Annegret. "La Guerre en dentelles: Women and the Prix de Rome in French Cultural Politics." *Journal of the American Musicological Society*, 51/1, 1998, 83-129.

Firestone, Shulamith. The Dialectic of Sex: The Case for Feminist Revolution. UK: The Women's Press, 1979.

Hensel, Sebastian . *The Mendelssohn Family (1729-1847): From Letters and Journals*. London: Sampson Low, Marston, Searle & Rivington, 1884 (2 volumes).

Jung, Carl G. *The Integration of the Personality*. London: Routledge and Kegan Paul, 1963.

Kurtz, Michael. *Sofia Gubaidulina: A Biography*. Bloomington and Indianapolis: Indiana University Press, 2007.

Leung-Wolf, Elaine. Women, Music, and the Salon Tradition : Its Cultural and Historical Significance in Parisian Musical Society. PhD diss., University of Cincinnati, 1996.

Peacock , Diana. *Women Composers: the Lost Tradition Found.* New York: The Feminist Press, 1988.

Reich, Nancy B. Clara Schumann: *The Artist and the Woman.* Ithaca: Cornell University Press, 1985.

Rosand, Ellen. "Barbara Strozzi, Virtuosissima Cantatrice: The Composer's Voice." *Journal of the American Musicological Society*, 31, 1978, 241-281.

Shahar, Shulamit. *Medieval Childhood.* Tel Aviv: Dvir, 1990 [Hebrew].

_____.The Fourth Estate: *A History of Women in the Middle Ages.* Tel Aviv: Dvir, 1990 [Hebrew].

Showalter, Elaine. *Speaking of Gender.* London: Routledge, Chapman & Hall, 1989.

Sirota, Victoria R. *The Life and Works of Fanny Mendelssohn Hensel.* PhD diss., Boston University, 1981.

Tuchman, Barbara W. A *Distant Mirror: The Calamitous 14th Century.* Tel Aviv: Dvir, 1995 [Hebrew].

Woolf, Virginia. *A Room of One's Own.* Tel Aviv: Miskal, 2004 [Hebrew].

Chapter One

Baird, Joseph L., and Radd K. Ehrman (trans.) *The Letters of Hildegard of Bingen.* Oxford: Oxford University Press, 1998 (2 Volumes).

Bar-On, Ya'arah. The Crowded Delivery Room: Gender and Public Opinion in Early Modern Gynecology. Tel Aviv: Zmora-Bitan, 2000 [Hebrew].

Beer, Frances. *Women and Mystical Experience in the Middle Ages.* Woodbridge: Boydell Press, 1992.

Flanagan, Sabina. *Hildegard of Bingen*, 1098-1179. London : Routledge, 1990.

Fox, Mathew (ed.) *Hildegard of Bingen's Book of Divine Works.* Santa Fe: Bear and Company, 1985.

Hart, Columba and Jane Bishop (trans.) *Hildegard of Bingen: Scivias*. New Jersey: Paulist Press, 1990.

Maddocks, Fiona. *Hildegard of Bingen: The Woman of Her Age*. London: Review, 2001.

Newman, Barbara. "Hildegard of Bingen: Visions and Validation." *Church History*, 54/2, 1985, 63-175.

Sacks, Oliver. *Migraine: The Evolution of a Common Disorder*. Berkeley: University of California Press, 1973.

Shahar, Shulamit. *Medieval Childhood*. Tel Aviv: Dvir, 1990 [Hebrew].

Silvas, Anna. Jutta and Hildegard: *The Biographical Sources*. Turnhout: Brepols, 1998.

Singer, Charles. "The Visions of Hildegard of Bingen." *Yale Journal of Biology and Medicine*, 78, 2005, 57-82. Reprinted from Magic to Science: Essays on the Scientific Twilight. London: Ernest Benn, 1928. http://www.ncbi.nlm.nih.gov/pmc/articles/PMC2259 136/pdf/16197730.pdf

Chapter Two

Cusick, Suzanne G. Francesca Caccini at the Medici Court: Music and the Circulation of Power. Chicago: The University of Chicago Press, 2009.

Kirkendale, Warren. The Court Musicians in Florence During the Principate of the Medici. Firenze: Leo S. Olschki, 1992.

Nagler, Alois M. *Theatre Festivals of the Medici, 1539-1637*. New York: Da Capo Press, 1976.

Chapter Three

Cowan, Alexander. "Women, Gossip and Marriage in Early Modern Venice." http://www.storiadivenezia.net/sito/donne/Cowan_ Women.pdf

Glixon, Beth L. "More on the Life and Death of Barbara Strozzi." *The Musical Quarterly*, 83/1, 1999, 134-141.

_____."New Light on the Life and Career of Barbara Strozzi." *The Musical Quarterly*, 81/2, 1997, 311-335.

Kuehn, Thomas. *Illegitimacy in Renaissance Florence*. Ann Arbor: The University of Michigan Press, 2002.

Magner, Candace (ed.) "Barbara Strozzi, La Virtuosissima Cantatrice: My Life in 1600s Venice." http://barbarastrozzi.blogspot.co.il/

Rosand, Ellen. "The Voice of Barbara Strozzi." In Bowers, Jane & Judith Tick (eds.) *Women Making Music: The Western Art Tradition, 1150-1950*. Urbana and Chicago: University of Illinois, 1987, 168-190.

_____. "Barbara Strozzi, Virtuosissima Cantatrice: The Composer's Voice." Journal of the American Musicological Society, 31, 1978, 241-281.

Selfridge-Field, Eleanor. "Venetian Orphans." *Early Music*, 34/4, 2006, 681-682.

Chapter Four

Buckley, Elizabeth. The Scriptural Cantatas "Esther" and "Jacob, et Rachel" of Elizabeth-Claude Jacquet de la Guerre: Historical Context and Performance Practice. Bibliobazaar, 2011.
http://books.google.co.il/books?id=oH8OywAACA AJ&dq=Buckley,+Elizabeth.+The+Scriptural+Canta tas+Esther+and+Jacob,+Et+Rachel+of+Elizabeth-Claude+Jacquet+de+la+Guerre:+Historical+Context +and+Performance+Practice.+Bibliobazaar,+2011.& hl=en&sa=X&ei=-fggU-CrFqGxywPYuoCQAg&ved=0CCgQ6AEwAA

Jerold, Beverly. Fontenelle's Famous Question and Performance Standards of the Day. College Music Symposium, 43, 2003, 150-160.
http://www.jstor.org/stable/40374475

Montespan, Madame La Marquise. *The Complete Memoirs of Madame de Montespan*.
http://www.gutenberg.org/files/3854/3854-h/3854-h.htm

Neuls-Bates, Carol. "Elizabeth-Claude Jacquet de la Guerre: Composer and Harpsichordist." *Women in Music.* New York: Harper & Row, 1982.

Rose, Adrian. "Élisabeth-Claude Jacquet de la Guerre and the secular cantate françoise." *Early Music*, 13/4, 1985, 529-541.

Rosow, Lois. Cephale et Procris by Elisabeth-Claude Jacquet de La Guerre. *Notes (Second Series)*, 56/4, 2000, 1023-1026.

Schmidt, Carl B. "Elisabeth-Claude Jacquet de la Guerre. Céphale et Procris, edited by Wanda R. Griffiths." *Journal of Seventeenth-Century Music*, 5/1, 1999. http://www.sscm-jscm.org/v5/no1/schmidt.html

Chapter Five

Godt, Irving. Mariana Martines: *A Woman Composer in the Vienna of Mozart and Haydn.* Rochester NY: University of Rochester Press, 2010.

_____. "Marianna in Italy: The International Reputation of Marianna Martines (1744-1812)." *The Journal of Musicology*, 13/4, 1995, 538-561.

Robertson , Ritchie. "The Complexities of Caroline Pichler: Conflicting Role Models, Patriotic Commitment, and The Swedes in Prague (1827)." *Women in German Yearbook*, 23, 2007, 34-48.

Chapter Six

Arnold, Elsie & Jane Baldauf-Berdes. Maddalena Lombardini- Sirmen: Eighteenth-Century Composer, Violinist, and Businesswoman. Maryland: Scarecrow Press, 2002.

Pincherle, Marc. "Vivaldi and the Ospitali." *The Musical Quarterly*, XXIV/3, 1938, 300-312.

Chapter Seven

Dobrzanski, Slawomir. "Maria Szymanowska and the Evolution of Professional Pianism." http://www.chopin.org/articles/Maria%20Szymanow ska%20and%20the%20Evolution%20of%20Professi onal%20Pianism.pdf

Kijas, Anna E. Maria Szymanowska (1789-1831): *A Bio-Bibliography*. Langham: The Scarecrow Press Inc., 2010.

Łabuński , Feliks R., "Poland's Contribution to Music." *Polish Music Journal*, 5/2, 2002. http://www.usc.edu/dept/polish_music/PMJ/issue/5. 2.02/polandlabunski.html#[1]

Valera, Terry de. "Maria Szymanowska (1790- 1831): A Pupil of John Field." *Dublin Historical Record*, 56/1, 2003, 53-55.

Chapter Eight

Ellis, Katharine. Music Criticism in Nineteenth-Century France: La Revue et Gazette musicale de Paris, 1834-1880. Cambridge: Cambridge University Press, 1995.

Fauser, Annegret. "La Guerre en Dentelles: Women and the Prix de Rome in French Cultural Politics." *Journal of the American Musicological Society*, 51/1, 1998, 83-127.

Friedland, Bea. Louise Farrenc, 1804-1875: Composer, Performer, Scholar. Ann Arbor: UMI Research, 1980.

Chapter Nine

Citron, Marcia J. (ed.) *The Letters of Fanny Hensel to Félix Mendelssohn*. New York: Pendragon Press, 1987.

_____. *Gender and the Musical Canon*. Cambridge: Cambridge University Press, 1993.

Gates, Eugene. "Fanny Mendelssohn Hensel: A Life of Music within Domestic Limits." *The Kapralova Society Journal: A Journal of Women in Music*, 5/2, 2007. http://www.kapralova.org/journal9.pdf

Hensel, Sebastian . *The Mendelssohn Family (1729-1847)*. London: Sampson Low, Marston, Searle & Rivington, 1884 (2 volumes).

Hertz, Deborah S. How Jews Became Germans: The History of Conversion and Assimilation in Berlin. New Haven: Yale University Press, 2007.

_____. Jewish High Society in Old Regime Berlin. New Haven: Yale University Press, 1988.

Higgins, Paula. "In Her Brother's Shadow: The Musical Legacy of Fanny Mendelssohn Hensel," In *The Changing Patterns of Our Lives: Proceedings of the Sesquicentennial Symposium*. Durham: Duke University, 3-5 March, 1989, 37-49.

Kimber, Marian Wilson . "The 'Suppression' of Fanny Mendelssohn: Rethinking Feminist Biography." <u>19th-Century Music</u>, 26/2, 2002, 113-129.

Lowenstein, Steven, M. The Berlin Jewish Community: Enlightenment, Family and Crisis 1770-1830. USA: Oxford University Press, 1994.

Mercer-Taylor, Peter. *The Life of Mendelssohn*. Cambridge: Cambridge University Press, 2000.

Sirota, Victoria R. *The Life and Works of Fanny Mendelssohn Hensel*. PhD diss., Boston University, 1981.

Tillard, Francis. *Fanny Mendelssohn*. Portland: Amadeus, 1992.

Todd, Larry R. *Fanny Hensel: The Other Mendelssohn*. New York: Oxford University Press, 2010.

Chapter Ten

Burton, Anna. "Robert Schumann and Clara Wieck: A Creative Partnership." *Music and Letters*, 69/2, 1988, 211-228.

Chissell, Joan. Clara Schumann, a Dedicated Spirit: A Study of Her Life and Work. London: H. Hamilton, 1983.

Gerig, Reginald R. *Famous Pianists and Their Technique*. Bridgeport: Robert B. Luce, 1974.

Litzmann, Berthold (ed.) *Letters of Clara Schumann and Johannes Brahms 1853-1896*. London: Longmans Green , 1927.

Mazuz, Aya. "The Nations in Thy Womb": A Biblical Allegory on Stylistic Duality in Clara Schumann's Piano Music. PhD diss., Bar-Ilan University, Israel, 2008.

Nauhaus, Gerd (ed.) and Peter Ostwald (trans.) The Marriage Diaries of Robert and Clara Schumann: From Their Wedding Day through the Russia Trip. Boston: Northeastern University Press, 1993.

Owen, Barbara. *The Organ Music of Johannes Brahms.* Oxford: Oxford University Press, 2007.

Reich, Nancy B. *Clara Schumann: The Artist and the Woman.* Ithaca: Cornell University Press, 1985.

Reich, Susanna. *Clara Schumann: Piano Virtuoso.* New York: Houghton Mifflin Company, 1999.

Sams, Eric. "Brahms and His Clara Themes." *The Musical Times*, 112/1539, 1971, 432-434.

Chapter Eleven

Atwood, William G. The Lioness and the Little One: The Liaison of George Sand and Frédéric Chopin. New York: Columbia University Press, 1980.

Azoury, Pierre A. Chopin Through His Contemporaries: Friends, Lovers, and Rivals. Portsmouth, NH: Greenwood, 1999.

Barbier, Patrick. *Opera in Paris, 1800-1850: A Lively History*. Portland, Oregon: Amadeus Press, 1995.

Beaumont, Barbara. Flaubert and Turgenev: A Friendship in Letters: The Complete Correspondence. London: Athlone, 1985.

Blount, Paul Groves. *George Sand and the Victorian World.* Athens: University of Georgia Press, 1979.

Chorley, Henry Fothergill. *Music and Manners in France and Germany*. New York: Da Capo Press, 1984.

Cofer, Angela Faith. Pauline Viardot-Garcia: The Influence of the Performer on Nineteenth- Century Opera. PhD diss., University of Cincinnati, 1988.

Duncan, Alastair. The Paris Salons, 1895-1914. Woodbridge Suffolk: Antique Collectors Club, 1994.

Edwards, Jennifer R. Pauline Viardot's Song Settings of German Poetry: The Relationship Between Music and Text. PhD diss., University of Missouri, Kansas City, 1997.

Eisler, Benita. *Chopin's Funeral*. New York: Alfred A. Knopf, 2003.

Everist, Mark. "Enshrining Mozart: Don Giovanni and the Viardot Circle." *19th-Century Music*, 25/2-3, 2001-2, 165-189.

Fitzlyon, April. *Viardot's Correspondence with George Sand*. London: Calder, 1964.

_____. The Price of Genius: A Life of Pauline Viardot. London: Calder,
1964.

Harris, Rachel M. *The Music Salon of Pauline Viardot: Featuring Her Salon Opera*. PhD diss., Louisiana State University, 2005.

Hunsaker, Amy J. *Pauline Viardot's Russian Compositions*. PhD diss., University of Nevada, 2010. http://digitalscholarship.unlv.edu/cgi/viewcontent.cgi?article=1665&context=thesesdissertations

Kendall-Davies, Barbara. *The Life and Work of Pauline Viardot-Garcia*. Cambridge: Cambridge Scholars Press, 2004.

Knowles, A.V. *Turgenev's Letters*. London: The Athlone Press, 1983.

McCormack, Jessica. *The Influence of National Style on the Compositions of Pauline Viardot*. PhD diss., University of North Texas, 2009. http://digital.library.unt.edu/ark:/67531/metadc9923/m2/1/high_res_d/diss...pdf

Schapiro, Leonard. *Turgenev, His Life and Times*. New York: Random House, 1978.

Steen, Michael. *Enchantress of Nations: Pauline Viardot, Soprano, Muse and Lover*. Thriplow, Cambridge: Icon Books, 2007.

Waddington, Patrick & Nicholas G. Žekulin (eds.) *The Musical Works of Pauline Viardot-Garcia (1821-1910): A Chronological Catalogue*. New Zealand & Canada, 2011. Online edition: http://dspace.ucalgary.ca/bitstream/1880/48502/3/Viardot_catalogue_2011.pdf

Chapter Twelve

Feldman, Ann E. "Being Heard: Women Composers and Patrons at the 1893 World's Columbian Exposition." *Notes*, Second Series, 47/1, 1990, 7-20.

Leung-Wolf, Elaine. Women, Music, and the Salon Tradition: Its Cultural and Historical Significance in Parisian Musical Society. PhD diss., University of Cincinnati, 1996.

Myers, Rollo. "Augusta Holmes: A Meteoric Career." *The Musical Quarterly*, 53, 1967, 365-376.

Pasler, Jann. "The Ironies of Gender, or Virility and Politics in the Music of Augusta Holmes." In *Writing through Music: Essays on Music, Culture, and Politics*. Oxford University Press, 2007, 213-249.

Rockwood, Rebecca L. *Augusta Holmes: "Les Argonautes" and "La Montagne Noir."* MA Thesis, Rice University, 2002.

Theeman, Nancy S. *The Life and Songs of Augusta Holmes*. PhD diss., University of Maryland, 1983.

Chapter Thirteen

Citron, Marcia J. *Cécile Chaminade: A Bio-Bibliography*. Westport, Conn.: Greenwood Press, 1988.

Moegle, Steel. *Cécile Chaminade (1857-1944): The Context of Her Music*. http://www.mmc.edu.mk/IRAM/Conferences/StrugaIII/pdf/17Steel.pdf

Smith, Robin. *The Mélodies of Chaminade: Hidden Treasures for Vocal Performance and Pedagogy*. PhD diss., Indiana University, 2012. https://scholarworks.iu.edu/dspace/bitstream/handle/2022/14331/Smith_Robin_2012.pdf?sequence=1

Chapter Fourteen

Clements, Elicia. "Virginia Woolf, Ethel Smyth, and Music: Listening as a Productive Mode of Social Interaction." _College Literature_, 32/3, 2005, 51-71.

Collis, Louise. _Impetuous Heart: The Story of Ethel Smyth_. London: W. Kimber, 1984.

Cook, Blanche W. "Women Alone Stir My Imagination: Lesbianism and the Cultural Tradition." _Signs_, 4/4, 1979, 718-739.

Kertesz, Elizabeth J. Issues in the Critical Reception of Ethel Smyth's Mass and First Four Operas in England and Germany. PhD diss., University of Melbourne, 2001.

Marcus, Jane. _Suffrage and the Pankhursts_. London: Routledge, 2010.

Raitt, Suzanne. "The Tide of Ethel': Femininity as Narrative in the Friendship of Ethel Smyth and Virginia Woolf." _Critical Quarterly_, 30/4, 1988, 3-21.

Vicinus, Martha. _Intimate Friends: Women Who Loved Women, 1778-1928_. Chicago: University of Chicago Press, 2004.

Chapter Fifteen

Block, Adrienne F. _Amy Beach, Passionate Victorian: The Life and Work of an American Composer, 1867-1944_. New York: Oxford University Press, 1998.

_____ "Amy Beach as a Teacher." _American Music Teacher_, 48, 1999, 22-25.

_____ "Amy Beach's Music on Native American Themes." _American Music_, 8, 1990, 141-166.

_____ "A 'Veritable Autobiography?' Amy Beach's Piano Concerto in C-Sharp Minor, op.45." _The Musical Quarterly_, 78, 1994, 394-416.

_____ "The Child is Mother of the Woman: Amy Beach's New England Upbringing." In Susan C. Cook & July S. Tsou (eds.) _Cecelia Reclaimed: Feminist Perspectives on Gender and Music_. Urbana and Chicago: University of Illinois Press, 1994, 107-133.

_____ "Why Amy Beach Succeeded as a Composer: The Early Years." *Current Musicology*, 36, 1983, 41-59.

Block, Adrienne F. and Carol Neuls-Bates. *Women in American Music: A Bibliography of Music and Literature*. Westport, Connecticut and London: The Greenwood Press, 1979.

Eden, Myrna Garvey. Anna Hyatt Huntington, Sculptor, and Mrs. H.H.A. Beach, Composer: A Comparative Study of Two Women Representatives of the American Cultivated Tradition in the Arts. PhD diss., Syracuse University, 1977.

Elder, Dean. "Where Was Amy Beach All These Years? An Interview with Mary Louise Boehm." *Clavier*, 15, 1976, 14-17.

Falconer-Salkeld, Bridget. The MacDowell Colony: A Musical History of America's Premier Artists' Community. Lanham MD: Scarecrow Press, 2005.

Feldman, Ann E. "Being Heard: Women Composers and Patrons at the 1893 World's Columbian Exposition." *Notes: The Quarterly Journal of the Music Library Association*, 47, 1990, 7-20.

Flatt, Rose & Marie Chisholm. Analytical Approaches to Chromaticism in Amy Beach's Piano Quintet in F# Minor." *Indiana Theory Review*, 4/3, 1981, 41-58.

Gerk, Sarah. *A Critical Reception History of Amy Beach's Gaelic Symphony*. M.A Thesis, California State University, Long Beach, 2006.

Jenkins, Walter S., John H. Baron (eds.) The Remarkable Mrs. Beach, American Composer: A Biographical Account Based on Her Diaries, Letters, Newspaper Clippings, and Personal Reminiscences. Detroit: Harmonie Park Press, 1994.

Robinson, Nicole M. *"To the Girl Who Wants to Compose": Amy Beach as a Music Educator*. MA thesis, Florida State University, 2013. http://diginole.lib.fsu.edu/cgi/viewcontent.cgi?article=7599&context=etd

Tick, Judith (ed.) "Amy Beach, Composer, on 'Why I Chose My Profession'". *Music in the USA: A Documentary Companion*. New York and Oxford: Oxford University Press, 2008, 323-329.
http://www.hennikerhistory.org/genealgy.htm
http://www.pianowomen.com/books.html

Verissimo, Laurel Keddie. *Amy Beach: Her Life, Times and Music*. MA Thesis, San Jose State University, 1993.

Chapter Sixteen

Article author query.

Books, Jeanice. "Nadia Boulanger and the Salon of the Princesse de Polignac." *Journal of the American Musicological Society*, 46/3, 1993, 415-468.

Dopp, Bonnie J. "Numerology and Cryptography in the Music of Lili Boulanger: The Hidden Program in Clairieres dans le ciel." *The Musical Quarterly*, 78/3, 1994, 556-583.

Fauser, Annegret. "Lili Boulanger's La princesse Maleine: A Composer and her Heroine as Literary Icons." *The Journal of the Royal Musical Association*, 122/1, 1997, 68-108.

Potter, Caroline. *Nadia and Lili Boulanger*. Burlington: Ashgate Publishing, 2007.

_____. Nadia and Lili Boulanger: Sister Composers. *The Musical Quarterly*, 83/4, 1999, 536-556.

Rosenstiel, Léonie. *Nadia Boulanger: A Life in Music*. New York: W. W. Norton, 1982.

_____. *The Life and Works of Lili Boulanger*. Rutherford, New Jersey: Fairleigh Dickinson University Press, 1978.

Spycket, Jérôme. A la recherche de Lili Boulanger: essai biographique. Paris: Fayard, 2004.

_____. *Nadia Boulanger*. Lattès: Payot Lausanne, 1987.

Chapter Seventeen

Brown, Linda & Shirley Wayne (eds.) *Florence Price: Symphonies nos. 1 and 3.*
http://books.google.co.il/books?id=9lzwS6YzrG8C&pg=PR28&lpg=PR28&dq=florence+price+diary&source=bl&ots=noTmp4dUwy&sig=AvY7f5K9o-Snc4-1WfeqyPwKfTE&hl=en&sa=X&ei=CzHuUvC_OIbwhQf5woHAAg&ved=0CDYQ6AEwAw#v=onepage&q=florence%20price%20diary&f=false

Brown, Rae L. "The Woman's Symphony Orchestra of Chicago and Florence B. Price's Piano Concerto in One Movement." *American Music*, 11/2, 1993, 185-202.

_____. Selected Orchestral Music of Florence B. Price (1888–1953) In the Context of Her Life and Work. PhD diss., Yale University, 1987.

Peebles, Sarah Louise. The Use of the Spiritual in the Piano Works of Two African-American Women Composers - Florence B. Price and Margaret Bonds. PhD diss., University of Mississippi, 2008.

Smith, Bethany Jo. Song to the Dark Virgin: Race and Gender in Five Art Songs of Florence B. Price. PhD diss., University of Cincinnati, 2007.

Chapter Eighteen

Shapiro, Robert. *Germaine Tailleferre: A Bio-bibliography.* Michigan: Greenwood Press, 1994.

Germaine Tailleferre. In *Famous People* online http://www.thefamouspeople.com/profiles/germaine-tailleferre-346.php

Chapter Nineteen

Aouizerate-Lveni, Jenny. *Verdina Shlonsky – A Story of a Composer.* MA thesis, the Hebrew University, Jerusalem, 2006.

Hirshberg, Jehoash. "The Vision of the East and the Heritage of the West: A Comprehensive Model of Ideology and Practice in Israeli Art Music." http://www.biu.ac.il/HU/mu/min-ad/8-9-II/06-Hirshberg_The%20Vision.pdf

Hitron, Haggai, "You are not a flower of this land". *Haaretz* literary supplement, 24.6.2007.

Peles, Joseph. "The Many Faces of Israeli Music" http://www.imi.org.il/Article.aspx?id=220cf375-2013-4b9d-aa38-35b8bfbc6ea1

Seter, Ronit. "Verdina Shlonsky: The First Lady of Israeli Music." http://www.biu.ac.il/hu/mu/min-ad/07-08/Seter-SHLONSKY.pdf.

Chapter Twenty

Kurtz, Michael. *Sofia Gubaidulina: A Biography.* Bloomington and Indianapolis: Indiana University Press, 2007.

Lukomsky, Vera. "'The Eucharist in My Fantasy': Interview with Sofia Gubaidulina." *Tempo, New Series,* 206, 1998, 29-35.

Lukomsky, Vera." 'Hearing the Subconscious': Interview with Sofia Gubaidulina." *Tempo, New Series,* 209, 1999, 27-31.

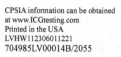
CPSIA information can be obtained
at www.ICGtesting.com
Printed in the USA
LVHW112306011221
704985LV00014B/2055